SEA

PACIFIC OCEAN

PORT HEIDEN

ANIAKCHAK CRATER

CHIGNIK

CASTLE CAPE

Mt. VENIAMINOF

PORT MOLLER

PERRYVILLE

SANDPOINT PIRATE COVE

KUPREANOF POINT

KOROVIN I.

WEST NAGAI STRAIT

POPOF I.

MIST HARBOR

BIG KONIUJI I.

UNGA

LITTLE KONIUJI I.

EAGLE HARBOR

SIMEONOF I.

NAGAI I.

CHERNABURA I.

SHUMAGIN ISLANDS

McCAUSLAND 6-2006

THE ALASKA PEN
An Illustrated History of UNGA

Unga High School

Compiled and Edited by:
Thor Lauritzen

Peggy Arness

and

Edward Melseth

BOOK PUBLISHERS NETWORK

Book Publishers Network
P.O. Box 2256
Bothell • WA • 98041
PH • 425-483-3040

10 9 8 7 6 5 4 3 2

Printed in the United States of America

LCCN 2006933634
ISBN 1-887542-43-4

Editor/Proofreader: Julie Scandora
Cover Design: Laura Zugzda
Interior Layout: Stephanie Martindale

Dedication

IN THE FALL OF **1934**, a small group of students and their faculty advisor gathered together to form a high school in Unga. At the same time, the students embarked upon a venture: to publish a monthly paper that would chronicle the activities of the entire school and would provide a source of information on happenings in the greater Shumagin region. Thus was born THE ALASKA PEN, a publication whose circulation eventually reached most of the states in the Union, and one that would continue for the lifetime of the Unga High School.

The vision, the skill, and the perseverance of this unique group of self-described "Penmakers" are attributes that honor their service and their memory. To Elizabeth and Marie and Clara and Catherine and John and Christine, to Thomas and Andrew and Hubert and Daniel — and to all of those who followed in their long shadow — we humbly dedicate this book.

Contents

Acknowledgements

THE ALASKA PEN AND ITS surrogate, PEN WHISPERS—125 issues in all, spanning the years 1934-1951, form the foundation upon which this latter-day history of Unga was built. In our Dedication, we honored the original ten "pen makers," and we again wish to acknowledge their pioneering achievement in recording the history of Unga and its environs. Their foresight in that first year gave guidance to the many students who followed them to continue the task of presenting school and local news for sixteen additional years.

Clearly, this book could not have been written without the historical input that these two papers provided. Neither could the work have proceeded without the good fortune of recovering virtually all of the issues that were published. And for that, we are indebted to the late Zenia Rodgers Foster and her daughter, Elizabeth Gronholdt, for offering their collection of the first eight years' issues to the Alaska State Library for preservation. The remaining issues (1943-51) were already available in one of our collections and were loaned to the library for reproduction. We offer our heartfelt thanks to these donors and to Anne Laura Wood, Historical Collections Librarian, Alaska State Library, for guiding the microfilming of this collection.

From the beginning, the intent of this project was to identify articles of historical interest from these student publications and to reproduce them verbatim with accompanying illustrations such as drawings, charts, and photographs. This turned out to be a daunting task, and we were only partially successful in our quest for these kinds of illustrative material. Many people were simply reluctant to loan precious photographs, and we understand their concern. To those who did share their photographs, we hereby acknowledge with utmost appreciation their contribution: Roberta Hill Allen, Jennie Johansen Berntsen, Robert Berntsen, Polly (Mrs. Peter) Calugan, Judy Casey Cross, Sharon Gronholdt Dye, Ruth Lauritzen Ekren, Andy Endresen, Martha Hunt Fletcher, Harry Foster, Mary (Mrs. Russell) Foster, Robert Galovin, Flossie Brandal Gilbert, Ruth and Robert D. McCausland, Lynelle Gronholdt McDaniels, Barbara Melseth, Nora Berntsen Newman, Jacquelin Ruth Benson Pels, Frank Siemion, Carol Larsen Smith, and Evert Tigner.

A special acknowledgement is due, posthumously, to Mr. Allan L. Petersen, who, over the first thirteen years of the period covered by this book, served as Unga's unofficial photographer. His signature panoramic prints and snapshots have graced the pages of numerous family photo albums and are prominent in the present work.

Credits for specific items used in the book are given in the section "Credits for Photographs and Illustrations." We apologize for any omission or for any credit improperly given.

Finally, as the person who has shepherded this project over the past three years, I would like to acknowledge the invaluable contributions of my coworkers. Peggy Arness, working closely with the Alaska State Library, was instrumental in building a virtually complete file of THE ALASKA PEN and PEN WHISPERS. At this writing, all but three issues of the 125 issues published have been located and incorporated into the library's microfilm. Peggy has been a tireless researcher in the often thankless job of locating photographs from sources in addition to her own extensive collection. The information she compiled from historical discussions with her husband, Jim (who unfortunately did not live to see the final product: Jim died in February of 2006), provided essential input into the book.

Edward Melseth's letters to Alice Nilson and to this writer served as the initial inspiration for undertaking this project. Ed has spent much of his life (since his birth in Unga in 1943) in or around Unga, and his familiarity with virtually all of the players in this drama made him an indispensable ally. Like Peggy, Ed has spent countless hours gathering pictures and information from former Ungaites, and his prodigious memory has enriched the history of this period for us all to appreciate and enjoy.

A Special Remembrance...

As we go to press, word was received that Bob McCausland has died. Bob was an early proponent of this history project and he supported it generously with pen-and-ink drawings that enriched this book. Bob reviewed the draft of the book early this summer and recommended we add a map of the area covered in the book, and he eagerly offered to draw the map. His inside cover illustration was his last completed art project.

Although he never visited Unga, Bob spent the war years as a young seaman in the Aleutians where he began his career sketching his unique impressions of the joys and the foibles of life. In 1941, Bob married Ruth Bjornstad, a grand-niece of Andrew Grosvold of Sand Point, which led fifty years later to his association with this writer, a grand-nephew of Grosvold, and with other former Ungaites through the "I Remember Unga" reunion held in Westport and Tokeland, Washington, in 1973.

Bob McCausland was truly an inspiration to all who knew him, and he will be sorely missed but never forgotten.

Thor Lauritzen (July 2006)

Frontispiece

Our Town

I AM WRITING THIS STORY to tell you about our town of Unga. There are about 200 people in Unga. There are 5 bicycles in our town. We do not have any cars. There is a gold mine near Unga. It is the old Apollo Mine. We can walk from Unga to Squaw Harbor. It is about 7 miles to go by boat. Unga is on the Pacific Ocean. When we look out of our school window we can see a point called "Elephant Head." It looks like pictures of elephants. We have a library in Unga. There are two stores and one post office. We had a dock but a storm came and the waves knocked it down. There is a round dance hall in Unga. All the houses are built of lumber. The school-house is on a hill. Sometimes it is hard to get to school when the wind blows. The people burn wood and coal in their stoves. We wear the same kind of clothes you do. We order our clothes from the catalog. We have no doctor or hospital. There is a doctor at the cannery in Squaw Harbor in the summer time. A traveling dentist came to Unga this fall. The people of Unga fish codfish and salmon in the summer. Many people work in the cannery. The men go trapping in the winter. Unga is an old town.

[This article was written by fourth grader, Evelyn Whittaker, in response to questions from stateside students, and was printed in Unga Newsletter, dated November 1, 1938. Unga Newsletter was published annually for three years by the students of the primary room. Ed.]

The Sjoberg & Casey warehouse

Foreword

THE VILLAGE OF UNGA IS nestled along the northeast shore of Delarof Harbor on the island of Unga—the largest island in the Shumagin archipelago. Delarof Harbor is a shallow inlet roughly three miles in length, running in an east-west direction. The outer harbor is framed by high monolithic cliffs and mountains, its entrance guarded by a headland called Elephant Head on its southern flank and the Uglamia-Cross Island highlands on the north. The harbor entrance fronts on West Nagai Strait, an oceanic waterway that separates the islands of Unga and Nagai and contains in its depths the fabled Shumagin Banks of North Pacific fishing lore. It is the resource provided by the Shumagin Banks that sparked the growth of Unga through the turn of the 20th century from an isolated Aleut/Russian fishing and hunting site to the prominence it attained in the early 1900s as the hub of the Alaska codfishing industry. In 1920, the 14th US Government Census reported a village population of 308, comprising 31 families and 111 individuals, most of whom were bachelor codfishermen. Two San Francisco-based salteries and a number of privately owned stations dotted the perimeter of the harbor and were in full-scale operation through much of the decade.

By 1930, both large salteries continued operations, but on a substantially reduced scale and under private ownership. Despite the turndown in codfishing fortunes and the approaching worldwide depression, the village thrived. The 15th US Government Census pegged Unga's population at 163 persons, comprising 28 families and the aging remnants of the codfishing crews. Thus, in the intervening ten years, in spite of a large drop in individual numbers, the family units changed only slightly. This relative stability was reflected in the initiation of a number of community activities—a women's club, a Girl Scout troop, a community library, and a Sunday-school—that lent support to a vibrant Territorial school system that by 1934 had expanded to twelve grades.

Despite the economic factors that plagued the village through much of the '30s, Unga continued to serve as the dominant settlement in the islands. But that was about to change. As salmon fishing overtook codfishing as the major economic engine in the Shumagins, the movement toward much larger and more sophisticated processing facilities required deeper harbors and more secure anchorages—sites that were better filled by locations such as neighboring Squaw Harbor and Sand Point. This reality, plus the disruption of traditional lines of commerce during the war years, the uncertainty and anxiety of living near a war zone, and the closure of the US Marshal's office shortly thereafter prompted a rapid decline in Unga's population. In the early 1950s, businesses and organizations that served the community were forced to close. Decommissioning of the US Post Office and the closure of Unga Territorial School later in the decade sealed the fate of Unga as a viable community. In the 1960s, only a few families remained, and by the decade's end they, too, were forced to leave, and Unga Village ceased to exist.

This is a story about the last four decades in the life of a village. It is a story about a hardy people who eked out a living from the sea, whose lives were constantly challenged by the harsh environment in which they lived, whose isolation bred independence, whose joys were generously shared, and whose heartaches were felt by all. That they persevered under these conditions, particularly when faced with the collapse of their little world, is a testament to their character. This is

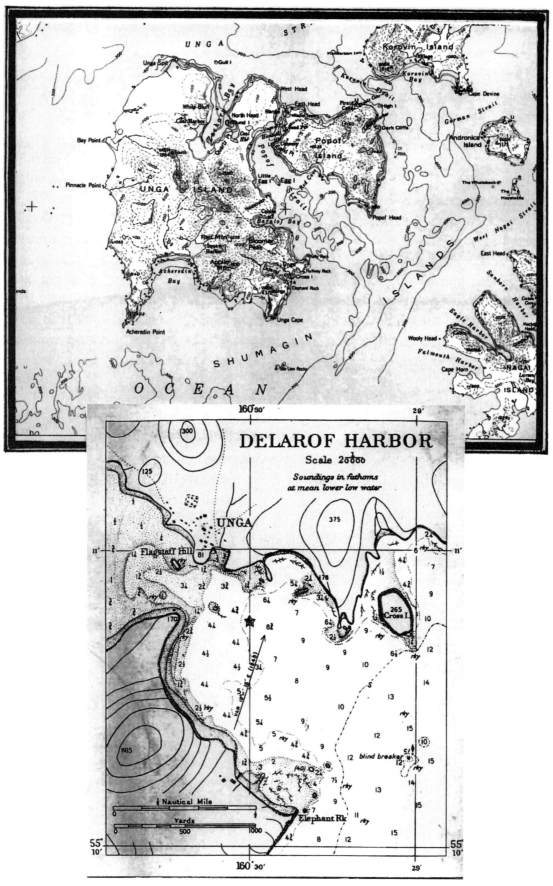

Top: Unga Island from USGS Chart for Port Moller, Alaska, N5500-W16000/60×120 (1953)
Bottom: Delarof Harbor from USCGS Chart for Shumagin Islands, No. 8900, Plate No. 3560 (1944)

a story about Unga, but a similar tale could be told about many of its Aleutian neighbors, which suffered the same fate. It is, most of all, a 20th century Alaskan story.

We were fortunate in our case to have first-person accounts of many of the events that shaped the times. It is these reminiscences, along with the historical articles lifted from the pages of THE ALASKA PEN—Unga High School's monthly newsmagazine—that provided the foundation upon which this "illustrated history" was built. Our book is organized into three chronological sections: Part I covers the 1930s and is appropriately titled "The Thirties"; Part II covers the early 1940s—"The War Years"—and Part III the postwar period and Unga's precipitous decline, dubbed "The Aftermath."

Unga Village, ca. 1945

PART I
THE THIRTIES

Codfishermen and their catch

Principal Editor:
Thor Lauritzen

Co-editors:
Peggy Arness
Edward Melseth

INTRODUCTION

THE DECADE OF THE 1930S represented a crucial turning point in the latter life of Unga. The decade was framed by the Great Depression, the precipitous decline in codfish stocks, the explosive growth of the salmon industry, and the uncertainties accompanying the drift toward war. The Depression and the social upheavals that wracked the country and the world weren't felt quite so dramatically in isolated areas such as Unga, whose inhabitants depended largely on subsistence hunting and fishing. A far more significant happening was the severe decline in the one industry that built the village in the late 1800s and peaked in the first two decades of the 20th century. Codfishing was largely responsible for opening up the village to outsiders—principally northern Europeans and New Englanders who shared similar livelihoods with their Alaskan counterparts. When codfishing waned, many of these itinerant fishermen moved on, but a large number remained, married, raised families, and became stalwarts in their adopted community.

Another source of livelihood—trapping—was also on the decline in the '30s, due largely to the social rejection of animal furs as a commodity in trade. Trapping became little more than a winter diversion for villagers who took this opportunity to gather game for the family table.

Despite these ominous signs of economic collapse, the village enjoyed a resurgence of community spirit, brought on in large part by the territorial school system, the establishment of a four-year high school, and the resurgence of the salmon fishing industry.

The school system in Unga had evolved from a mission-run school in the 1880s to an Alaska Native Service facility at the turn of the century and, finally, to the Unga Territorial School. In 1930, the school boasted an enrollment of 35 students in grades one through eight. By 1934, the number of high school-age students had increased to 14, and Unga High School and its mouthpiece, THE ALASKA PEN, the school's monthly periodical, were born.

These opportunities for the area's children would not have occurred without the enthusiastic support of the townspeople who had long shown their community spirit by cooperating to develop a central water supply system for the village, a network of boardwalks throughout the town, and a community hall that was the envy of the entire Shumagin area. The pride at work in the village was evident in the gaily painted houses and gardens scattered throughout the town. And there was more, much more, to come in the '30s. These advances were due in large part to those who contracted to journey to this isolated corner of Alaska to teach. Most taught for periods of one to three years before moving on to their next assignment, but one stayed on for 13 years and set a pattern of excellence in teaching and community service that has never been approached. For many students, Mrs. Petersen was the only teacher they ever had, and for this writer, she was easily the most unforgettable person I've ever met. Mrs. Allan (Jettie) Petersen arrived in Unga in 1934, the wife of Deputy US Marshal Allan L. Petersen, whose headquarters was located in Unga. She began teaching that fall and continued without interruption until 1947 when the marshal's office was closed. Mrs. Petersen may not have been the prime mover in the community activities that were initiated in the 1930s, but her inspiration was surely instrumental in their organization and their success.

In 1936, following an informal gathering of women into sewing circles, the Unga Women's Club was organized. That was followed shortly by the investiture of a girl scout troop and a community library. Other civic groups that were instituted during this period were Sunday School, the Unga Improvement Club, a city council, and a waterworks. Having reasserted its prominence as a social center of the Shumagins, Unga continued its role as the economic center of the area, with two general stores, a US Post Office, and a wireless station.

Obviously, the success of these social services reflected the eagerness of the entire community to provide an environment for progressive growth, and the initial cooperation was impressive. For example, out of a village population of only 163 persons, the Unga Women's Club began with an enrollment of 34 ladies—virtually the entire population of adult women in town. The Girl Scouts were similarly successful: more than 30 young ladies benefited from the activities of Unga Troop No. 1 over the 12 years that the troop was active. However, similar organizations involving their male counterparts did not meet with much success, due largely to their adoption early in life of the livelihood of their fathers. Teenage sons assumed the role of hunter, trapper, and fisherman, many before their formal education was completed. Thus, the carefree life of the adolescent male was relatively brief.

It was in this environment that the Unga High School was born. For the first time, the youth of the community were given the opportunity to continue their education without the trauma of family dislocation or the expense of attending a remote boarding school.

The decision to publish a monthly newsletter concurrent with the organization of the high school was a bold step in uniting the community behind its students and one that would provide a lasting historical account of what turned out to be Unga's twilight years. THE ALASKA PEN was the result of close cooperation between students and faculty and a strong commitment to serve not only the school but the greater community, this being the only printed periodical in the entire Alaska Peninsula district. Thus, the PEN reported on daily activities at school, provided a vehicle for students to exercise their journalistic skills, served as the local newspaper, and editorialized on such far-flung concerns as the problems in Ethiopia, national politics, and the perennial problems of local mail service or lack thereof. The foundation upon which THE ALASKA PEN was built was so strong and the commitment so devoted that the paper continued publishing through most of the war years and into the 1950s. Its legacy is the basis for the present work—one that seeks to meld the history of this period with comparable photographic images. Here, then, is Part I: The Thirties.

Introducing THE ALASKA PEN

We hope that you'll
   Be happy when
It is time for a new
   Alaska Pen.
It's your paper, you know,
And the news you see there
Is your news and our news
That we want you to share.
We'll have puzzles and jingles
And maybe some jokes,
Our very own stories
To read to home folks.
We'll try to draw pictures,
We'll tell what is new,
So please help us to learn
What has happened to you.
We know you're all with us;
We'll do our best, then,
So you can't do without
   THE ALASKA PEN.

TO THE POINT

THE ALASKA PEN

On September 14, at the close of the school period, the election of staff officers was announced. The officers were selected by the teachers because of the difficulty in choosing the ones best adapted to the various positions. The names of those selected for the different tasks are listed above.

THE ALASKA PEN stands for the Alaska Peninsula, PEN being short for peninsula as well as indicating the literary nature of our efforts. The departments of the paper are named, as nearly as possible, in accordance with the PEN. The feather pen on the first page is a copy of the map of the Alaska Peninsula from Lake Iliamna to Unimak Island. The location of Unga is indicated. We realize, of course, that we are not living on the Peninsula, itself. Perhaps we should consider ourselves as bits of ink dropped by the SUPREME WRITER.

(TAP I, 1, p. 2, September 1934)

HISTORICAL HIGHLIGHTS

❧ September 1934 ❧
THE ALASKA PEN: A BIRTH

On September 14, at the close of the school period, the election of staff officers was announced. The officers were selected by the teachers because of the difficulty in choosing the ones best adapted to the various positions. The names of those selected for the different tasks are listed above [see THE ALASKA PEN, the first issue of which is appended].

THE ALASKA PEN stands for the Alaska Peninsula, PEN being short for peninsula as well as indicating the literary nature of our efforts. The departments of the paper are named, as nearly as possible, in accordance with the PEN. The feather pen on the first page is a copy of the map of the Alaska Peninsula from Lake Iliamna to Unimak Island. The location of Unga is indicated. We realize, of course, that we are not living on the Peninsula, itself. Perhaps we should consider ourselves as bits of ink dropped by the SUPREME WRITER.   (TAP I, 1, p. 2)

SJOBERG-CASEY WEDDING

Mrs. Sjoberg, wife of Gustaf E. Sjoberg, local merchant, who recently returned from a visit to San Francisco, announces the marriage of their daughter, Viola, to Mr. Edward F. Casey.

Mr. and Mrs. Edward F. Casey

The wedding took place July 28, at the Grace Methodist Church in the presence of a few close friends and relatives.

The young couple will make their home in San Francisco where Mr. Casey is engaged in the insurance business. Viola's many Unga friends wish her much happiness.   (TAP I, 2, p. 9)

[Ed and Viola shortly tired of life in the big city and joined her parents in Unga, where Ed went into partnership with Mr. Sjoberg. In the early 1950s, Ed returned to San Francisco and resumed his insurance career. Sjoberg & Casey's continued operation until 1953. Viola's sad departure from Unga is documented in Part III. Ed.]

LAURITZEN-BENSON WEDDING

Announcement of the marriage of Miss Ruth Lauritzen to Mr. N. J. Benson has been recently received in Unga.

Mr. and Mrs. N. J. Benson

Miss Lauritzen is the daughter of Mr. and Mrs. Hjalmar Lauritzen, local merchants. She was educated in the Unga school and has been working in Seward for some time.

Mr. Benson is an employee of the Alaska Railroad and has been a resident of Alaska for several years. He is president of the Seward Athletic Club.

Ruth's many friends in Unga wish the couple much happiness. (TAP I, 4, p. 9)

THE WRECK OF THE *ST. ANDREW*

A tragic accident occurred this morning (the eighth of October) when the *St. Andrew* from Mist Harbor dragged anchor and went on the rocks, and five men were found to be missing. The missing men are: Harold Lauritzen, Edward Hausman, Jalmar Hirve, Edward Haime and Andrew

Kristensen. The accident happened to the men when they were going out to the boat in a skiff. The body of Edward Haime has been found and frequent searches have been made for the other four men. The men surviving of those who came on the *St. Andrew* are: Albert Reeve and John Kristensen. Their purpose for coming to Unga was to get freight and mail. (TAP I, 2, p. 8)

[See "Crossings," this section, for additional information on this tragedy. Ed.]

❧ 1935 ❧
"STARR" BIRTHS

FEBRUARY 16—Among the passengers on the MS *Polar Bear* for Unga were Mrs. Harry Hunt and twin daughters, Martha and Marjorie. The stork, assisted by Captain Ryning and a lady from Akutan, brought the twins to the SS *Starr* while enroute to Unalaska. Mrs. Hunt's many friends are happy to have her safe in Unga again. The Twins are getting along splendidly. (TAP I, 7, p. 9)

Lena & Martha and Harry & Margie

[Lena and Harry Hunt were longtime residents of Unga. Lena was the daughter of Fred Pomian, a turn-of-the-century immigrant from Germany, and Harry a 1920s emigrant from California. Martha attended Unga Territorial School and is now living in retirement in Minnesota with her husband, Keith. Marjorie did not survive infancy. Ed.]

OUR NEW RESIDENTS: THE PETERSEN FAMILY

When Allan Petersen was offered the position of Deputy US Marshal at Unga, he gathered his apprehensive family together and asked them to consider the opportunity as an adventure. It was an adventure that was to last for thirteen years. It all began in the spring of 1934 with a telegram from the US Marshal's office in Anchorage asking if Mr. Petersen would be interested in taking over a remote district that stretched from Chignik to King Cove, an area accessible only by sea. His response was immediate and affirmative. Shortly thereafter, he received a second wire instructing him to proceed to Unga on the first available boat to relieve the retiring Mr. Charles Woberg. He arrived in Unga on June 24, 1934.

His wife, Jettie, and his children, Jimmy and Peggy, followed on the August run of the mailboat S. S. *Starr*, arriving on the 14th after a trip that was highlighted by a harrowing grounding in the dark of night off tiny Egg Island, some 60 miles from their destination.

The Petersen family settled into the large three-story Victorian-style house in the center of town and immediately became involved in the activities of the community. Jettie joined the faculty of the Unga Territorial School as primary grades teacher and Peggy (9) and Jimmy (11) enrolled in the fifth and seventh grades, respectively. Mr. Petersen was soon immersed in his duties as the only law enforcer in the 200-mile-long district. He took these responsibilities very seriously and was known to pore over medical books to better serve his district, one that lacked even the most rudimentary professional medical services.

S. S. Starr *hard aground*

As the years passed, the family acquired Laddie, a large black retriever, and Mr. Petersen a small motorboat, the *Ranger*, that

Allan Petersen and Laddie

Jimmy and his catch

allowed him to better serve the adjacent islands. The family chose to remain in Unga throughout the war, Mr. Petersen assuming leadership of the local contingent of the Alaska Territorial Guard, and Mrs. Petersen the role of school principal, while Jimmy served out the duration of the war in the US Navy. A showcase of this period was the "victory garden" that Mr. Petersen maintained and which provided the family with fresh vegetables—a precious commodity when supply lines from the "States" were haphazard at best. Peggy graduated from Unga High School in 1942 and assisted her mother the following year as primary grades teacher. As a result of Unga's post-war decline, the Unga headquarters of the marshal's district

was closed in 1946 and the Petersens resettled in Kenai.

Peggy, the lone survivor of the family, remembers their years at Unga with great fondness. Indeed, she has returned to visit the townsite on several occasions, the last being in 2004. Her childhood home is no longer there—it was razed in 1950—but, as she reminisced in 'I Remember Unga': "If given the chance to return to my childhood years and select the place, without a heartbeat I would say UNGA !"

[Ed. Note: The Petersens' arrival in Unga occurred prior to the publication of the first issue of THE ALASKA PEN, and was inadvertently omitted from that issue's local news. Hopefully, this article corrects that omission.]

❧ 1936 ❧

MISS KOMEDAL VISITS HOMETOWN

Miss Evelyn Komedal, daughter of a well-known merchant and property owner in Unga years ago, returned on the SS *Starr* to her hometown.

Her last visit here was ten years ago when she stayed for the summer.

Miss Komedal first went to the States when she was twelve years old, and some years later her father, Mr. A. Komedal sold his store and other holdings to Sjoberg and Mentzer and moved to Seabold, Washington, their present home.

Miss Komedal is a registered nurse having attended a training school in Seattle. After her graduation, she spent two years at Point Barrow.

She traveled the entire coast of Alaska in her trip to Point Barrow. On her return, she flew to Nenana and came down the Alaska Railroad to Seward, thus seeing from the air, on a train, and from a boat many different sections of Alaska.

Returning to the States, she entered the Seattle Pacific College where she took Christian Workers and Academic subjects for three semesters.

She has spent nearly a year in Valdez acting in the capacity of a missionary nurse. Miss Komedal has stated that she intends to aid in Christian work here and to do any necessary nursing during her stay here.

Unga is fortunate in having Miss Komedal as there has not been a registered nurse here for years and the people of Unga are glad to welcome her. (TAP II, 6, p. 4)

The Komedal Family in 1934

THE WRECK OF THE *EDNA WATTS*

On the morning of July 1, 1936 the town of Unga was awakened by a loud explosion which entirely wrecked the gasboat *Edna Watts*.

Captain Lauritz Pedersen and Harry Brugman both sustained serious burns about the hands and face. Other members of the crew, Alex Calugan and Tom Foster, escaped injury by quickly jumping into the bay.

The large gasboat had been on the beach being scraped and painted in preparation for the fishing season. One of the tanks in the after hold had been leaking and the odor of gasoline was not noticed by any of the crew. Harry Brugman, upon arising, struck a match to light a fire in the galley and immediately found himself enveloped in flames. Captain Pedersen rushed to the aid of the unfortunate man and it did not take long before he too was ablaze.

The fire spread rapidly throughout the boat, reached the gas tanks and then little was left of the *Edna Watts*.

Harry Brugman is at present in the cannery hospital at Squaw Harbor and his condition is serious. Captain Pedersen is on the road to recovery and he and other members of the ill-fated *Edna Watts* have been able to gain employment, fishing on the *Easter* at Squaw Harbor and in that way will not miss out entirely on the fishing season.

[This article was copied verbatim from the Seward Gateway *and is presented here for its historical significance. All crewmembers of the Edna Watts, including Mr. Brugman, recovered from their injuries. The remains of the vessel could be discerned in the middle of the lagoon many years after the unfortunate accident. Ed.]*

POE-MARTIN WEDDING

Mr. G. C. Martin and Miss Frieda Poe, who arrived on the SS *Curacao*, were married at Squaw Harbor on March 22 by Judge F. C. Driffield. They hiked over to Squaw Harbor via Cape Horn, passing the dam that once supplied the [Apollo] mine with water, on the ice. As they rounded the Horn, snow covered hills greeted their eyes, and there in the distance lay the little town of Squaw Harbor where they were going to take their marriage vows. After the simple ceremony, they hiked back the seven miles to Unga.

Mrs. Martin is greatly impressed with the beauty of the island. We hope that she will enjoy her stay here.

Everyone joins in wishing the couple happiness.
(TAP II, 8, p. 4)

[Glenn Martin accepted a teaching position at Unga in September 1935. In addition to his teaching obligations, Mr. Martin served as scoutmaster of the newly-founded but short-lived Boy Scout troop. The newlyweds left Unga at the end of the 1935-36 school year. Ed.]

BERNTSEN-HANSEN WEDDING

APRIL 18—Judge F. C. Driffield, US Commissioner, arrived from Squaw Harbor to join Mr. Carl Hansen and Miss Irene Berntsen in wedlock. Miss Berntsen is the daughter of Mr. and Mrs. John Berntsen, Sr. Mr. Carl Hansen has made his home here for the last six years. The wedding ceremony took place at the home of Mrs. Angelo Damalt, with relatives of the bride and groom attending.

Later in the evening a wedding dance was held at the Public Hall and refreshments were served at Mrs. Damalt's home.

Friends join in wishing the newlyweds much happiness.

(TAP II, 9, p. 5)

CLUBS FORMED

The town women organized the Unga Women's Club this fall. The officers elected were: Mrs. Edward F. Casey, president, Mrs. Lena Lauritzen, vice-president and Mrs. John Evets, secretary-treasurer....   (TAP III, 1, p. 6)

[A Girl Scout troop was also organized, but this historical event somehow failed to make a headline in THE ALASKA PEN. Its colorful history was not lost, however. The histories of both organizations are presented in separate essays elsewhere in this publication. Ed.]

❧ 1937 ❧
FORMER HIGH SCHOOL STUDENT WEDS

Miss Frances Pearson, who was formerly a student of the Unga High School, was married on April thirteenth to Norman Larsen.

The student body of the Unga High School wishes to congratulate Mr. and Mrs. Norman Larsen. We hope that they will celebrate their fiftieth anniversary.   (TAP III, 8, p. 8)

KNUTSEN-LAURITZEN WEDDING

Miss Alice Sophia Knutsen of Kupreanof Harbor, daughter of Mr. and Mrs. Knut Knutsen, married Mr. Arthur Hjalmar Lauritzen of Unga on August 21, 1937.

The Knutsen-Lauritzen wedding party

The ceremony was conducted at the home of Mr. and Mrs. Hjalmar Lauritzen at 3:30PM by US Commissioner Fred C. Driffield. Mrs. Edward F. Casey was matron of honor and Edward Holtness of Cordova, cousin of the bride, was best man. Many guests were present. A wedding dinner was served at six o'clock to about thirty guests. In the evening the public was invited to a wedding dance. The Squaw Harbor crew was invited over. The cannery orchestra played for the dance. Refreshments were served to everyone. The jolly party lasted until four o'clock next morning.

The teachers and students of the Unga High School wish Mr. and Mrs. Arthur Lauritzen all the joy possible in their married life.

R. G. (Reynold Gilbert, Society Editor)
(TAP IV, 1, p. 3)

[Alice was a prime mover in the initiation of this history project and reviewed some of our early writings for historical accuracy. Both Alice and Arthur were born and raised in Unga, and although they and daughter, Arlene, left the islands early in their lives, Alice retained many ties with Unga and its inhabitants. Late in life, she returned twice to Unga, her last visit occurring in 1997 when she was 82 years old. Alice died at home in Mukilteo, Washington, in 2004. Ed.]

THE APOLLO MINE

The Apollo Mine in past years has been a very progressive mine, and when it was shut down there were many people in town and people from out of town who were out of work.

The Apollo Mine, ca. 1900

Last spring, Mr. (Frank) Brown came up from "outside" with a couple of men and did some repairing. While they were repairing, they employed several of the town men. Most of them liked the work and they all have the hope that it will re-open and be successful.

This past summer, there were a couple of mining engineers up there who looked over the mine.

These men who were working and those who were looking the mine over have left, and only Mr. Brown is up at the mine.

If the mine does re-open, it would be a great benefit to Unga. Many more people would be building their homes here and we would probably get better mail service than our present system.

(TAP IV, 2, p. 4)

[Mr. Frank Brown died in the late '30s— before his dream of re-opening his beloved mine was realized. In the years since, a number of explorations were conducted, but none resulted in further commercial mining. A historical review of the Apollo Mine is presented in Part III. Ed.]

WEDDINGS

A double wedding was held at Squaw Harbor on the 18th of October. Those who were married were Albert Krone, son of Mr. and Mrs. Fred Krone, to Miss Olga Foster, daughter of Mrs. John Foster. Ivar Wallin and Miss Luba Osbekoff of Chignik were also married. After the newlyweds returned from Squaw Harbor, a dinner was given by Mr. and Mrs. Fred Krone at their home. A dance was held in the evening. The students and teachers of the Unga High School wish both couples all the happiness attainable.

The other marriages that have occurred during the past months have been Mrs. Esther Hansen to Raymond Rodgers and Mrs. Dolly Woberg to Harry Foster. [THE ALASKA PEN reports on September 17th that] Mr. Raymond Rodgers and Mrs. Esther Hansen were married and left for a deer hunt... [and on October 4th, THE PEN reports that] Mr. Harry Foster took Dolly Woberg for his wife. (TAP IV, 2, p. 6)

BLUE FOX WRECKED

Word came that the *Blue Fox* had been wrecked on Koggion Point last week. It was said that the helmsman got off his course because of thick falling snow. One of the men that was on it said that the boat hit the beach going full speed ahead and pushed a big hole in the starboard side which caused the boat to go down in 10 minutes. The men on the boat were fortunate enough to get off without being drowned and being unfortunate also because of having to row all the way to Sand Point. A few days after the disaster, some men went over to the *Blue Fox* with empty gas drums to put in it in order to float it and tow it to Sand Point. We hope the owner is fortunate enough to save a lot of it. (TAP IV, 4, p. 4)

The Blue Fox *in Seattle, ca. 1935*

[The Blue Fox *was owned by Ralph Grosvold of Sand Point. Attempts to salvage the boat were unsuccessful. Ed.]*

NURSE FOR UNGA

Mrs. Laura Elkins, a public health nurse, arrived on the *Starr*. She was sent from the Public Health Office in Juneau... (TAP IV, 4, p. 5)

[Mrs. Elkins' visit is discussed in greater detail in the Women's Club essay, in Part II. Ed.]

❦ 1938 ❦

UNGA COMMUNITY LIBRARY

The Unga Community Library is the most recent institution of community improvement organized in our town... (TAP IV, 5, p. 4)

[A comprehensive history of the Unga Community Library is presented elsewhere in this publication. Ed.]

GALOVIN-NELSON WEDDING

On the tenth of March, Mr. Alex Nelson and Mrs. Margaret Galovin, daughter of Mr. and Mrs. Fred Krone, were married in Squaw Harbor. After the wedding ceremony, they went to Sand Point and remained until the 16th of March. The student body of the Unga High School wishes to congratulate Mr. and Mrs. Nelson and wish them many happy years together. (TAP IV, 7, p. 5)

CODFISHING

On April third, eleven codfish dories reported a catch of approximately one thousand fish. High boat was one hundred and ten. (TAP IV, 7, p. 8)

REVENUE CUTTER VISITS

Fine weather on May 4th brought the revenue cutter *J. C. Spencer* in port. Doctors and dentists were ashore. Quite a few teeth were pulled. The doctors went to the homes where colds were worst. Two cases of flu were reported. (TAP IV, 8/9, p. 6)

DR. TORBET VISITS

[The September 1938 visit of Dr. Torbet is discussed in detail in the essay "Unga: Methodism's Fragile Foothold in Alaska" in Part II.]

THE CATTLE???

Yes sir! The cattle! Especially the bull! When he came to town he came all by his lonesome but, believe you me, it wasn't long before he had plenty of company. He could do nothing but run, for the mob of children that were behind would scare almost anything. Most of the children had never seen a bull before! Then when the cow came to town it was almost too bad for her. Can you imagine why? It was the first time the children had ever seen a cow. At the present time, the animals are living quite peaceably in the town. (TAP V, 1, p. 4)

SOMETHING NEW (CARLSON-GRONHOLDT WEDDING)

Yes sir! Something new! Mr. Norris had his first experience performing a marriage ceremony. He deemed it an honor and a privilege to be able to join in holy matrimony the young couple...Miss Clara Christine Carlson of Sanak, Alaska and Mr. Peter Gronholdt of Sand Point, Alaska. Everyone wishes them lots of happiness.

DAMALT-COWDEN WEDDING

Rev. R. J. Welsh, our new minister, has also had his first experience in joining a couple in holy matrimony. They were Marie Ruby Damalt and Frank George Cowden, both of Nelson Lagoon, Alaska. Good cheer and good luck is our wish for their happy future.

TOWN'S GROWING

The town is getting bigger every year. Raymond Rodgers is building a house. It will be finished this winter.

Conrad Lauritzen has built a chicken house for his chickens to live in this winter. The chickens have already moved in and they seem to like their new home.   (TAP V, 1, p. 5)

DENTIST HERE

Dr. (Robert D.) Livie has been in Unga for some time now. He has been extracting teeth, putting in new fillings, new plates and what not. Unless there is more dental work to keep him here, he will be leaving on the October *Fern*.

(TAP V, 1, p. 7)

[Dr. Livie's dental practice was located in Valdez, Alaska. Ed.]

PLETNIKOFF-MATHIEWS WEDDING

On October 14th, Mr. Alex Mathiews and Mrs. Doris Pletnikoff from Sand Point arrived to be married. They started over and had to land at Kelly's Rock and hike over from there. They said it was an enjoyable trip, but it seems they didn't like Unga, for right after the ceremony they went back to Sand Point.   (TAP V, 2, p. 5)

MURPHY-SHANGIN WEDDING

Tim E. Shangin from Perryville brought Tootsie Lena Murphy from Kanatak on the M. S. *Fern* to get married. When Tim arrived he had on a big ten-gallon hat. We didn't know why he wore it, so we decided they wore them in Perryville. After the commissioner married them, they went to Sand Point to spend their honeymoon.

(TAP V, 2, p. 5)

THE *HAMILTON* ARRIVES

On Monday, when nobody expected any boat to be in, the US Coast Guard Cutter *Hamilton* arrived.

It was about two o'clock when it came in. Who should be on board but Mr. Anthony Dimond. When he came ashore, he came up to the school and when he entered the High School room, the first thing he said was, "The room is altogether too small."

Mr. Dimond plans on visiting all the westward towns.

We were very pleased to have him visit Unga.

(TAP V, 2, p. 5)

[At the time of his visit, Mr. Dimond was Alaska's delegate to the US Congress. Hs visit and comments regarding the cramped quarters undoubtedly played a role in the authorization and building of a new school in Unga just a year later. Ed.]

TREE PLANTING

We have been celebrating the 150th anniversary of the Constitution by planting trees, which have been sent here by Mrs. Curtis of Seldovia, Alaska.

The Women's Club have sesquicentennial tree markers which were placed on the trees.

The Girl Scouts sang two songs, "America the Beautiful" and "The Star Spangled Banner".

The trees—two cottonwood and three spruce—have been planted near the center of town. Rev. R. Welsh and Mr. Allan L. Petersen helped with the planting.   (TAP V, 2, pp. 5 & 6)

EARTHQUAKES

First a rumble, then a good shake, which lasted long enough to remind folks of the good shakings they used to get when they were youngsters. This came on the tenth of November at about ten o'clock in the morning when all the children were in school.

It seemed that the High School students were more excited than any of the Primary children. Aren't we ashamed?

When the desks began to rock to and fro, all of the children looked at the teacher—wonderingly. The teacher gasped and said, "Earthquake!" Several of the High School students began to run for the door, but the teacher asked that they walk out quietly. There were quite a few pale-faced folks walking out slowly. Some of them were frightened speechless. Regardless of all this, everyone got out of doors where they stood and waited for the quake to stop.

While we were outside, we noticed that across the bay there was a great falling of rocks, but it really sounded like thunder to some.

It seemed that not only school students were frightened, but many of the parents at home were worried as to whether it would last very long or if it would do any damage.

Since this first shake on the tenth of November, we have had quite a few. It seemed that every day or so we got a little shake.

There is said to be an Italian scientist in Europe who has predicted that there were to be many earthquakes during the month of November. We are all hoping that the quaking is almost over because we don't particularly like it at all.

(TAP V, 3, p. 2)

GYMNASIUM OPENS

The Unga Gymnasium, which is the recently-renovated old pool hall, was opened for games, Tuesday, December 13th.

Many of the men in town generously gave their time and much appreciated hard work to the needed repairs on the building.

The membership fees are small and entitle the members to play with any gymnasium equipment for six months. The only purpose of collecting money at all is to buy new materials and games.

There is a class with instructor to include everyone in town. Come out and play with us and watch your waistline grow slim!   (TAP V, 4, p. 5)

[The gymnasium was a great but short-term happening. The building was converted in 1939 into the Unga Methodist Church. Ed.]

❧ 1939 ❧

MOVIES

Most of the people in Unga were found spending all the evenings down at the gymnasium where the talking movies were featured. It has been many years since the people of Unga have had a chance to see movies. Everyone seems to be making up for lost time now.

The movies were directed by Mr. W. E. Goss, who travels from place to place showing pictures. The admission was fifty cents for children and a dollar for adults. At first many objected to the price but, after going the first time, they couldn't help going the next three nights.

Mr. Goss was here for four days and each night he showed a different picture. The main feature for the first night was "The Man Who Was Called Back". The second night it was "Aloha". The third night it was "Black King". The fourth night it was Slim Summerville in "Troopers Three". They were all greatly enjoyed by all and it seems everyone wants to see more from the conversations at school.   (TAP V, 8, p. 6)

[Following are excerpts of student comments regarding Mr. Goss and his movies. The remarks were made in response to an article written by Mr. Goss following his visit to Unga. Ed.]

WHAT WE THINK OF THE MOVIE MAN GOSS

...We have seen an article in a paper which Goss wrote and he said that at Unga he had to let dogs in the theatre... He also said that he was sometimes paid with furs, ivory and sometimes with smoked salmon. We in Unga never paid him with stuff like that. We know what money is just as well as anyone else...   NL (Norman Lauritzen)

...I guess he's ashamed of himself charging so much for rotten shows so he went out further and said that people brought dogs and gave him smoked salmon and ivory to pay for their tickets. In fact, no one had any salmon that time of year... There are about 5 dogs in town and he may call us people dogs who were good enough to pay...to see his shows... He took us for dumb, I guess. But we'll make him dumb when he sees how untruthful he is and not only he will see it but many others...   IC (Isabel Calugan)

...People who went to see the shows all paid money and didn't bring one single dog along with them. Besides, most of the people here haven't any dogs. That's just Goss' imagination...
AF (Alma Foster)

...We all came the first night and there wasn't much to see because the old machine kept breaking down and it wasn't much to see after all.
PC (Peter Calugan)

...He made enough money on the two bit shows and went out of Unga about $350.00 richer for showing four shows ten or fifteen years old.
NL (Norman Lauritzen)
(TAP VI, 2, pp. 4-6)
[Mr. Goss never returned to Unga! Ed.]

DOUBLE WEDDING

On September 27th, two young couples from Chignik were married by the US Commissioner.

Miss Minnie Wallin and Mr. William Matthews with Miss Stella Brun and Mr. Edward Wallin took their wedding vows at 9 o'clock in the evening at the home of Mr. and Mrs. D. W. Norris.

Everyone wishes them the best of luck and happiness for their future.   (TAP VI, 1, p. 4)

LUDVICK-OSTERBACK WEDDING

The *Falcon* came in today (November 8th) bringing a lot of folks from Sand Point to attend the wedding of Margaret Ludvick and Alvin Osterback. Lots of luck, Margaret and Alvin.
(TAP VI, 3, p. 3)

TO EKLUTNA

This is the first year that any of our students have had a chance to go to Eklutna. Peter and Isabel Calugan and Billy Berntsen were the ones who received the opportunity to go to such a fine school. We all wish them good luck and hope that they will show the people of Eklutna that the students from Unga can really do things.
(TAP VI, 3, p. 6)

UNGA'S VISITORS

Unga enjoyed spending Christmas holidays with her visitors from the neighboring communities. She invites them to visit her more often.

The people who came from Sand Point to spend Christmas holidays were: Mr. and Mrs. R. Garlow, Mrs. Fritz Bjornstad, Miss Pauline Gunderson, George, Paul and Andrew Gronholdt, Johnnie Gunderson and Agnes Endresen.

The people who came from Squaw Harbor to spend Christmas holdiays were: Mr. and Mrs. Martin Gilbert, Mr. and Mrs. Charles Christiansen, Mr. Peter Harris, Mr. Peter Gilbert and daughter, Emma, Eddie and George Gilbert, Betty Jacobsen, Esther, Ada and Reynold Gilbert. We hope they all had a good time.   (TAP VI, 4, p. 3)

CODFISHING

Codfishing dories riding at anchor, Delarof Harbor, Alaska, 1930s

Codfishing is almost a thing of the past. Yet once it was the main industry of the Shumagin Islands. Perhaps it might interest people to know a little of this "lost industry."

The first record of commercial codfishing dates back to 1863—that is on the Pacific coast. This fishing was done in the Okhotsk Sea by the brigantine *Timandra* from California. In 1865 the schooner *Porpoise* sailed from California to fish in the Shumagin Banks. This was the first fare of codfish from the Shumagin Islands, a locality since famous in the annals of the Pacific codfishery. From 1865 to 1920 codfishing was the main industry of Unga.

At first the fishing was done in dories, which after a haul would return to a schooner nearby. This schooner was used as a saltery and carrier for both the fish and the dories. When their season's catch had been made, they would return to their home port. In the early seventies, a shore station with nine men was established at Pirate Cove, which is about 18 miles from Unga. This station was the pioneer codfish station of Alaska. Many of these stations were established as time went on, due to the fact that it was found advantageous both for the fishermen and the companies. In 1915 there were about 20 of these shore stations in the vicinity of Unga; about 8 were situated on Unga

Island. Most of these stations were owned by large concerns in San Francisco. At times, as many as forty men were employed at the larger stations. A few independent stations were established by local people. At the present time there are about 8 of these small stations operating on Unga Island—the large companies have gone a long time ago.

Some of you may not know a lot about codfish and how they are caught, so I'll try and give you some idea about this fish of the past, (but which is coming into its own again).

The fishermen set out for the grounds or banks early in the morning in small power dories and upon reaching their favorite spot or fishing hole, drop their anchor. Each dory had two sets of cod lines, each line had two hooks. One set of lines is dropped from each side of the dory for about 60 fathoms. Each one of the hooks is baited, and lucky is the fisherman who can haul up the fish, "pair by pair". As soon as the fish reach the gunwales of the boat they are cut at the throat. This throating causes the fish to bleed in order that the meat remains white after curing.

As soon as the fisherman gets his day's catch, which averages around 200, he sets out for his shore station, where after a quick meal, he must "dress" his fish. The dressing operation consists

The Knut Knutsen saltery, Delarof Harbor

the process of canning codfish has been perfected, the average housewife will find it easier to prepare. Codfish is rich in food value and makes a delicious dish whether fried, boiled, creamed or made into fish balls.

Why, if this fish is so good and was so plentiful at one time, has it lost its popularity? Salmon was taking its place, inasmuch as salmon is easily canned and easily prepared for a meal. Salmon, in a way, is also to blame for the diminishing for codfishing, due in

of heading and splitting the fish, the removal of the backbone. The fish are then placed meat side up in large tanks and partly covered with rock salt. After a period of 24 to 48 hours the fish produce a brine pickle and after five to seven days are completely cured and ready for shipment to the market. Codfish vary in size, running from 40 to 11 or less pounds and are from 43 to 26 inches in length, anything smaller is called a "snapper" and generally not used for market purpose, but are excellent for home use.

Often before the codfish are headed, the tongues are taken out. The tongues are cured in the same manner as the fish itself. They are put up in small kits. Codfish tongues are delicious, having a taste similar to oysters, when fried.

Codfish is salted, frozen or dried, the dried fish being known as "stock-fish". Codfish in the salted or dried form required considerable time in preparing, inasmuch as it had to be soaked in water for some time. Now that

On the Shumagin Banks fishing grounds

A codfish haul, Gus Sjoberg Saltery

The above article on codfishing was written about ten years ago by Mrs. Edward F. Casey and is now published for the informational value that it may hold for those unacquainted with the industry, and may it bring back memory to those that witnessed the Golden Age of Unga.

(TAP XI, 9, p. 8, May 1947)

[The shore-station codfishing industry in Unga was controlled largely by two companies: the Alaska Codfish Company, which was located on the village side of Delarof Harbor, and across the harbor, the Union Fish Company, both of San Francisco. Although the Union Fish Company ran the majority of stations in the Shumagins, including the Pirate Cove saltery on Popof Island, the first shore station in Alaska, its Unga operation was dwarfed by the Alaska Codfish Company. The 1920 US Government Census reports 98 "residents" in the Alaska Codfish Company bunkhouse, versus 18 in the Union Fish Company's bunkhouse.

Unga's two retail merchants were closely associated with the codfish industry - Gustav E. Sjoberg with Alaska and Hjalmar Lauritzen with Union. (Sjoberg was the father of Viola Casey, the author of the above ALASKA PEN article.) Both gentlemen operated their respective salteries after the parent companies divested interest in the operations and continued to provide codfish products into the early 1940s. Despite the long-held hope that a resurgence would occur, codfishing in the Shumagins languished through the '40s, as salmon fishing flourished. It wasn't until the 1980s that commercial codfishing resumed, and it thrives today. Ed.]

Cutting codfish tongues, 1934
Reynold Gilbert and Clara Pearson

part to the large number of codfish caught each year in the many salmon traps and destroyed, and the fact that ofttimes the gurry or offal from the salmon canneries finds its way out to the feeding grounds of the codfish, which either destroys them or makes them inedible.

The people here at Unga, where codfishing is one of their means of livelihood, hope that someday, codfish will make a "comeback" and we all hope it won't be in the too far future.

Alaska Codfish Company shore station at Unga, early 1900s

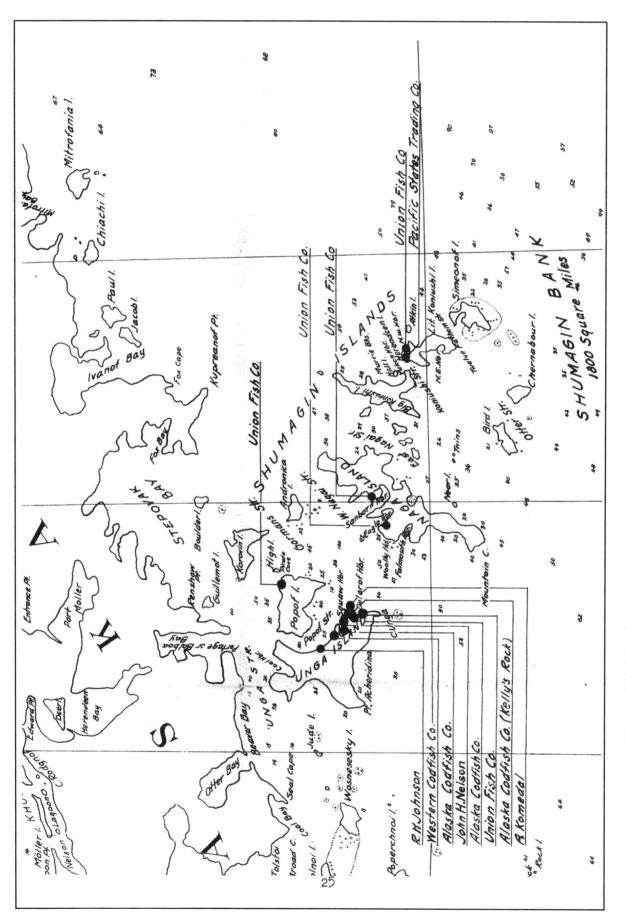

Shumagin Island Shore Stations in 1916 (From Pacific Cod Fisheries, Bureau of Fisheries Document No. 830, GPO 1916)

COMMUNITY ORGANIZATIONS AND ACTIVITIES

Growing up in Unga in the 1930s, one had a variety of extracurricular activities from which to choose, to while away the long months of winter. The Unga Community Sunday School, under the direction of Mrs. Anna T. Lauritzen, provided religious instruction throughout much of the '30s. This service in later years was supplemented by the Epworth League, a Methodist youth organization, and finally by the Methodist Youth Fellowship. Several sewing clubs were active during this period, including the Small Girls' Sewing Club, the Junior Girls' Sewing Club, and the Women's Sewing Club, all sponsored by the women of the community and led largely by Mrs. Zenia Rodgers. Other organizations that came and went during the course of the decade were the Young People's Society, the Boy Scouts, and the Unga Improvement Club. In the end, three organizations outlasted the '30s and continued through much of the '40s and, with the Unga Methodist Church, became centers of community involvement during this period.

The girls' sewing clubs were the precursors of Unga Girl Scout Troop No. 1, which gained national recognition soon after it organized in September of 1935. Similarly, the Women's Sewing Club evolved into the Unga Women's Club in 1936 and affiliated with the National Federation of Women's Clubs shortly thereafter. The third organization—the Unga Community Library—was initiated by the Unga Women's Club in 1938, thrived through the '40s and was the last organization to serve the community in the '50s until the community itself ceased to exist.

While the Girl Scouts groomed the young ladies of the village for responsible adulthood and the library offered everyone a window to the world, the Women's Club served as the conscience of the village, using its considerable clout to influence decisions regarding the town's well-being. Finally, the Unga Methodist Church, the only active religious organization in the area, served the spiritual needs of the villagers. Although the Russian Orthodox Church offered only sporadic priestly services to the predominantly Orthodox villagers, the church's lay leaders were a continuous presence and, in conducting services on specific occasions, assured the continuity of Orthodoxy in the lives of the faithful. All of these organizations functioned in a cooperative manner with each other and with the Unga Territorial School.

The histories of each of these several organizations are presented in essays elsewhere in this publication: the Girl Scout and Russian Orthodox stories in Part I, the Women's Club and Methodist stories in Part II, and a review of the Unga Community Library in Part III.

SCHOOL NEWS

Unga Territorial School 1930-1940

The Unga Territorial School in 1930 was housed in an imposing three-level building that sat atop a hill overlooking the village. In the short modern history of Unga, this is the second school building to have occupied this site, the first having been a single-story structure built before the turn of the 20th century. Built in the late teens or early '20s to accommodate a growing student body, the structure contained a manual training facility and a coal-fired furnace at ground level, two large classrooms on the main floor, and living quarters for teachers on the top floor. Access to the upper levels was provided by a broad external staircase, a covered porch and double doors leading into a central hallway. An interior staircase from the hall led to the third floor. The hallway extended through the building to an exit at the rear. Each of the two classrooms, entered from the hallway, contained five tall windows on the side and three on the front to provide illumination, there being no electricity in the building. Gasoline lanterns were used for evening functions. Like most of the dwellings in Unga, the school contained no indoor plumbing. A privy at the rear of the building provided the necessary facilities.

<hr />

Since its inception early in the 20th century, the Unga Territorial School offered eight grades of elementary education. In 1930, Mr. and Mrs. William Brown, teaching their second year at Unga, welcomed 40 students into the school. Mr. and Mrs. C. W. Graham replaced the Browns in 1931 and were assisted in 1932-34 by Miss Lena Yarnell (the future Mrs. A. E. Reeve). Little information is available for this four-year period, it having preceded the publishing of a school paper. The Grahams were succeded in 1934 by Mr. and Mrs. Leroy J. Maas and Miss Yarnell by Miss Ernestine Brass and Mrs. Allan Petersen.

The Unga Territorial School student body, 1929-30, William Brown, Principal

The first graduates of Unga High School, Elizabeth Rodgers (L) and Marie Gronholdt

The 1934-35 school year was a milestone in the history of the Unga Territorial School system, for it heralded the inauguration of a four-year high school curriculum and, with it, the student publication, THE ALASKA PEN. It is unclear what prompted the establishment of a high school in Unga, although the fact that at least ten students were to be graduated from the eighth grade in 1934 may have been a principal factor. Also, community support for a high school was strong, as evidenced by the success of local civic functions to raise money for the school. (See for example, TAP I, 1, p. 3 in the appendix.) Of course, the willingness of the teachers to assume a larger role and the support and concurrence of the Alaska Commissioner of Education, Mr. A. E. Karnes, cannot be overlooked. In the final analysis, the Unga High School began its historic first year with an enrollment of 14 students: ten in grade 9, three in grade 10, and Elizabeth Rodgers, who became editor-in-chief of THE ALASKA PEN, in grade 11.

When Mr. and Mrs. Maas arrived in Unga, they brought with them all the equipment necessary to produce a school paper: a typewriter with an 18-inch carriage, a state-of-the-art mimeograph, and the auxiliary gear for cutting stencils. Hardly had the school year begun before the high school student body embarked on an ambitious program to print and publish a monthly newsletter—one that would continue virtually unchanged in appearance and scope for as long as the Unga High School existed. Thus was born THE ALASKA PEN: a vehicle for expounding not only on activities at school but on daily happenings in the village and the greater Shumagin area. To emphasize the uniqueness of this endeavor, THE ALASKA PEN being the only periodical published in the entire Alaska Peninsula-Aleutians region, we have here reprinted in its entirety the first issue of THE ALASKA PEN, published within a month of the inauguration of the Unga High School. (See Page 209.)

The Maas' tenure was foreshortened in its second year, and Mr. and Mrs. J. Gerald Williams arrived to complete the remainder of the 1935-36 school year and the subsequent year. Mr. Williams' tenure was highlighted by the graduation of the first students from Unga High School: Elizabeth Rodgers and Marie Gronholdt, in May, 1936 and John Nelson and Thomas Lauritzen the following May. Elizabeth, John, and Thomas hailed from Unga and Marie from Sand Point.

Mrs. Petersen continued to teach the primary grades with the assistance, initially, of Miss Brass and Mr. Glen Martin, who also taught music to upper classmen. But after the 1935-36 year, Mrs. Petersen was the sole teacher of grades 1 through 4 and would remain so throughout the last of the '30s and the beginning of the '40s.

Mr. and Mrs. Dwain W. Norris replaced the Williamses in 1937 and continued in that capacity until 1941, a tenure that earned them the accolade of serving Unga High School the longest. However, that distinction was clouded by the fact that the high school graduated no students during those four years. Thus, the promise of a vibrant high school student body based upon the undergraduate population in 1934 failed to materialize: of the 18 students enrolled in grades 6 through 9 in that year, none choose to graduate from Unga High School.

As the decade neared its end, an ambitious movement was begun to seek support for a new school, one of the reasons being a lack of adequate space in the existing facility for a growing high school student body, the dwindling number of potential graduates notwithstanding. The movement was ultimately successful and ground was broken in April of 1940 for a new school, to be located at the foot of Violet Hill, a site at the north end of the village that, it was hoped, would protect the facility from the vicious southeast gales that plagued the old building. The 1939-40 school year was thus the swan song for the venerable school on the hill. The building was ultimately sold and razed, and the lumber recycled into a newly constructed house in Sand Point.

Unga Village, ca. 1935

OUR SCHOOL

I am telling you about our school. The name of our school is the Unga Territorial School. We have three rooms and three teachers in our school. Mrs. Petersen teaches the Primary, Mrs. Norris teaches the Upper Grades and Mr. Norris teaches the High School. Mr. Norris is the principal. There are 23 pupils in the Primary Room, 18 in the Upper Grades and 11 in the High School. Our school house is old. We hope to have a new school house next year. There is a furnace down in the basement to heat the rooms. On our school ground there is a slide, see-saw, giant stride and a jumping bar. We celebrate many holidays in our school. We celebrate Christmas. Everybody comes to the Christmas program. We have a Christmas tree and presents. Yesterday we had a Halloween party. We always have a Valentine Box. Every month we have an assembly. Each room tries to win the Honor Room pennant for best attendance. We have 9 months of school. School starts at nine o'clock in the morning and is out at 3:30 in the afternoon.

[This article was written by fourth grader Mary Galovin, and was printed in Unga Newsletter, dated November 1, 1938. Ed.]

Mrs. Petersen's honor room

UNGA TROOP NO. 1:
THE GIRL SCOUT STORY

The First Investiture
Back row: Mmes. Jettie Petersen, Mary Sharpe, Irene Cushing, Bertha Siemion, Esther Hansen, Zenia Rodgers, Anna T. Lauritzen, Cecilia Foster, Annie Gilbert, and Sarah Haaf. Front row: Elizabeth Rodgers, Esther Gilbert, Margaret Berntsen, Emily Rodgers, Pearl McCallum, Peggy Petersen, Florence Cushing, Alma Foster, and Ruby Cushing

The dream of girl scouting in Unga was conceived during a meeting of a group of girls and Mrs. Allan Petersen on June 30, 1935. Shortly thereafter, the group sought and gained recognition as Unga Girl Scout Troop No. 1 by the national organization, Girl Scouts of America. This entitled them to wear the well-recognized green uniforms of the club. Thus, one of the first functions of the troop was to seek funds for the purchase of uniforms. THE ALASKA PEN reported the call for support:

> Save your Libby Milk labels and help some Girl Scout obtain scout paraphernalia free of charge. Any scout will appreciate receiving them or will call in person to remove labels from empty or full cans.

> Plan on attending the Bazaar....on October 12th [1935], proceeds of which will go toward purchasing Scout uniforms and other necessities...   (TAP II, 1, p. 3)

> The...bazaar was held at the Public Hall. Admission was 25 and 10 cents. The flowers and embroidery work made by the girls were raffled and auctioned....   (TAP II, 2, p. 12)

> Total receipts of the evening were $75.45. Uniforms for the nine Scouts and two Scout Lieutenants have been ordered, as well as other Scout equipment. A balance of five dollars has been given the Young Girls' Sewing Club, the majority of whom are also Girl Scouts...   (TAP II, 2, p. 3)

The now official Unga Girl Scout Troop No. 1, led by Captain Mrs. Allan Petersen and Lieutenants Elizabeth Rodgers and Mrs. Bertha Siemion, invested the first nine girls in a solemn ceremony on November 22, 1935. The girls included: Margaret Berntsen, Isabel Calugan, Florence Cushing, Ruby Cushing, Alma Foster, Esther Gilbert, Pearl McCallum, Peggy Petersen, and Emily Rodgers. The new uniforms arrived on December 17, 1935, and with them, the troop was formally outfitted. The uniforms were donned each week for the troop's regular meetings and for special community functions.

Unga Girl Scouts Troop No. 1, ca. 1943. From left: Evelyn Foster, Ruth Lauritzen, Ester Cushing, Mary Galovin, Virginia Brandal, Mildred Hansen, Alice Cushing, Ethel Cushing (?), Meryl Hansen, Bertha Berntsen, Nora Berntsen and Carolyn Haaf.

Over the next 12 years, nine additional investiture ceremonies were held: May 9, l936 for Olive Krone, Ada Gilbert, and Betty McCallum; February 4, 1938 for Budilia Rodgers and Thelma Lauritzen; March 10, 1939 for Evelyn Whittaker and Esther Cushing; March 8, 1940 for Mary Galovin, Ruth Lauritzen, and Karen Skulstad; December 20, 1940 for Virginia Brandal and Ruth Olsen; October 28, 1941 for Ethel Cushing and Esther Olsen; October 29, 1943 for Nora Berntsen, Meryl Hansen, Mildred Hansen, Alice Cushing, Bertha Berntsen, and Carolyn Haaf; February 9, 1945 for Martha Hunt; and January 23, 1947 for Jennie Johansen.

Throughout the 13 years of its existence, the girls of Troop No. 1 were heavily involved in village activities, ranging from volunteer work in the Unga Community Library to upkeep of Unga's two cemeteries. They knitted socks and sweaters and quilted during the war years, they honored school graduates with parties, and they were always available to participate in village celebrations.

The primary role of the Girl Scouts, however, was to provide guidance, training, and inspiration to young ladies preparing to enter the adult world. One particular function of scouting is to instill into its members an appreciation for the natural world and, in the local environment, there was much to honor. The Scouts participated in numerous hikes to historical and geological sites surrounding the village. They organized picnics in the summer, gathered berries in the fall, did a bit of trout fishing, and in winter, enjoyed ice skating. Their most anticipated jaunts, however, involved a brisk three-mile hike to a small, sturdily-built structure on the shore of the upper bay. Dubbed "The Little House," this cabin was bequeathed to the troop by long-time Apollo miner, Frank Brown. The scouts assumed ownership of the cabin shortly after Mr. Brown's death in 1939. The cabin had three rooms: one large outer room and two small bedrooms—adequate space to cook spaghetti dinners and to spread sleeping bags on overnight retreats. The girls considered their isolation to be particularly advantageous since they could make as much noise as they wished, singing and dancing to music from a wind-up phonograph. THE ALASKA PEN reported on this important acquisition:

> The latest and most interesting activity this year has been work on a cabin which was donated for camping purposes by Mr. Brown. Many people have been helping us repair and furnish the cabin. A stove was donated by Conrad Lauritzen. Mr. Petersen and some boys from the jail made necessary repairs on windows, doors, and foundation. Other friends have helped in different ways. Mrs. Petersen, our captain, has taken a few of the girls up (at various times) to do some cleaning and painting. On days when it was too stormy to go up to the cabin, we have worked on such things as curtains, rugs, dish towels, and flower pots.

> ...All Girl Scouts are looking forward to many happy times in our "Girl Scout Little House".
>
> (TAP V, 8, p. 6)

The Girl Scout Cabin: "The Little House"

A common thread joining these activities throughout the scouting years was the pursuit and awarding of merit badges. The theme of these various badges encompassed the values of the true American girl. Physical exercises included sports, hiking, camping, and learning to cope under difficult conditions, the latter being particularly important in the isolated environment of Troop No. 1. Thus, learning to tie basic knots, to communicate using the Morse Code, and to practice first aid were considered essential skills. Other badge pursuits were geared toward homemaking and involved cooking and how to serve a proper meal, including table setting and etiquette. In addition, the girls learned to sew, to dress attractively, to practice cleanliness, to acquire social skills, and even how to make a bed correctly. The girls pursued the badge requirements seriously and knew that, in the end, the pins, badges, banners, and certificates were truly earned. The subsequent awards banquets were eagerly anticipated and were highlights of the scouting years.

In May of 1947, scouting in Unga approached a critical crossroad, one that ultimately had a profound effect on the viability of Troop No. 1. THE ALASKA PEN reported:

> During the past year many things have happened of interest [to] the Girl Scouts. Besides Mrs. Petersen, who is the troop leader, there were several assistant leaders. Mrs. Garlow helped the girls in earning badges, particularly those who specialized in the homemaking field. Mrs. Lauritzen gave the girls a wider spread of knowledge in sewing, and Mrs. Casey in knitting. Mrs. Petersen aided the girls in various ways...
>
> The Girl Scouts were organized by Mrs. Petersen in 1935 and have been active for twelve years under her leadership. Even though she is leaving, we hope this organization will be carried on. This will depend largely upon the interest and cooperation of the girls.   (TAP XI, 9, p. 10)

The Unga Girl Scouts did "carry on" for a short time. Although there were no formal investitures reported, the troop did initiate several new members. They included Ann Lauritzen, Joan Cushing, and Nellie and Flossie Brandal. In the end, however, the great exodus of residents in the late '40s reduced the number of members and leaders to such an extent that the activities and responsibilities could no longer be sustained. The last reported meeting occurred on May 7, 1948.

More than fifty years later, memories of scouting years in Unga are precious indeed. Most former scouts can still give the salute, recite the Girl Scout Law, tie a proper bowline or square knot, and remember with great fondness their years as Unga Girl Scouts.

> On my honor I will try: to do my duty to God and my country,
> to help other people at all times, and to obey the Girl Scout Laws.

The Girl Scouts and their new uniforms

Berry picking

Hiking

Volley ball playing

Wood gathering

"A Skating We Will Go."

Ice skating

Some typical activities of Unga Troop No. 1

RUSSIAN ORTHODOXY IN UNGA

Church of the Virgin Mother of Vladimir

Religion has always played a prominent role in the village life in Unga. At the very beginning of the Russian occupation of Alaska, Russian orthodox churches and chapels were established in villages stretching from the western Aleutians to Kodiak and beyond. The native population accepted this western religion eagerly and devoutly. Whether by choice or coercion, this aspect of Russian culture became firmly entrenched in the several communities and continues to the present. The people of Unga and the greater Shumagins were no exception. According to the definitive historical accounts of Black*, a chapel was established in Unga before the turn of the 19th century. As the village grew with the Russian exploits, so also did the chapel. By 1843, it became the Church of the Virgin Mother of Vladimir. The final chapel—the ruins of which exist today—was built in 1874.

Although for much of its active life the Unga church had no resident priest, it was serviced by visiting priests from regional parishes and by lay members of the community. This handicap did not deter members from observing religious holidays and participating in church functions. The principal holidays, of course, were Easter and Christmas, the latter of which was celebrated on the traditional dates corresponding to the Julian calendar. Thus, Christmas was always observed on January 7th. A major part of the Christmas celebration (see sidebar) was the observance of starring, wherein an elaborately decorated multi-pointed star, representing the star that guided the magi to the Christ Child, was carried to all the homes in the village. The star was mounted on a central axis that allowed it to be spun. In the procession, it would normally be carried by a lay person who would twirl the star, marking time to a Russian carol, as it moved through the village. The star was followed by a crowd of

* Lydia T. Black, *The History and Ethnohistory of the Aleutian East Borough*, The Limestone Press, Kingston, Ontario (1999), page 113.

villagers singing carols. The mood was definitely festive. At each house, the star would be carried into the living room and the ceremony repeated in front of the Russian icon lighted by an oil lamp (lampala) that was an integral part of the living room decor of all Orthodox houses. The ceremony was not restricted to those of the Orthodox faith, however. Several of the houses contained no shrines, but the ceremony proceeded nonetheless, generally toward the corner of the living room that would normally have housed the shrine. According to the senior Mr. Flore Lekanof of St. George (Pribilof Islands), in Orthodox houses, the shrine is placed such that the worshipper faces the east when confronting it.

The more somber aspects of the Russian Christmas celebration were followed by a period of masquerading. THE ALASKA PEN describes, in separate articles, the masking ceremony:

> ...This [starring] is kept up for three nights in succession and it is followed by seven nights of masquerading. The latter is the time when the people disguise themselves and try to get rid of Jesus...   (TAP I, 5, p. 2)

> ...Masquerading follows on January 9 and is carried through New Year's Eve, January 13. This masquerading is symbolical of the dress of the wisemen, although the custom has lost its true meaning and has proved to be merely a funfest...   (TAP X, 5, p. 3)

Obviously, the above articles give somewhat conflicting dates during which masquerading is carried out following the procession of the star, but as a general rule, this ceremony occurred in the evenings before Russian New Year. The religious significance of masquerading, or masking, as it was generally called, is also the subject of some uncertainty, as the reports indicate. But what is clear is that masking was a time of great merriment, somewhat akin, as Mr. Lekanof relates, to the carnival atmosphere of a Mardi Gras, the festivities of another Christian culture preceding the observance of Lent. Both starring and masking were eagerly embraced by the entire village and particularly the youngsers, who reveled in creating often outlandish costumes and filling their bellies with the refreshments that greeted them at each door. Russian Christmas thus offered a welcomed break from the gloominess of a Shumagin winter.

For much of the 1930s and 1940s, Mike (Miska) Galovin served as Russian Orthodox lay leader (or reader) in Unga. Miska was scion of one of the major Russian-Aleut families whose lineage can be traced to the early generations of the Chebetnoy family, who populated much of the Shumagins throughout the 19th and early 20th centuries. Miska maintained the church with the help of the community at large, conducted church services and funerals, and led the annual Christmas procession of starring. Mike and Mattie Galovin and their children, George, Mary, and Ray, left Unga in 1946 and settled in Bellingham, Washington. Although Mike never returned to Unga, the church continued to offer inspiration to those who remained, but eventually, the structure collapsed and today lies in ruin. The only Russian Orthodox church that exists in the Shumagins today is the little chapel of St. Nicholas in Sand Point. The chapel was built in the late 1930s and continues to offer religious guidance to area Christians. Nora (Berntsen) Newman, who was born and raised in Unga (and served as editor-in-chief of THE ALASKA PEN in late 1950), currently serves as reader.

Miska guiding the star

St. Nicholas Chapel, Sand Point

RUSSIAN CHRISTMAS -
A Celebration

The Greek Orthodox religion is one of the oldest forms of Christian worship in the world. This religion is quite prevalent in Alaska. Most Alaskan Orthodox churches carry on their services in the Slavonic tongue. However, some churches are breaking away from the tradition since English is spoken in all the communities. In Greece, the native language is used in the church as well as the Russian tongue in Russia.

Every native village along the Alaskan Peninsula has its Orthodox church. Priests visit the churches whenever possible, but in the smaller communities, generally some local individual takes charge of the services.

At this time of the year, it is one of the greatest seasons on the church calendar. January 7 is Christmas Day. At this time, the followers of the church follow the star and visit the many homes in the village. This goes on for three days, or until all the homes are visited.

Every community has its own star patterned after its own design. Some have six, eight, ten, twelve, or even sixteen points. Some are decorated and lighted by electric bulbs, others by candles, and still others by various reflecting ornaments. This star is symbolical of the "Star of the East" and the search of the wise men in quest of the Christ Child. The last or third day, the services in relation to the star are often held in the cemetery.

As the followers of the star go from home to home, they sing songs of glorification, songs of how the Christ was found, and songs relating to the birth of Christ.

Masquerading follows on January 9 and is carried through New Year's Eve, January 13. This masquerading is symbolical of the dress of the wise men, although the custom has lost its true meaning and has proved to be merely a funfest for the many communities.

At midnight on January 13, the faithful hold services in their homes and thank God for the successful past year and pray for divine guidance for the new year.

On January 18, holy water is sprinkled in the homes after the two o'clock service. January 19 represents the baptism of Christ. (TAP X, 5, pp. 2-3)

CROSSINGS

Crossing the Bar

Sunset and evening star,
  And one clear call for me,
And may there be no moaning of the bar,
  When I put out to sea.

But such a tide as moving seems asleep,
  Too full for sound and foam,
When that which drew form out of the boundless deep,
  Turns again home...

1934

HAROLD LAURITZEN

The funeral of the late Harold Lauritzen, who lost his life at sea October 8, was held Tuesday, October 23, at 3:30 P.M., his body having been found early that morning.

Harold was a local young man, son of Mr. and Mrs. Hjalmar Lauritzen, Unga merchants. He had spent the greater part of his life in Unga where he was in business with his father and brothers.

Harold was loving and loyal to his parents. He made many friends, as he was sincerely liked for his kindly and generous attitude toward all. These friends share in the bereavement, and wish to extend the greatest sympathy to those dear ones whom he left behind.   (TAP I, 2, p. 9)

JOHN FOSTER

Mr. John Foster, aged 45 years, a long time resident of Unga, passed away suddenly on November 19 after a short period of illness.

Mr. Foster was born in Unga in 1889 and spent a few years at school in Carlysle, Philadelphia, Pennsylvania.

He is survived by his widow, Mrs. Cecilia Foster, and eight children; his mother, Mrs. Richard; and four brothers, Nick of Seattle, William and Charles, of Philadelphia, and Tom, of Unga.

Mr. Foster was devoted to his family and was very helpful toward his neighbors. He will be greatly missed by all.   (TAP I, 3, p. 8)

Harold Lauritzen

John Foster, Sr.

1935

FRANK FUKUSHIMO

Frank Fukushimo passed away quietly at his home across the bay. Mr. Fukushimo, who has spent the last few years of his life here, had been ill for some time.

February 1—the funeral of the late Frank Fukushimo was held at 3:30 PM. Hymns were sung at the cemetery and Deputy US Marshal, A. L. Petersen read a parting prayer.   (TAP I, 6, p. 9)

EARNEST JOHNSON

Earnest Johnson, aged sixty years, passed away quite suddenly during the night at his home. Mr. Johnson was born in Sweden and came to this country about forty years ago. He served in the U. S. Navy and enlisted in the Spanish-American War. He has been in Alaska about twenty years, making a living codfishing and salmon fishing. During his stay in Unga, he has been employed as a storekeeper at E. F. Casey's General Store. He is survived by two sisters who live in Sweden.

(TAP II, 3, p. 6)

CHARLES WOBERG

December 6th—The U. S. Coast Guard Cutter *Haida* made a flying trip from Cordova coming to the aid of Mr. Charles Woberg, who has failed to recover since his arrival on the SS *Starr* from Golia Island. He was taken to the Seward General Hospital, where all are hoping he can find relief from his suffering.

December 14th—News came over radio station KFQD at Anchorage that Mr. Charles Woberg had passed away at the Seward General Hospital. The bereaved family has our sympathy.

(TAP II, 4, p. 8)

1936

NICK PALUTOF

February 7th—The MS *Blue Fox* arrived in port with the body of Mr. Nick Palutof, who had been found dead on the beach near his cabin. Mr. Palutof had been trapping alone at Eagle Harbor, the only companion being a dog that he had taken along with him. Several weeks ago, Mr. Louis Berntsen went down to bring him home

but could not find any trace of him. Two weeks of storm prevented further investigations until a day ago when Deputy Allan Petersen went to Eagle Harbor on the *Blue Fox*.

Mr. Palutof was fifty-nine years of age and was born on Korovin Island. He is survived by a sister, Mrs. Hansen of Squaw Harbor, and a son, Jimmy Palutof.   (TAP II, 6, p. 12)

1937

ROBERT GALOVIN

Mr. Robert Galovin passed away at his home on the morning of March 6th, after a long period of illness.

Robert Galovin, Sr.

Mr. Galovin was born in Unga and has lived in and around this district most of his life.

He was engaged in fishing, both cod and salmon, and in trapping.

He is survived by his wife, the former Miss Margaret Krone; his two sons, Robert, Jr., aged 6, and Clarence, aged 2; his mother Mrs. A. Lindquist and his brother, Mr. Mike Galovin. All reside in Unga.

Funeral services were conducted by Miss Elna Bard at the family home. The services were attended by all the citizens of Unga. School was dismissed during the services and the funeral.

Robert was well liked by all and is very much missed by his friends and relatives. May He Rest In Peace.   (TAP III, 7, p. 3)

1938

CHRISTINE CUSHING

Miss Christine Cushing passed away at her parents' home on March 13th, after two years illness.

Miss Cushing was born in Unga and was very much liked by her friends in the school and community. We all join in mourning with the Cushing family. May She Rest In Peace.   (TAP IV, 7, p. 6)

JOHN OLGIN

On Sunday morning, May 1st, at 5 A. M., Mr. John Olgin, the oldest resident of Unga, passed away. Mr. Olgin was 85 years of age. The funeral services were held at 3 P. M. May 2nd. May He Rest In Peace.   (TAP IV, 8 & 9, p. 6)

ALBERT HAAF

On September 14th, the boat *Icy Point* was picked up near Sand Point and Albert Haaf was supposed to have been on it. Evidently, he wasn't there.

It was reported to the U. S. Commissioner, D. W. Norris, that Mr. Haaf was missing and Mr. Norris appointed Mr. Alexander Calugan to organize and take charge of a searching party. Mr. Calugan and his party searched all one night and until noon the next day and was unable to find the missing person. The party reported that they thought that he had been drowned.

A few days later, it was reported that Albert Haaf's body could probably be secured by dragging the ocean bottom where it is thought that he fell overboard while in a drunken state of mind. Mr. Norris appointed Mr. Alvin Osterback to organize and take charge of another search party. The weather that day and the next was quite unfavorable and even though they did what they could, they were unable to find the body.

Mr. Haaf's relatives have also spent a considerable amount of time trying to locate him, but all has been to no avail.

Albert was very well liked by everyone and heartfelt sympathy is felt for his folks.

(TAP V, 1, p. 6)

PETE ANDERSON

Mr. Pete Anderson, an old man who has lived in Sand Point for many years, passed away on the 28th of September at the Unga jail.

He was brought to the jail during the summer because of his eyes, which were failing him and he couldn't work.

The funeral was held the next day at 11 A. M.

(TAP V, 1, p. 6)

MAGGIE LINDQUIST

The people of Unga regret the passing of Mrs. Maggie Lindquist. She was one of the oldest people in Unga and very well liked. Micky Lindquist, her grandson, is now attending high school and we all join with him and Mrs. Lindquist's son, Mike Galovin, and other relatives in mourning her loss.   (TAP V, 4, p. 4)

1939

MANUEL VINCENT

March 10th marked the passing away of one of our Unga residents. We are all sorry that Mr. Manuel Vincent had to go and we know that his friends will miss him.

Peter Vincent, who is Mr. Vincent's adopted son, wishes to thank everyone who helped in the funeral services and in preparing the body for burial. The school joins in mourning the loss of Mr. Vincent.   (TAP V, 7, p. 4)

HELGI MAGNUSON

It was November 21st when Charlie Lind and Helgi Magnuson left Unga and started over the hill trail to Squaw Harbor. The night was so bitter cold and there was such a strong wind that only Charlie Lind was able to reach their destination. Helgi Magnuson, unable to make the trip, froze to death on the trail. He had been a resident of Squaw Harbor for a number of years.

(TAP VI, 3, p. 6)

("CROSSINGS" continue at the conclusion of Part II: The War Years.)

The John Nelson codfish station at Squaw Harbor, ca. 1920

PART II
THE WAR YEARS

Mr. Petersen's victory garden

Principal Editor:
Peggy Arness

Co-editors:
Edward Melseth
Thor Lauritzen

INTRODUCTION

IN THE FALL OF 1940, much of the world was engulfed in war. Although the United States was technically at peace, there were ominous signs that the Atlantic Ocean would not shield the country from World War II for long. Canada had entered the war in September 1939, the covert land-lease program in support of the USSR and the UK was well underway, and the Japanese Empire, by now a formidable Axis power, was flexing its military muscle in Eastern Asia and the South Pacific. Political and military leaders such as Ernest Gruening, Alaska's territorial governor, and General William "Billy" Mitchell had begun warning a reluctant and skeptical Congress of the potential threat facing Alaska from Japan and emphasized the urgency of establishing defensive positions in the Territory and especially along the chain of Aleutian Islands that stretched ominously close to the Japanese Archipelago. It was none too soon that calls for military installations in the Aleutians were heeded and ships and planes began flooding the islands with men and materiel. From Kodiak in the east to Adak, more than a thousand miles westward, many of the Aleutian Islands were being rapidly transformed from isolated villages and fishing sites into bastions of defense.

Although no military, aside from a volunteer Alaska Territorial Guard unit, was billeted in Unga, a small naval station with airfield and mooring facilities was established on the spit at Sand Point, a mere 14 miles away. The largest village in the Shumagins, Unga in 1940 had a population of some 200 people, a brand new school, two churches, a large community hall, and most important, a lively group of young people who loved to dance. As a result, Unga, long the focal point of area social gatherings, was soon to become a popular rest and recreation destination for the military.

As the new decade advanced, the US was drawn into both the Atlantic and Pacific theaters of the war and, for Unga, life would never be quite the same again. Many of the young men of the community joined or were drafted into the military, leaving voids that, in some cases, were never refilled. A few families moved to safer locations while teaching positions that were normally filled by "outsiders," i.e., ministers and teachers, were vacated. Despite these dislocations, church and school continued, the former with local volunteers and the latter with resident teachers, who continued to provide excellent educational opportunities for the youth of Unga and the greater Shumagin area.

The Unga High School continued to publish THE ALASKA PEN during the 1940-41 and 1941-42 school years, but lack of a student body during the following year forced the publication to take a breather. In September of 1943, a new publication was begun. Echoing the small high school student body, the paper was called "Pen Whispers" and, although smaller, it continued the tradition of THE ALASKA PEN in presenting news of the community as well as the school and was published monthly through the school year. The PEN resumed normal publication in September of 1944 and continued through the remainder of the war. Appropriately, Part II of *The Alaska Pen: An Illus-trated History of UNGA*, is dubbed "The War Years."

Despite the disruptions in mail service and critical supplies during the war years, THE ALASKA PEN and PEN WHISPERS continued to gather and disseminate news from the greater Shumagin area and to exchange publications with a number of schools elsewhere in Alaska and the States. However, news items involving the military were often expressed in generalities so as to not inadvert-ently pass information on military movements and activities to the enemy. We are now able to discuss these activities in some detail and are fotunate, for example, to present here the account of one such happening—the wreck of the *FP-33*—by an eyewitness who participated in the salvage of the vessel.

Unga, February 19, 1944 (Official US Navy Photograph)

HISTORICAL HIGHLIGHTS

❦ February 1940 ❦

THEATER IN UNGA

Unga was fortunate enough to be the place chosen by Mr. and Mrs. J. Fletcher of Unalaska as a place to spend a vacation. They were kind enough to bring some movies with which to treat folks here. The movies were enjoyed by all and we sincerely hated to see the Fletchers leave.

Due to the fact that Unga residents enjoyed the shows so much, Mr. and Mrs. E. F. Casey purchased the projector and are now making arrangements with film companies for films. We are all waiting very anxiously for the next show and the first one to be Unga-operated.   (TAP VI, 6, p. 4)

[That "next show" happened in July of 1940; see below. Ed.]

❦ April-May 1940 ❦

UNGA'S NEW SCHOOL

Everyone in Unga is very pleased to see the construction of the new school building going ahead. Some of the materials arrived on the *North King* about the 20th of April and more are expected on another boat sometime in May.

Mr. Graves, the contractor, arrived on the M. S. *Fern* and has been very busy ever since getting things going. He reports that he is getting along quite well and making rapid progress.

Some of the men in town have been working in rain and sunshine and they don't seem to mind at all. Fortunately, they have been lucky enough to have quite a few good days so far. Raymond Rodgers and George Foster report that their arm muscles have become considerably stronger, which is a result of their excavation work for the building!

Mr. Graves says that he thinks the new building will be ready for the opening of school next fall. In the meantime, we are all looking on anxiously as the work progresses.   (TAP VI, 8, p. 4)

[The new school was opened for classes in October of 1940. A description of the school and its amenities is given in the School News essay elsewhere in this section. Ed.]

DEDICATION

The heirs of Frank Brown, formerly of Unga and one-time superintendent of the Apollo Mine here, sent recent information announcing that the cabin at the head of the bay has been turned over to the Girl Scout Organization of Unga.

The dedication of this property they wish to be made in memory of their father, who lived here for so many years and was greatly respected and beloved by all who knew him.   (TAP VI, 8, p. 7)

[Photos of the cabin and its description are given in The Girl Scout Story in Part I. Ed.]

❦ October 1940 ❦

THE SHOW IS THE THING

The month of July inaugurated the regular weekly showing of moving pictures in the town of Unga. In the past, itinerant exhibitors have brought

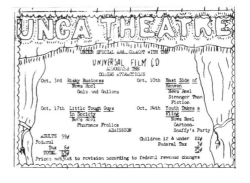

equipment and set up in dance halls and pool halls and we have had a brief taste of movies.

Sjoberg & Casey have altered one of their warehouses, installed an oil burning hot air furnace and turned over one complete floor to the cinema...

Mr. John Berntsen, Jr., has been assisting with the projection. As time goes on, Mr. Casey promises further improvements...including modern seating for the comfort of all... (TAP VII, 1, p. 9)

❧ November 1940 ❧

OUR NEW CITIZENS

Full citizenship was granted to Olaf Melseth and Harold Pedersen by Judge Hellenthal, District Judge, at the District Court while in session at Anchorage. Witnesses for both men were Allan L. Petersen and Ralph Grosvold.

Both men passed their final examinations in good shape and seem very pleased to be American citizens. They both realize what a privilege it is to be an American citizen, and how necessary it is in order to obtain work. They are both very happy and glad to be home again with their friends and families.   (TAP VII, 2, p. 4)

Olaf Melseth and daughter Jeanette

❧ January 1941 ❧

SIFTED FROM SAND POINT

Elizabeth Grosvold was selected to be Sand Point's reporter. Here is some news she sent:

BEEF HUNTING

Captain Ralph Grosvold with the help of Robert Bear recently went beef hunting. The cattle on Captain Grosvold's island are very wild and have to be hunted like caribou. With an approximate herd of two hundred, this should be exciting sport. Captain Grosvold says they are stampeded into a narrow pass and then counted and separated. This helps him choose some good beef. He brought back some fine beef and had no trouble getting rid of it. There is nothing like beef, especially in this country where we get so little.

Captain Grosvold and friend

BUILDING BOOM IN SAND POINT

We are all very proud of the fact that Sand Point is growing. Russian Town, or over the hill, as most people call it, has four new homes in the last year or so. Alvin Osterback is building a large home and Paul Gronholdt has his almost finished. Alec Kelsen and Peter Gronholdt have been living in their new homes for quite some time and say they are very comfortable. Sand Point will be as large as Unga if it keeps on growing so fast!

LOCAL NEWS

Mrs. Don Fadden nee Gronholdt is making a visit with her parents. A recent bride of Seattle, Washington, Mrs. Fadden plans on being here until January.

The Sand Point Sewing Club, recently organized, enjoyed an evening with Mrs. Fadden entertaining at the home of her mother, Mrs. Peter Gronholdt.   (TAP VII, 4, p. 6)

[Mrs. Fadden was the former Marie Gronholdt, one of the two first graduates of Unga High School. Ed]

❦ Febuary 1941 ❦

MAGIC

About 10 AM, January 26, Mrs. Petersen came in the intermediate room and invited us in to a special program she had arranged for her room. The high school students were invited to the program, too.

Mr. Michael Reddy, who was here aboard the M. S. *Pansy* from Seldovia, was at school to do some slight-of-hand [sic] performances. He did such things as cut a rope and then make it one rope again, making one ball become three balls, the shell game, pulling a rope through his neck, and a great many card tricks. Many of us are still wondering how some of the tricks were done and some of us think we know some of the tricks.

We enjoyed the brief half hour's entertainment very much and wish we could see some of the tricks again. We were glad to have Mr. Reddy with us.   (TAP VII, 5, p. 5)

❦ March 1941 ❦

BEAR-PLETNIKOFF WEDDING

On February 8th, Miss Martha Bear and Mr. Johnny Pletnikoff came over to Unga from Sand Point with a few of their friends. They went up to the school house where they were married by Mr. Norris (U. S. Commissioner).

After the wedding, the married couple left for Sand Point, where they will make their home.   (TAP VII, 6, p. 4)

GILBERT-HARRIS WEDDING

Miss Esther Gilbert was a student of the Unga High School a couple of years ago and had since moved to Squaw Harbor with the family... February 26th she came over with Mr. Peter Harris on the *Ellen* and they were married by Mr. Norris. After the ceremony, they went back to Squaw Harbor and came back later in the evening and gave a free dance.   (TAP VII, 6, p. 4)

MORE MOVIES

We hadn't had movies for about three months and everyone was happy when the movies came again. Mr. Casey had sent his machine out to get it repaired and now it works fine. The first movie we had was "Mad About Music". Deanna Durbin was the main actress and Boy! can she sing. The second movie was "The Merry-Go-Round of 1938". The third movie was "The Law of the Tombstone". The main actor was Buck Jones. We also have seen one of Bob Baker's and are now looking forward to another of Deanna Durbin's— "That Certain Age".

Everyone enjoys the pictures and looks forward to the next almost before the present one is over.
(TAP VII, 7, p. 5)

❦ May 1941 ❦

GREETINGS TO MR. AND MRS. NORRIS

The Primary Room extends best wishes to Mr. and Mrs. Norris for a good trip and vacation this summer. We regret that you will not be back for next year, but hope you will enjoy being students and going to school again. Learn a lot and come back to Unga again.

Reporter: Thorwald Lauritzen (TAP VII, 8, p. 4)

"Ship's comin'! Ship's comin'!" Cannery crew arriving in Squaw Harbor in the mid-1940s

❧ May 1941 ❧

We are all glad to welcome the cannery people back again, and to know that the cannery is to operate this year. It looked for a while as though they would not be able to operate, due to labor troubles. It would be a blow to us all here if the P. A. F. Cannery at Squaw Harbor did not operate, as so many of our people depend on the canneries for their summer's work.

The M. S. *Howkan* arrived the latter part of April. Captain Bill Howell was, of course, in command of her and had the same crew as last year. The *Howkan* also brought Mr. Isaac Johnson, the Outside Foreman, and most of the pile driver crew. They lost no time in getting started driving the trap at Kelly Rock.

April 30th was the day the S. S. *Delwood* came to Squaw Harbor bringing more of the crew. Among them was Dick Peasley, who is assistant bookkeeper this year, also Dr. Schneider, who is new up here. We are always glad to see the Doctor come.

On May 16th, the S. S. *Aleutian* arrived bringing the rest of the crew. We are sorry Mr. Lee is not back with us, but we are especially glad that the new Superintendent is Mr. Stanley Tarrant. Most of us remember him from 1935, when he was bookkeeper at Squaw Harbor.

Mr. Hawkins is back again as bookkeeper, we are glad to say. We will miss Mr. and Mrs. Moore in the kitchen, but know we will like the new cooks. Many of the same mechanics and outside men are back but we also see many new faces. We are glad to see all of them.   (TAP VII, 8, p. 6)

❦ September 1941 ❦

THE WRECK OF THE *PATMOS*

On the night of the 22nd, a strong wind arose and blew Mr. Knutsen's boat, the *Patmos* ashore on a sand beach across the bay from Unga. Luckily, the boat missed hitting a wharf (at the Hjalmar Lauritzen saltery) by a few yards.

The Patmos *in Unga*

The next morning, some men tried to get it off, but they were not successful. They took the *Elmer* over and tried to pull it off but only succeeded in pulling off a part of the deck. Then it started to leak and they could not bail it fast enough to keep it from sinking. Now they have no hope of saving it, and so are taking off everything they can. They have already taken out the engine. Everyone was sorry to hear of this incident.

Lawrence Petersen's boat, the *Katie*, was also blown ashore, but was taken off without damage being done.   (TAP VIII, 1, p. 1)

THE FRED KOSCHMANNS ARRIVE

This year Unga School welcomed two new teachers. They are Mr. and Mrs. Fred Koschmann, who have taught the last several years in Fairbanks and who were married just last spring.

They arrived here on Labor Day on the *Cordova*. The next day school started and it seemed only a short time until we felt well acquainted with them.

We found that they are both musical and so are looking forward to an interesting year in that department.   (TAP VIII, 1, p. 3)

COUPLE ADOPTS BABY

On the 15th of September, Mrs. Lena Hunt went to Sand Point and returned with a six weeks old baby. He was the son of Mr. and Mrs. Carl Erickson. As Mrs. Erickson died soon after the birth of this baby and since there were several other children in the family, the father decided he could not take care of them all. Several people in Sand Point have taken in the other children so that they will have nice homes, too. Mr. and Mrs. Hunt are going to adopt this boy.   (TAP VIII, 1, p. 5)

[He was given the name, "Freddy." Ed.]

❦ October 1941 ❦

S. S. *VICTORIA* AT SQUAW HARBOR

The S. S. *Victoria*, straight from Seattle, docked in Squaw Harbor the night of October 11. The freight from Unga, of which there was a great deal, was hauled here by the *Elmer* and the *Vis*.

Mr. and Mrs. Koschmann, Mr. Casey and Mr. Petersen went over on the *Elmer* to meet it. Mr. and Mrs. Koschmann and Mrs. Brittel of Squaw Harbor, hiked back to Unga on Sunday. The others returned on the *Elmer*.   (TAP VIII, 2, p. 1)

WIND DAMAGES SCHOOL

During the night of the sixteenth of October, Unga experienced one of the hardest blows ever felt here. The raging wind pushed over a number of small shacks and, worst of all, blew one-fourth the tar paper off the school roof and caused a flood in the building. Looking over things the next morning, the teachers decided it was too wet to hold school, so the pupils were dismissed until things could be dried up.

During the day, the roof was repaired by some of the boys after several hours of tacking the old roofing paper together again. When the weather moderated, new paper was put over the part that had been patched. The paper was also tacked down, a job that had not been done when the roof was originally put on (hardly a year earlier!). The boys came down pretty well smeared with compound, but hopeful that the leaks had been stopped.

(TAP VIII, 2, p. 1)

❧ November 1941 ❧

TRAPPERS LEAVE

Last Thursday, November 13, most of the trappers from Unga left for the mainland and their trap lines. They had been waiting for fine weather for some time. The men who went were Fred Pomian, Conrad Lauritzen, Johannes Olsen, Harry Hunt, Aleck Calugan, Albert Cushing and Daniel Wilson. Raymond Rogers left for the mainland almost two weeks sooner than the rest of the trappers. John Berntsen and his son Henry left Saturday. We all wish them good luck. (TAP VIII, 3, p. 1)

A typical trapper's cabin

S. S. *CORDOVA* TAKEN OFF THE MAIL RUN

The S. S. *Cordova* made its last trip for the year 1941 the first part of November. The S. S. *Lakina* will take the place of the faithful *Cordova* while she is being overhauled in Seattle.

We take this opportunity of thanking the officers and crew of the *Cordova* for the friendly, dependable way they served the Westward.

(TAP VIII, 3, p. 3)

[There is no indication in later issues of THE ALASKA PEN that the Cordova ever returned to the Westward mail run. It is known that the ship was requisitioned by the US Government for service in the Aleutians shortly after December 7, 1941 and was involved in the evacuation of civilians from Dutch Harbor. She was sold shortly after the war. Ed.]

MUMPS STILL ABOUT

The mumps epidemic is still going. At the time this paper goes to press, there are three sick with it, two of school age and one younger. Those who have it now seem to be sicker than the ones who had it earlier in the year. As yet there have been no serious results, and we hope there will not be any.

So far, the adults have been spared but they are 'knocking on wood'. (TAP VIII, p. 3, p. 5)

❧ January 1942 ❧

WHEN THE CODFISH COME BACK TO UNGA

Due to the fine weather the last few days, a number of fellows have gone out for the first codfish of the season. Catching a few good cod seems to be a great thing. They are known to many people as the Alaska turkey and surely make a good dish.

It's rather early in the year for any amount of fish. Later on during the year, about March, codfishing starts as a business. The fish are taken to a saltery and salted for market. The salting stations in this locality are owned by individuals. The first one to catch 60 or 70 fish starts everyone else fishing. Codfishing lasts for a few months and then salmon fishing starts. (TAP VIII, 5, p. 3)

[A comprehensive illustrated essay on codfishing in the Shumagin Islands region is presented in Part I of this work. Ed.]

RODGERS-GRONHOLDT WEDDING

On January 21st, Elizabeth Rodgers and Andrew Gronholdt were married at the home of Mr. and Mrs. Raymond Rodgers. A party of friends and relatives were present to give best wishes to the young couple. A reception was held immediately after the ceremony.

The bride and groom left for Sand Point, where they will make their home, at nine o'clock the same evening. (TAP VIII, 5, p. 1)

[Elizabeth was the first editor-in-chief of THE ALASKA PEN and shared first Unga High School graduate honors with her future sister-in-law, Marie Gronholdt Fadden. Ed.]

Mr. and Mrs. Andrew Gronholdt

❧ January 1942 ❧

SQUAW HARBOR BOYS TO COLD BAY

During the week of January 18, five men left Squaw Harbor to go to work in Cold Bay on the Army field there.

They were William, Martin and Raymond Gilbert, Peter Harris and Jimmy Palutof. The construction company chartered the M. V. *Vis II* to take the men to their new jobs.

(TAP VIII, 5, p. 6)

[This is one of the few indications that WWII was beginning to impact the area. In another instance—reported in this issue of THE ALASKA PEN—the Unalaska military district disallowed the M. V. Penguin from accepting civilian passengers on their Westward run, but the order was subsequently recanted. The article follows. Ed.]

MRS. CASEY TO UNALASKA

On the 18th of December, Mrs. Casey left Unga to go to Sand Point in hopes of getting a boat there to take her to Seward. It wasn't, however, until January 15th that a boat finally came along. The *Penguin* had stopped in Sand Point on its way to Unalaska, but they had orders not to take any passengers. However, when they were halfway there, they received a wire from the commanding officer of the district to turn back and take Mrs. Casey. She is now safely landed there.

(TAP VIII, 5, p. 3)

[Although she didn't get to Seward, Mrs. Casey's ordeal was concluded satisfactorily in Unalaska. She returned to Unga in March 1942 with a brand new baby! Judith Ruth was born on February 12th. Ed.]

SKULSTADS TO SIMEONOF

On the 27th of December, Harry Sharpe took Mrs. Skulstad and her children, Karen, Thorwald, Fern and Kenneth down to Simeonof Island on the *Pansy*. Mrs. Skulstad had not been down to her home since the latter part of November. They returned about five days later with the report that everything was fine there. Phenny Grassamoff returned with them. She is now staying with Mrs. Skulstad.

(TAP VIII, 5, p. 3)

[Mrs. Skulstad's husband, Tom, died in a tragic accident in November 1941. His obituary appears in the

"Crossings" portion of Part II. The Skulstad family operated a fox farm on Simeonof Island for many years. Ed.]

MAIL!

Unga's Christmas mail seems to be coming in dribbles. Two installments have arrived so far and we hope for the rest soon...

With the coming of war, the old phrase, "The mail must get through", seems to have been forgotten.   (TAP VIII, 5, p. 1)

❦ February 1942 ❦

WINDCHARGER CRASHES

On January 29, a raging wind came over town and caused another casualty at the Unga School, probably the worst of all. It blew over a forty-foot tower, which held the windcharger and which, in falling, made a small hole in the roof of the living quarters.

The framework of the tower was bent out of shape, and the charger was badly damaged, making it impossible to repair it in town. The parts were gathered up and put away with the hope of being fixed in the future. As the batteries were low, a motor generator was borrowed to restore their charge, so they would not be damaged by sitting unused so long.   (TAP VIII, 6, p. 1)

[Harnessing the wind to provide electrical power was a brilliant idea, but not in a region such as Unga where gale-force winds were the rule, not the exception. Needless to say, the charger was never rebuilt. Ed.]

MURDER IN BELKOFSKY

In February, Mr. Petersen (Deputy US Marshal) received word that he was wanted at Belkofsky, as there had been a murder out there. It so happened that the M. S. *Pansy* was in port that evening so the Marshal left almost immediately. The next evening he returned quite late with the prisoner and several witnesses.

This is the second murder that has occurred around here this winter and we certainly hope it is the last.   (TAP VIII, 6, p. 3)

CHICKEN POX EPIDEMIC?

We thought we had our share of contagious diseases this winter, but it seems we have missed one which is now paying us a visit. Ray Galovin has Chicken Pox! Where it came from, we can't say. We have had practically no communication with the world outside, so we must blame it on our neighbor communities. No doubt we have [*sic*], or will return the favor someday.
                              (TAP VIII, 6, p. 3)

A SCHOOL THAT LEAKS—AGAIN.

The fact that our school has a leaky roof causes quite a noise each day in the upper grade room. There are at times two five-gallon cans and a wash tub there to catch the water. When these have water in them, the drip, drip, drip is barely noticed, but when they're empty, the ping as each drop hits bottom is quite musical.

If the floor of the room only leaked as much as the roof, there would be nothing to worry about, but we'd rather have the roof as tight as the floor.

We are hoping that sometime soon we will have enough dry, sunny days in succession to allow repairs to be made, but at the present the outlook isn't optimistic. It seems that the roofing compound won't harden as long as the roof is wet and it hasn't been dry since October, and then only for a day or two at a time.

Perhaps by next year we'll have a shingle roof and our troubles will be over. (TAP VIII, 6, p. 6)

[Another brilliant idea gone awry. This was the first and last flat-roofed building constructed in Unga! Read on. Ed.]

❧ March 1942 ❧

MORE ON THE LEAKY ROOF

To those who have been following the articles concerning our leaky roof, we would like to say that the leaking has stopped—almost. First, it hasn't been raining the last few days, and second, the warm weather is allowing the roofing compound to work into the tears and cracks.

We hope its good behavior is mainly due to cause two, but fear it is chiefly because of the first. (TAP VIII, 7, p. 4)

RODGERS-FOSTER WEDDING

Mrs. Zenia Rodgers became the bride of Mr. George Foster on the evening of March 27. Mr. Foster came down from Unalaska about a week ago and will be returning again soon to his work. A dance was given in their honor on Friday and turkey sandwiches were enjoyed by all. Congratulations, Mr. and Mrs. George Foster! (TAP VIII, 7, p. 5)

US DEFENSE BONDS

Defense bonds are selling so fast that neither the Post Office nor the school has been able to keep a supply on hand for very long. Since incoming mail is rather slow, this has meant that much of the time there have been none available. However, another mail is expected soon, so keep your money ready! (TAP VIII, 7, p. 5)

❧ May 1942 ❧

CANNERYMEN ARRIVE

On the 26th of April, a number of the cannerymen at Squaw Harbor arrived. Immediately, arrangements were made for the fishermen and workers from local communities [to be employed]. Due to the war, many local men are working on government projects, but it is thought that there will be a sufficient number available to put up the catch. Many fishermen will undoubtedly stop other work to do the regular season's work.

(TAP VIII, 8, p. 4)

THE KOSCHMANNS BID FAREWELL

"As our year in Unga draws to a close, we would like to express our appreciation to the many, both students and patrons, who have cooperated with us, and by their friendly help, made this a happy, worthwhile year. We have especially appreciated the fine help of the students in publishing the PEN and in the Young People's work at the church. We wish for you all only the best in the future."   Mr. and Mrs. Koschmann
(TAP VIII, 8, p. 4)

Note: THE ALASKA PEN was not published during the 1942-43 school year. A somewhat abbreviated version was produced during 1943-44 and was called PEN WHISPERS. THE ALASKA PEN's original format and normal publication schedule resumed in September of 1944.

❧ September 1943 ❧

LOCAL IMPROVEMENTS

Many property owners are busy painting and repairing their homes this fall. Several houses with new coats of paint add to the town's appearance. Repaired foundations and shingled roofs make more comfortable homes for the winter.

The "House of Blazes" reborn

Joe Alisto moved his house several feet east of the Mike Galovin property. Albert Krone is making practically a new house out of the old "House of Blazes". Albert Cushing bought the cabin on Flag Pole Hill from Mr. Casey and plans to build an addition to his house.   (PW I, 1, p. 3)

[Historical Note: The "House of Blazes" was built around the turn of the 20th century by Alfred Komedal and served originally as a general store. It was partially destroyed by fire some years later. Ed.]

HEALTH EXAMINATION

On the fourteenth of September we had our first health examination at school. Dr. Heath, U.S.N.R., kindly came over here to check us over. He listened to our heartbeat with an instrument called a stethoscope. He tested our eyes by having us stand at a certain distance from the chart of letters that we could read.

After he got through examining everybody from the first grade through the ninth grade, he made a little talk. He told us he was especially impressed with the cleanliness of all the children (the mothers of the children will have to be thanked for that). He said that the pupils of the Unga School were very healthy. He found that several children had bad eyes and some enlarged tonsils.

We're very grateful to Dr. Heath for taking time to come over here [from the Naval facility at Sand Point]...   (PW I, 1, p. 4)

❦ October 1943 ❧
CRUISER *ALASKA* FUND

On September 21st, our school started to collect money for the Cruiser Alaska Fund, which will be used to buy a gift to present to the new USS *Alaska.* The plan was suggested by [Alaska's] Governor Gruening and he hoped people in Alaska would contribute enough money to buy a fine gift for the new warship. Everyone in school donated and then the pupils collected money from the people in town.

The school gave $27.65 and the town people $188.60, making a total of $216.25. Every family in town made a donation. The money and a list of the names of the contributors was sent to the governor's office on October 16th.

Mildred Hansen, Grade 6
(PW I, 2, p. 1)

❦ November 1943 ❧
SCHOOLS AT WAR PROGRAM

The Unga Territorial School has joined the Schools-at-War Program. We have entered the "Triple-Threat Jeep Campaign". By buying war bonds and stamps, we "purchase" jeeps or smaller equipment for the armed forces. The goal which we chose from the Junior Unit is the Life Raft for the Navy, value $250.00. This is supposed to be "bought" by December 7th, "Pearl Harbor Day".

Any school may fly the Minute Man Flag if 90% of the pupils buy at least one stamp a month. We are trying for 100% record. We think that every child in the school should buy at least one stamp a month!

Arthur Hansen is chairman of the Schools-At-War. Helpers are Aleck Cushing and Ray Galovin. The committee is in charge of the Stamp Sale in school... Enough sales were made during November to make an average of 97%, which entitles our school to fly the Minute-Man Flag during December...

Arthur Hansen, 8th grade
(PW I, 3, p. 1)

A FUR-TRAPPING UPDATE

Every year about this time the men of the town go to their trapping grounds on the Mainland. The trapping season opens November 15th and closes January 15th. The main furs the trappers get are mink, land otter, red fox, cross fox, silver fox and weasel. Once in awhile they get wolf and wolverines. Sometimes silver fox are caught on Unga Island.

The men who went trapping this winter are Tom Fox and John Foster, Fred Pomian, Olaf Melseth, Fred Krone, Raymond Rodgers and Norman Larsen and John Berntsen, Sr. Trapping has been an important occupation in this place since the early sea otter days.

Robert Galovin, 6th Grade
(PW I, 3, p. 4)

❧ 1944 ❧

[Historical Note: The major story for 1944—the grounding of the Army freight and passenger vessel, the FP-33, *in Unga's outer harbor on the night of January 25th and its eventual salvage—was couched in intentionally vague language in* PEN WHISPERS, *ostensibly at the request of the military. The 33 was always referred to as simply "the stranded vessel." We have attempted to re-create the story as it unfolded in the seven-month salvage operation. That story is presented elsewhere in Part II. Ed.]*

❧ January 1944 ❧

THE VOYAGE OF THE *PANSY*

The M. S. *Pansy* arrived in Unga on January 18th from a trip to Anchorage and Seldovia. Harry Sharpe, "skipper", brought his family and they plan to stay in Unga the rest of the winter and next summer. They are living with Mrs. William Peters, Mrs. Sharpe's mother. Others coming on the *Pansy* were Louis Berntsen, Eddie Gilbert, Thorwald Skulstad and Nick and Aleck Saracoff. The *Pansy* left Anchorage December 1st. The party spent three weeks in Seldovia waiting for suitable weather before heading westward. It has been six years since Mrs. Sharpe visited relatives and friends in Unga. We are glad to have Harvey and Lila in school.

Barbara Jean Berntsen, 6th Grade
(PW I, 5, p. 4)

The *Pansy* *tied up in Squaw Harbor along with, from left:* Southland, Vis, *and* Easter

❧ February 1944 ❧

NEWS FROM THE CALUGANS

We were glad to hear from Isabelle, Peter and Pauline Calugan, who are patients in the Cushman Hospital at Tacoma, Washington. Peter is getting along fine. He said there are 143 patients on the second floor where he is. Peter sent us pictures of the hospital. Isabelle is still in bed. She had two operations in January but found it is not necessary for the third operation. We all send best wishes to our former classmates and wish them a speedy recovery.

Carolyn Haaf, 5th Grade
(PW I, 6, p. 2)

❧ March 1944 ❧

JACK BENSON INJURED

Lt. Cmdr. Jack Benson, who had been on leave here and was later put in charge of the salvaging job here, suffered an accident while at work on March 2nd. He was picked up and taken to Kodiak in a plane later in the day. Word received from him later said he had suffered a dislocated hip and was improving but will still need a month or more hospitalization. We are glad that Jack's injury was not too serious and that he will soon recover.

Mrs. Benson and children, Jackie and Jerry, left here on March 17th for Kodiak to be near Mr. Benson. We are sorry to have them leave but enjoyed their visit and hope to see them back again sometime.

Ruth Lauritzen, 9th Grade

KOSBRUK-SHANGIN

Nick Shangin and Mary Kosbruk, both from Perryville, were married on March 25th by Edward F. Casey, U. S. Commissioner.

Howard Berntsen, 8th Grade

FLU EPIDEMIC

The flu epidemic hit Unga the first part of March. In school, there were 23 cases of which seven had had perfect attendance up to that time.

Esther Cushing, 9th Grade
(PW I, 7, p. 3)

UNGA VISITORS

Rev. J. Dean King, pastor of the Methodist Mission at Unalaska, made a short visit in Unga the evening of March 24th. While in town, he inspected the Methodist Church and parsonage as he plans to return here soon to take up the work of the church—at least during the summer.

Rev. King has been in charge of the Unalaska parish for the past eight years. He is now returning from the States where he has been on leave for the past six months.

Tom Fox had a surprise visit with his daughter, Mrs. May Koski, and grandchildren who are returning to their home in Unalaska. They have been living in Berkeley, California since the evacuation of Unalaska in 1942.

Arthur Hansen, 8th Grade
(PW I, 7, p. 4)

❧ April, May 1944 ❧

CANNERY CREW ARRIVES

On April 22nd, the cannery crews arrived for the Pacific American Fisheries Co. at Squaw Harbor and Alaska Pacific Salmon Co. at Sand Point. Mr. Williams is the new superintendent at Squaw Harbor and Mr. Farrell returned as superintendent at Sand Point. Several of the old crew members returned and seem glad to be back for another salmon season.

Best wishes for a "big run" and "a full pack"!
Esther Cushing, 9th Grade

TRAVELERS RETURN

Mr. and Mrs. George Foster and daughters Budilia and Emily, returned home from Bellingham where they spent the winter. The girls attended business college there. All enjoyed their visit with friends and relatives in Seattle and Bellingham. They say they are glad to be home.

Meryl Hansen, 6th Grade.
(PW I, 8, p. 7)

❧ October 1944 ❧

THE GALE

The people were taken by surprise on October 16th when a gale suddenly came up. The sou'wester [sou'easter ?] was so fierce that it lifted the fish box off Casey's dock, sank a dory, and forced the *Alice* between two rocks up at Skinner's Point. The dory was shattered to splinters but the *Alice* was unharmed. The sound of the waves was like the sound of an erupting volcano. Sometimes the waves were dashing forty to fifty feet high. It reached its greatest intensity at two in the afternoon. Many iron girders that were buried in the bay since the last gale from the southeast in 1937 were dashed against the warehouse at Casey's. At one time, it looked as if the dock might go down with the waves. Many boulders as big as a double fist were cast about like snowflakes.

Casey's dock in a similar storm

Many braved the waves to take their dories to safer waters. Some of the Unga dogs that followed the children nearer the edge of the water were forced to lie down due to the intensity of the wind. School was dismissed one-half hour early so that the children could watch the gale.

Some pictures were taken of the storm and watchful eyes were first directed to look at one breaker and then another. One's attention was attracted towards Elephant Rock, then to the opposite cliffs.   (TAP IX, 3, p. 6)

❧ November 1944 ❧
GILBERT-HANSON WEDDING
The marriage of Miss Ada Gilbert, a former Unga student, and Charles Hanson of Squaw

Harbor has been announced. Mrs. Hanson is making her home with her mother while her husband is in the service.   (TAP IX, 3, p. 6)

Mr. and Mrs. Charles Hanson

❧ January 1945 ❧
RODGERS-ENDRESEN WEDDING
A beautiful wedding was solemnized Sunday, January 14th at 3:00PM when Miss Emily Rodgers, daughter of Mrs. Zenia Foster, became the bride of Andy Endresen, son of Ed Endresen.

The single ring ceremony was read by U. S. Commissioner Robert Garlow, before a beautifully decorated altar of ferns, potted plants and lilies, and aglow with candlelight.

Preceding the ceremony, Miss Budilia Rodgers, sister of the bride, and Mrs. Laura Berntsen sang "I Love You Truly", accompanied by Mrs. Allan Petersen on the piano.

For the entrance of the bridal party, Mrs. Petersen played the "Bridal Chorus" from Lohengrin by Wagner on the organ.

Cpl. and Mrs. Andy Endresen

Mrs. Elizabeth Gronholdt, sister of the bride, was matron of honor. She wore a printed Jersey dress ornamented with a corsage of sweet peas and roses. Best man was Ray Rodgers, brother of the bride.

In the evening, a dance was held at the dance hall and a reception for the community was held at the home of the bride's mother. Delicious refreshments were served around a table centered with two silver bells. Mrs. Rodgers' piano was moved from her home to the dance hall. Music for the dance was furnished by Miss Budilia Rodgers and Mrs. A. Petersen.

Afer a short honeymoon up the bay, the bride will continue her studies in the Unga High School and Cpl. Andy Endresen will return to his military base.   (TAP IX, 5, p. 3)

———◆———

WELCOME HOME

On January 21st, a boat brought Speros Kaboures home from a Seward hospital, where he had spent several weeks suffering with a serious illness. His condition is much improved and he is swiftly regaining his health.

Mrs. Jenny Melseth and children have returned to their home here after spending several months at King Cove.   (TAP IX, 5, p. 5)

———◆———

PROUD AS A PEACOCK

The Unga School is very proud of the recognition it received in the December [1944] issue of the Reader's Digest in the article "The World's Biggest Selling Job".

They are pleased to announce their total of bonds and war stamps, for the period beginning with the close of school last spring and ending December 3l, l944, is $2,022.50.

$25.00 United States Savings Bond

In December, the Post Office and school had a complete sell-out of War Savings Stamps. A period of fifty-four days passed before a boat arrived with mail and a new supply of stamps.

Since the stamp supply was received late in January, it was necessary to launch a one day's selling campaign in order that the school may continue to fly the "Minute Man Flag". The flag is flown by schools with 90% or more of the pupils regularly buying War Savings Stamps each month.

The record of the community, as well as the school, is one that any community may justly be proud. The town of Unga had a quota of $1,000 for the Sixth War Loan drive. The total sales amounted to $2,043.75. This is over 204%. Can any community boast of a better record?

(TAP IX, 5, p. 6)

———◆———

❧ March 1945 ❧

FOSTER-RUDOLPH WEDDING

Miss Alma Foster, daughter of Mrs. Cecilia Foster and [former] student of Unga High School, recently married Paul Rudolph of Juneau, Alaska.

The bride has been living in Juneau since the evacuation of Unalaska.

The students of Unga High School extend our sincere wishes to the bride and groom for a happy marriage. (TAP IX, 7, p. 8)

❧ April 1945 ❧

TOWN NEWS

On April 10th, a boat arrived bringing Tom Fox home after paying a visit with his family out west.

On April 16th, Johannes Olsen surprised friends and relatives by coming home on a 45-day furlough. The following night, a dance was held at the Community Dance Hall for the benefit of the "Fleet" that was in.

On April 18th, Andrew Foster arrived here from Seattle on his new boat, the *Bogdan.* Skinner and Eddy boats, the *Gloria* and the *Beryl E* also arrived from Seattle. Harold Pedersen, Olaf Swenson, Ralph Grosvold, captain of the *Beryl E,* and Nick Saracoff are a few of the many that arrived. Another dance was held for a group of sailors on shore leave from their ship. John Foster has gone to Sand Point to work for Skinner and Eddy.

Hans Hansen has moved into the house which he purchased from the [John] Iversen estate.

Budilia Rodgers, 11th Grade
(TAP IX, 8, p. 7)

❧ May 1945 ❧

EDUCATOR VISITS

Violet S. Hear, health educator and supervisor from the office of the Commissioner of Education, called on the Unga School on May 16th. Since her arrival was after school hours, the pupils assembled at 8PM in order for her to see them in school.

She made a thorough inspection of the building and has promised that when the pupils return in the fall to school they will see a newly decorated building. (TAP IX, 9, p. 2)

MINERS VISIT

Joel M. Moss and Burr S. Webber, two mining engineers working for the Department of Interior of the United States Government, have arrrived and are making their headquarters in Unga for the next few days.

They are working on the Apollo and Sitka mines at present and are endeavoring to discover the extent of the gold vein.

Their work is to make a survey of the mineral deposits on the peninsula and the islands along the Aleutian Chain. (TAP IX, 9, p. 6)

❧ September 1945 ❧

A MOVIE!

For the first time in over a year a movie was shown in Unga. "Song of Russia", starring Robert Taylor and Susan Peters, was shown by servicemen from a boat that was in port. The entire community turned out for the movie and all expressed their appreciation for the opportunity to see it. Following the movie, the high school held a dance for the sailors and served refreshments.

(TAP X, 1, p. 3)

COMINGS AND GOINGS - SUMMER 1945

Mrs. Nellie Krone arrived home during the summer after spending some time with her son in Bellevue.

Mrs. Ida Bjornstad and two children returned home [to Sand Point] from Seattle during the summer.

Other people who made trips to the States and returned are: Mrs. Allan Petersen, Mrs. Opal Lawvere and Andrew Krone.

Edward F. Casey has returned to Seattle after spending the summer in Unga.

Mike Galovin and Mr. and Mrs. Daniel Wilson have left to spend the winter in Bellingham.

Victoria Kay Garlow was born in the Seward General Hospital on July 30th. She is the daughter of Mr. and Mrs. Robert Garlow. Mr. Garlow visited Southeastern Alaska while on his summer vacation. He manages the Sjoberg & Casey store, is US Commissioner for this district and is the local [Unga] Postmaster.

Harriet Krone was born on August 17th to Mr. and Mrs. Albert Krone.

The fishermen who have returned from Bristol Bay have reported a very profitable season. Speros Kaboures went to Cordova instead of returning to Unga, since he sold his property here. Henry Berntsen flew to Anchorage after the fishing season and now has returned home.

Many of the high school students were employed at the cannery during the summer. Unga was very much deserted during the canning season since several were employed by the cannery, and also some families moved there for the season.

Norman Larsen has just returned from Cold Bay where he received medical treatment.

Allan Petersen has returned from Anchorage. He went there on official business.

George Foster has returned home after spending much time in the Merchant Marines. His travels took him into the South Pacific War Zone.

Mary Larsen, who spent her life in Unga, passed away suddenly on Sunday, August 5th.

Knut Knutsen called in Unga. (TAP X, 1, p. 4)

SAND POINT TEACHERS ARRIVE

The Sand Point school has two teachers this year: Mr. and Mrs. Allen, from Arizona. They and their four sons arrived on the S. S. *Columbia* on Thursday, August 30th.   (TAP X, 1, p. 8)

❧ October 1945 ❧

VICTORY LOAN DRIVE

The War is over—but this is not the whole story. Let's finish the job! The government must have a victory loan

(1) to pay the bills for munitions still unpaid,

(2) to pay the cost of guarding Germany and Japan,

(3) to pay for the care of our wounded and disabled,

(4) to pay off and provide benefits for eight million veterans to be discharged by next July, and

(5) to keep the lid on inflation.

The Victory Loan Drive opens October 29th and extends through December 8, 1945. Its eleven billion-dollar quota includes a four billion dollar goal for individual Americans. A lot of money!

The school has been asked to shoulder the responsibility for this drive in Unga. Your pledge for the Victory Loan will be solicited by a school child. You will be called upon but once by some pupil to whom you may give your pledge. The bond need not be purchased on October 29th, but may be bought any day between October 29th and December 8th. ...those people who are purchasing bonds on a monthly savings basis will find this covers a period of three months' savings.

During the period of May 1941 through June 1945, the Territory of Alaska, with per capita E Bond sales of $317.08 ranked fifteenth in the nation. Hawaii was first. Let's support the Victory Loan Drive and raise Our rank!

The high school will sponsor a free dance on Friday, November 2nd, for all citizens who are interested in the Victory Loan Drive.

(TAP X, 2, p. 3)

WEATHERMAN BUSY

Last week the weatherman was quite busy handing out a variety of weather in this locality. He started the week with calm weather and then changed his mind and gave us quite a "blow" from the southeast with a great deal of rain. Hardly had he put this weather in motion until he changed his wind direction and gave us a stiff northwest gale with mild temperatures and rain squalls with pebbles of snow later in the day.

The high school had just finished the study of earthquakes in physical geography when the weatherman added his bit by giving a demonstration—an earth tremor that gave the accordion doors in the high school room considerable vibrations. At 4AM the next morning, he repeated with a more emphatic demonstration.

Then on Friday, the weatherman decided that several people who live here have never seen lightning nor heard thunder, so he threw in a touch of both. By Saturday, he became ashamed and gave us sunshine. (TAP X, 2, p. 8)

❧ November 1945 ❧
TRAGEDY CLAIMS ARMY VISITORS

T/5 Vernon E. Ashcraft, from Milan, Indiana, and T/5 John J. Dewdall, from Astoria, Oregon, lost their lives when the skiff in which they were riding capsized.

They and a companion, Edward J. Kambral, of Cleveland, Ohio, were rowing to their barge that was anchored below the bluff of Flagpole Hill when a terrific wind arose and upset the skiff as they were nearing their boat. The skiff and two of the soldiers were immediately swallowed by the heavy sea, but Mr. Kambral was thrown a line and pulled to safety.

Mr. Ashcraft had been in service in Alaska for 29 months. He was on his way to the States for discharge.

Mr. Dowdall, who was married, had served in the Pacific and the Canal Zone. He also was expected to be discharged when he arrived in the States.

A second probable disaster was averted when a soldier was swept up the bay in a skiff by a strong northeast wind. He was found the next day. (TAP X, 3, p. 4)

LET THERE BE LIGHT

The new light plant has proved to be of great value to the school for the last several days, since the weather has been cloudy and the mornings darker. The squinting of eyes in an effort to see is not as noticeable as previously among the pupils. (TAP X, 3, p. 3)

[The electrical generator was installed as part of the overall reconditioning of the school that occurred during summer, 1945. Ed.]

AN UPDATE ON THE CALUGAN CHILDREN

Isabelle Calugan writes from Cushman Hospital in Tacoma that she is an "up-patient" and has privileges to walk to visit Peter and Pauline and other patients in the hospital. (TAP X, 3, p. 3)

PETERSEN-ARNESS WEDDING

Mr. and Mrs. Allan Petersen announce the marriage of their daughter Peggy May to Jim Arness, on November 3, 1945. They are at home at 128-5th Avenue West, Kirkland, Washington. (TAP X, 3, p. 7)

WO j. g. and Mrs. Jim Arness

[Peggy was a 1942 graduate of Unga High School. She taught school in Unga during the period of the grounding of the F. P. 33. She met Jim in Unga, where he was dispatched to assist in the salvage operation. Peggy is a co-editor of this historical account. She and Jim have homesteaded in North Kenai since 1952. Ed.]

❧ December 1945 ❧

TRAPPER TROUBLES

When Andrew Foster and Lewis Berntsen started their trip to the trapping grounds, they didn't know they would have to play Robinson Crusoe. When they had reached the bay on the mainland, the *Bogdan* was so heavily iced down that it sunk. Both Andrew and Lewis made shore all right, but couldn't get any of their food off the boat because the hold was full of water. So they had to go without food for about three days. Meanwhile, they were busy getting the boat fixed.

They finally got the *Bogdan* to run again after chipping the ice off. After traveling toward home for awhile, they met the *Alasco*, whose captain decided that the *Bogdan* needed to be towed home.

The men recovered from their hardships and suffered with a few frozen fingers...

Emily Endresen, 11th Grade
(TAP X, 4, p. 7)

American National Red Cross Certificate of Service (courtesy Mary Foster)

OUR BOYS IN THE SERVICE

Like the Depression at the beginning of the 1930s, the effects of the nation's preparation for war ten years later made little impact on the life of the community of Unga. Throughout 1940, village activities continued unabated. A new school was being built, gardens were being planted and tended, salmon fishing during the summer season was not interrupted, and trappers continued their annual fall trek to the mainland for furs. The only indication that external events were beginning to be felt was the occasional availability of jobs in such strategic locations as Dutch Harbor, Cold Bay, Amchitka, and Sand Point, where a small Naval detachment had taken over much of "the Spit." But the drift toward war was ominous, like the fog rolling in over the headlands that guarded the harbor. THE ALASKA PEN reported in early February 1940 that a gathering was held at the school to pray for peace. The group was led by Miss Hazel Paramore, the local missionary, who asked the attendees to think "about the meaning of peace to our country, to the world, and to our own community." (TAP VI, 6, p. 3) Yet, it wasn't until January of the following year that the call for mobilization actually hit Unga, with the following announcement in the PEN:

SELECTIVE SERVICE

On registration day, January 22 [1941], Mr. [D. W.] Norris and Mr. [E. F.] Casey registered eleven men between the ages of twenty-one and thirty-five years for selective service. At a later date, two other men came over from Nelson's Lagoon and registered. The men are now looking forward to receiving the questionnaires from the local draft board at Unalaska. Thus far, we have no information as to when the first group shall be called.   (TAP VIII, 5, p. 5)

Indeed, it wasn't before another fishing season had passed that the first call-ups were announced:

UNGA SELECTEES CALLED

John Nelson, Thomas Lauritzen and John Haaf received orders last boat to report to Unalaska by November 15 [1941] for medical examination preparatory to being inducted into the Army. They plan on leaving on the next westbound boat. It has not been revealed where they will be stationed, should they be accepted. Rumor has it that Alaskans will be trained in Alaska, but this has not been verified. They are the first to be taken from this station.

They will be greatly missed by all, and the best wishes of everyone goes with them.
(TAP VIII, 2, p. 1)

In the ensuing months and years that the full complement of servicemen was selected and served, the PEN and PEN WHISPERS attempted to maintain monthly contact with them, publishing their military addresses when available and any activities that they were permitted to discuss. Under various headlines, but predominantly "UNGA BOYS IN THE SERVICE," the two publications reported continuously until the last of the conscriptees were discharged in late 1946.

As the war progressed, other men from the area were called to duty. They included Harry and Thomas Foster, Andy and Edmund Endresen, Albert Cushing, Jr., Mike Lindquist, Johannes Olsen, Alec Wilson, Jr., and Walter and Billy Berntsen from Unga; Barney and Aleck Grassamoff from

Simeonof Island; Hubert, Charles, and Donald McCallum, formerly of Unga; George Gronholdt, Fred Pletnikoff, and Nick Galovin from Sand Point; and George Gilbert, Peter Gould, Peter Harris, and Charles Hanson from Squaw Harbor. In addition, James Petersen, Adolph Rodgers, and George Fox enlisted from other locations. Jimmy served in the Navy, Adolph in the Army Air Force, and George in the Army.

All of the local draftees were skilled boatmen or shipwrights or carpenters. The Army, somewhat out of character, realized their value to the war effort and the particular needs of the Western Aleutian campaign, and utilized these men accordingly. Thus, George Gronholdt was assigned to captain small boats, and Johannes Olsen to run a power barge. Andy Endresen, who acquired a reputation for building dories and other small craft in Unga, continued in this line of work, along with the obligatory and infamous KP duty that he stood and about which he wrote home to friends and family eager to hear news from "the front." (See Sidebar.)

As had earlier been indicated, most of the area conscriptees did in fact receive their training, and spent their entire service years, in Alaska, where they enjoyed frequent and often lengthy furloughs. THE ALASKA PEN documents their many visits throughout the war, all of which were highlighted by community dances and parties. However, all were not so fortunate, and in the summer of 1944 the winds of war blew over the Shumagins with a vengeance. The first casualty was Lt. Adolph Rodgers who, late in the 1930s learned to fly and subsequently enlisted in the Army Air Force in 1941. Adolph, the son of Mrs. Zenia Rodgers, was killed in a plane crash in California. Adolph's obituary is printed in "Crossings," at the conclusion of Part II. During the same period, word was received by Mr. Tom Fox that his son George was killed in action in Italy, and later that year, Mr. and Mrs. John Berntsen were informed that their son Walter, a staff sergeant with the Alaska Transportation Service Harbor Craft, had died. No details of his death had ever reached the PEN.

—>»•«‹—

MY FIRST "K.P."

December 7 [1943] Harry [Foster] and I were finally inducted into the Army. The next day the Sgt. in charge of the barracks thought it would be fun to put us on for K.P. duty. In case you don't know what that means, I'll soon tell you. K.P. means a lot of hard work! At five thirty in the morning we got out of bed, mopped the floor, made up our beds and then started over to the mess hall where this wonderful job of K.P. was to be done.

The first thing we were introduced to was the floor which we scrubbed three times a day. The next thing on the list was to wash up a lot of aluminum trays, the kind used in most military camps to eat out of. We washed about five hundred of them after each meal, besides a lot of other stuff. Not so many, you say?

Once each day we would peel about fifty gallons of potatoes and other kinds of vegetables. By the time the day was over we sure didn't feel so ambitious.

This little game called K.P. wasn't so funny to us after the second time. So remember, my friends, don't ever say you're not going to do K.P. It's one of those jobs in the Army that catches up with you sooner or later.

Andy Endresen, Pvt., U. S. Army.
(PW I, 5, p. 5)

Thomas Lauritzen, Cpl., US Army

John Nelson, Pfc., US Army

Johnnie Haaf, Pvt., US Army

Harry Foster, Cpl., US Army

Andy Endresen, Sgt., US Army

Johannes Olsen, Sgt., US Army

Aleck Wilson, Pfc., US Army

George Gronholdt, US Army

Charlie Hansen, US Army

Jimmy Petersen, S.1/c, US Navy

While their sons, husbands, and brothers served abroad, the folks back home participated in numerous activities in support of the war effort. There were victory bond drives, victory gardens, fund drives for the Red Cross, entertainment activities for visiting servicemen, and knitting circles. The Alaska Territorial Guard organized a detachment of volunteers to provide local protection of the community in case of attack. The detachment consisted of 34 men, 15 years and older, under the command of Deputy US Marshal and Captain Allan L. Petersen.

Draftees were released one-by-one as the war ground to an end. Johannes Olsen was the first to receive his discharge papers, in the summer of 1945. By the end of 1946, all but two of the servicemen (who chose to reenlist) had been returned to the private sector. Most of those who chose discharge over an extended military career returned to the islands, and some semblance of normalcy had resumed. But Unga and the greater Shumagins would never be quite the same. For many of the servicemen, the war provided them with their first taste of freedom from the confines of the islands. Some simply did not return, thus becoming part of the exodus that punctuated the postwar years. The war was over and Unga no longer held the interest of the young. The demise of the village was underway, as Part III: The Aftermath concludes.

In Memoriam:
THEY GAVE THEIR ALL

Adolph Rodgers, Lt., USAAF

Walter Berntsen, S. Sgt., US Army

ALASKA TERRITORIAL GUARD

Unga Unit, Organized October 1943

On the 22nd of October a meeting of the men of Unga was called by Capt. Allan L. Petersen to organize the Unga unit of the Alaska Territorial Guard. The purpose of the ATG is to be ready to guard and protect our homes and community in case of invasion or attack. Units of the ATG have been organized in many parts of Alaska under the direction of Governor Gruening. The officers of the Unga branch are Capt. Allan Petersen selected by Governor Gruening, Lieuts. Harry Hunt and Olaf Swenson and Top Sergeant Harold Pedersen selected by the members. Every man who joins must take an oath. All members are volunteers and serve without pay. A member of the ATG must be a citizen of the United States, 15 years of age or over and of good character. Guns, ammunition and some clothing will be furnished.

Alisto, Joe
Andreason, Axel V.
Berntsen, John
Berntsen, Louis H.
Berntsen, John Jr.
Brandal, Andrew
Calugan, Alexander L.
Casey, Edward
Creevden, Nick
Cushing, Albert B.
Endresen, Edward
Foster, Andrew J.
Foster, Thomas D.
Foster, Tom
Fox, Thomas
Galovin, George P.
Galovin, Robert

Gilbert, Robert
Hansen, Hans
Hunt, Harrison C.
Kaboures, Speros
Krone, Fred W.
Larsen, Edward H.
Larsen, Norman X.
Lauritzen, Hjalmar
Melseth, Olaf P.
Pedersen, Harold
Pedersen, Lauritz
Petersen , Allan L.
Pomian, Fred W.
Rodgers, Raymond R.
Swenson, Olaf
Wilson, Daniel D.
Wood, Charles O.

(PW l, 2, p. 4)

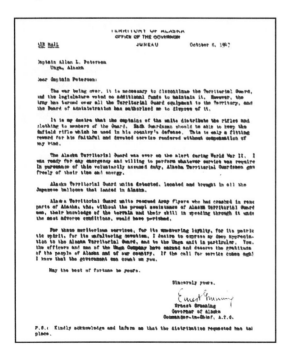

THE WRECK OF THE *33*

In the winter of 1944, the United States had been engaged in World War II for just over two years. In that time, the Japanese advance throughout the Pacific had been checked, and the tide of war had begun to recede. The Western Aleutians had been cleared of enemy forces after a vicious battle for Attu, and the so-called thousand-mile war was, for all practical purposes, over. The apparent relaxation in the Alaska theater of operations could be sensed by frequent and often lengthy furloughs for local servicemen and frequent visits by military vessels whose crews were starved for R&R activities. These visits were always welcomed with great enthusiasm because, in the absence of a regular mail boat during the war, the military provided mail service to the various villages scattered along the "chain." During the Christmas season, the vessels were also known to have distributed Christmas trees to the treeless islands.

Most of the vessels visiting Unga during the war years were small boats or harbor craft operating out of the small Naval shore station at Sand Point, some 14 sea miles due north of Unga. These were, in most cases, fishing vessels or tenders that had been condemned for wartime service as patrol boats. They carried identifications such as *YP-85*, *YP-154*, and *YP-155*. Larger vessels, predominantly Army freight and passenger ships such as the *FP-29*, *FP-32*, and *FP-41* were also common and welcomed visitors, whose crew often included servicemen from the Shumagin area. Unfortunately, the Unga harbor is a shallow, rock-strewn inlet that offers no safe anchorage for any size vessel, particularly during the frequent storms that blow out of the northeast and southeast. Absent docking facilities, virtually all vessels except skiffs and dories were required to anchor in the outer harbor and ferry passengers ashore by small boat. To escape storms, vessels would usually weigh anchor and seek shelter in Squaw Harbor or Sand Point where deep harbors and piers were available. But meteorological forecasts being what they were in the mid-'40s, storms would often build so rapidly that escape from their wrath was often problematic, especially when most of the crew was ashore enjoying an evening of merriment. Such was the case on a blustery evening in January 1944. The *FP-33*, one of a fleet of 12 sturdy wooden-hull vessels built especially for Alaskan coastal service, had arrived at the outer harbor during the day and found what was considered to be a secure anchorage: a narrow stretch of open water six to ten fathoms deep, between Elephant Rock, the harbor's distinctive southern headland, and a reef normally exposed at both high and low tide. Directly south of the anchorage lay a sheltered cove—sheltered, that is, from the predominant sou'easters—in the lee of Elephant Rock. Falling away to the northeast lay the open ocean and to the northwest the high headlands on the village side of the harbor.

In Unga, preparations were underway at the community hall in the center of town to welcome the prospective visitors. As PEN WHISPERS, the school's monthly news bulletin, reported, dances were organized, often at the drop of a hat, several times a month. These were occasions of full community involvement in which townspeople provided a variety of both solid and liquid refreshments and often live musical entertainment. It was to these festivities that the crew of the *FP-33* was invited and, according to some reports, most of the crew and passengers disemarked. They were ferried by small boat roughly one-half mile to shore. Daylight in January being of short duration, the ship was soon enshrouded in darkness.

Sometime during the evening of January 24th, a weather front came roaring through the area. The following cryptic entry appeared in PEN WHISPERS:

> January 25, 1944: a howling "Northwester"! Lt. Cmdr. [Jack] Benson, Marshal A. L. Petersen and Mike Galovin were busy caring for members of a stranded vessel. The "Unga Hotel" provided temporary shelter.   (PW I, 5, p. 3)

The "stranded vessel," the *FP-33*, had dragged anchor and had become impaled on the rocks in the lee of Elephant Head. Passengers and crew were forced to spend the night and many succeeding nights in the only public accommodations available in Unga: the federal jail! And thus began the long saga of the wreck of the *33*.

Through the waning days of January and into early February, high tides and a wind shift to the northeast eventually lifted the vessel off the rocks and threw her high and dry onto the gently sloping beach just under the sheer cliff of the headland. The temperature hovered near zero. The *FP-33* was temporarily abandoned to the elements.

Entries in journals kept by Mr. and Mrs. Allan Petersen during these harrowing days, supplemented by cogent eyewitness accounts of James Arness, who participated in the subsequent salvage of the vessel, tell the story of the wreck, the rescue, and the final days of the *FP-33*, unencumbered by wartime censorship. This is the gist of what was gleaned from these accounts: The *FP-33*, an Army freighter which normally ran between Seward and Adak, arrived off Unga the evening of January 24, 1944, ostensibly to deliver mail to the village. The vessel carried a complement of 23 servicemen, of which 14 or 15 were crew. Although the accounts did not indicate that entertainment had been arranged in town for the passengers and crew, it was more the rule than the exception that a dance would have been arranged and that much of the vessel's complement had gone ashore to attend the dance. One unconfirmed report suggests that all but the ship's cook had disembarked. How long they remained ashore is questionable, but Petersen's journal indicates that the crew had spent the first night aboard the *33* and were ferried ashore the following day. On January 26th, the *FP-32*, a sister ship of the grounded *33*, arrived with a Dr. Lester to treat some cases of frostbite and other minor injuries.

During their long weeks of "incarceration" at the "Unga Hotel," the crew of the stranded *FP-33* whiled away their time with a variety of community activities. The monthly gossip columns in PEN WHISPERS report on the week following the grounding of their vessel that a USO dance was held on the 27th, the President's Ball on the 29th, and on the 31st, a dance sponsored by local girls was held in honor of the "visiting servicemen." It was truly a rough incarceration. Between festivities, it was reported that on February 4th, "the dancehall floor was washed and polished by the 'boys' in the 'Unga Hotel,' " (PW I, 6, p. 3) just in time for another dance on the 5th. Then on February 8th, these same 'boys' began to paint the hall, which put a crimp on the usual activities, at least until the 12th—Lincoln's birthday. The month was rounded out with a dance on Valentine's Day and one on Washington's birthday. Needless to say, the jailbirds were becoming quite the popular guests. There is no indication that February 29th passed without incident, but this leap year date was the birthday of one of the most popular members of the crew—S. Sgt. Roy Camper—and it is rather unlikely that he celebrated his sixth birthday in his "cell." The *FP-33* crew began to disperse in March; shortly thereafter, the "Unga Hotel" reverted to its prior function, and all the while the *33* remained firmly grounded on the beach of Unga's outer harbor.

Part of the FP-33 *crew, billeted at the "Unga Hotel." S. Sgt. Roy Campen is second from the right.*

In the weeks and months that followed, several military support vessels such as the tugboat *LT-157* and the power scow *PB-868* converged on the scene to attempt to pull the *33* off the beach. The wreck was loaded with empty 55-gallon drums to increase buoyancy, but despite extremely high March tides, the *33* held fast. In mid-April, the steamship *Algonquin, YAG-29*, a veteran of years of service in the Bering Sea, was dispatched to Unga to serve as mother ship for Navy Lt. Bob Logan and his salvage crew. The salvage effort was now under the overall command of Capt. A. Paulson. As spring passed into summer with no apparent progress in the salvage, a second tug, the *LT-188*, skippered by Jim Arness, was called from its Chernofski station on the southwest coast of Unalaska Island to assist in the operation. The *33* hull was girded with cables and a towline attached near the stern. In Arness' account, "...at ten that night we [the *LT-188*] hooked outside in tandem but ahead of them [the *LT-157*]. When we pulled, she sheared to one side up onto the reef that she had first hung up on. The next day, they blasted away the rocks on part of the reef and that night we hooked on and pulled her into deep water." The date was August 2nd or 3rd, 1944, more than six months after her grounding. Arness reported that tug *LT-157* was selected to tow the hulk to Seward. She was first moved to Squaw Harbor where more buoyancy was added. She was at this point literally floating on oil drums. In this condition, she was towed without incident to Seward, where her engines were removed. She embarked on her final voyage shortly thereafter: a tow to Thumb Cove, an inlet on Resurrection Bay, eight miles southeast of Seward. Here she was beached once again and set ablaze.

The Algonquin, YAG-29: *Command vessel for the* FP-33 *salvage operation*

Thus ended the saga of the *FP-33*. But what of Unga? What lingering effect did this long ordeal have on the area? This writer visited the site of the grounding five years later and came across a heavy-duty stud link chain cable that extended from the shore in a northeasterly direction and ran into the sea. Nothing more remained. The effects on the village of Unga, however, were more subtle. The long and often frustrating recovery efforts were heady stuff for a small and lonely community suddenly thrust into the limelight. There hadn't been such a burst of activity on the harbor since the halcyon days of gold mining and codfishing at the turn of the century. Unga had become exposed to the rest of the world and in many respects liked what it saw. Unga would never be quite the same again. Lives were changed, but none so profoundly as that of James Arness, the tugboat captain who was called to service in the latter stages of the recovery. Jim served out the final months of the war in the Aleutians, married Peggy Petersen, a 1942 graduate of Unga High School and former grade school teacher in Unga (and our co-editor), and settled in Kenai after the war. He and Peggy live there still.

Endnote: During the entire period of the grounding incident, the local school paper—the only day-by-day published account of activities in and around Unga—never once referred to the grounded vessel as the US Army *FP-33*. We have herewith set the record straight. (TL:Ed.)

Salvage of the FP-33: *A Portfolio.*
Clockwise from upper left: Capt. Paulson and Lt. Logan; three views of the stranded vessel; passing oil drums to shore via a pass line.

SCHOOL NEWS
Unga Territorial School 1940-1945

OUR NEW SCHOOL

For more than two years the M. S. *Fern* has been traveling on a monthly schedule from Seward to Unalaska and on up to Bristol Bay, then returning to Seward to make another trip.

The *Fern* carries mail and most of the time it carries passengers. Last spring, on its April trip, it stopped in at Unga as usual. The mail and one passenger was left. The passenger was Mr. E. L. Graves, one of the contractors for the new school building. The new building was to be erected in Unga during the summer.

At about the time that Mr. Graves arrived, the cannery boats were beginning to arrive at the various fish canneries. Some of the cannery boats were big steamships and on one of these ships was a large supply of lumber and other materials to be used in the construction of our new school. The materials were unloaded at Squaw Harbor, which is about seven miles from Unga. A large scow and a fishing boat, the M. S. *Vis*, was used to transport the materials over to Unga. From the scow, the materials were unloaded into small codfish dories and taken ashore. Once on shore, it was loaded on a small car that was pulled up the hill, about 300 feet, by a winch to where the building was to be constructed. The gravel for the foundation was taken up the hill in the same manner.

Construction on the building started in early May and has been continued through the summer. Mr. Pond, a carpenter, arrived on one of the westward trips of the *Fern*, and has been helping all summer with the carpenter work. Mr. Osbo and Mr. Lechner, both from Seward, were here for a few weeks to put in the electrical work and plumbing.

The construction of the school building was far enough along so that we were able to move over from the old building and start school in the new building on the 1st day of October.

On the main floor there are four different classrooms: classroom I, classroom II, the Activity room and the Home Economics room. In classroom I, Mrs. Petersen teaches grades one to four. In classroom II and the Activity room are the students in grades five to eight and nine to twelve. These grades are taught by Mr. and Mrs. Norris. On the main floor, we also have the boys' and girls' lavatories and enough steel lockers so that each two students can have one locker.

Part of the basement is unexcavated and the rest is divided into the furnace room, coal room and the Manual Training room.

At the side of the school building the teachers' quarters are located. In it, there are two apartments: one for a single person and one for a married couple. The construction on the teachers' quarters will be finished in a few weeks and Mr. and Mrs. Norris will then move in.

The electric lights, the sanitary drinking fountain, the running water and the building in general is [*sic*] a wonderful improvement over the old building. The teachers and students are enjoying the advantages of the new building very much.

(TAP VII, 1, p. 2)

The 1940-41 school year spelled the optimistic beginning of a new period for the Unga Territorial School. Students were ushered into a flashy new building with more than adequate room for twelve grades of school, modern facilities including an efficient central heating system and electricity. The year also signaled the end of the tenure of Mr. and Mrs. Dwain W. Norris, who shepherded the school through the end of the '30s and successfully transferred operations to the new facility. Unfortunately, there were no high school graduates to crown their achievements. They were replaced in the fall of 1941 by a young, energetic couple, Fred and Leona Koschmann, who wrote some years later of the honeymoon year they spent in Unga.*

School enrollment in September 1941 was approximately 45. Mrs. Koschmann taught grades four through eight, Mr. Koschmann the nine high school students, and Mrs. Allan Petersen continued to teach the primary grades. Along with their school responsibilities, the Koschmanns participated eagerly in social activities of the village and were particularly active in church functions, Mr. Koschmann having organized and directed the church choir. THE ALASKA PEN published Volume VIII during the Koschmanns' short tenure. THE PEN sported a somewhat simplified format but continued its detailed reporting of school and village activities. In another change,

The Koschmann family, late 1940s: Carol, Leona, Fred, and Vic.

the editorial staff rotated among the high school student body, thus providing to more students the experience of publishing a monthly news magazine.

After a four-year drought, the Unga High School graduated its fifth and sixth seniors: Peggy Petersen and Norman Lauritzen. Peggy completed her first year of high school in Unga, returning from Seattle to attend her senior year at home. Peggy is the daughter of Allan and Jettie Petersen. All of Norman's school years were spent in Unga. Norman is the son of Conrad and Lena Lauritzen.

By the time the 1941-42 school year came to a close, the Second World War had been raging for some six months, and although this remote corner of the world seemed far removed from the hostilities, the effects of the mobilization for a protracted war had a profound effect on the village of Unga and its neighbors. Although the area's salmon canneries that provided the principal livelihood of the Shumagins continued operation, most of the single young men who contributed to their families' well-being were drafted into the military services. Contact with the outside world—the lifeline of all communities along the Peninsula—became haphazard and dependent largely upon military traffic among the islands. Mail, freight, and passenger service, that once maintained a monthly schedule out of Seward, would often stretch to several months' intervals, particularly during the long, stormy winter. And to make matters worse, the uncertainty of being evacuated from an approaching war zone hung over the village like a thick, dark fog. Under these circumstances, it was virtually impossible to entice teachers and other service providers to travel to the islands, and those itinerants whose contracts expired were more than anxious to move to more secure locations. So it was with the

* Fred Koschmann, "An Extended Honeymoon in Unga," *Alaska Magazine*, November 1978.

The Class of '42: Norman Lauritzen and Peggy Petersen

Methodist minister and his family and the young Koschmanns, who felt it prudent to move closer to medical facilities, both families being on the verge of enlargement.

Thus, the approaching 1942-43 school year was suddenly facing a dire predicament: a student body similar in size to the previous year's numbers but one lacking a full faculty. Fortunately, the Petersens decided to remain in Unga (they remained, in fact, for the duration of the war), and Mrs. Petersen assumed the dual role of principal and teacher. She was assisted the first year by Mrs. Daniel (Anna Cushing) Wilson of Unga and, in 1943-44, by her daughter, Peggy, who had spent the previous year attending the University of Washington. The only casualty during this period was the high school. Enrollment was insufficient to offer a full curriculum and, as a result, the high school and THE ALASKA PEN were temporarily suspended. Unga High School was reborn in September 1943 with five students—all freshmen—and to continue the tradition of publishing a monthly news magazine, the students introduced PEN WHISPERS. The following editorial, from Volume I, Issue 1, presents a brief mission statement describing the new publication.

Mrs. Allan Petersen, Miss Peggy Petersen, and the 1943-44 student body of the Unga Territorial School

EDITORIAL

Since our High School has always put out a school paper, we freshmen thought we'd like to put one out, too. Although we don't expect it to be as big and as good as THE ALASKA PEN, we're all going to do our best to make it worthwhile reading.

It was decided to change the name to PEN WHISPERS, as we believe this name will be more suitable. Our efforts will be "whispers" as compared with the original "Alaska Pen," yet we will keep you in touch with the happenings 'around town' through the whispers of our pens.

The paper will be published once a month with the subscription price of fifty cents a year. We solicit your interest and cooperation in this school activity.

Complimentary copies will be sent to the local boys who are in the service.

(PW I, 1, p. 2)

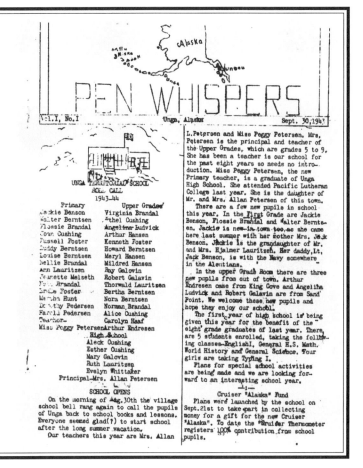

Like its predecessor, PEN WHISPERS reported on regional news as well as school activities. Evelyn Whittaker served as editor-in-chief for the entire eight-month run. She was assisted by Mary Galovin, Assistant Editor, Aleck Cushing, Business Manager, Thorwald Lauritzen, Art Editor, and Peggy Petersen, Typist and Technician. Ruth Lauritzen and Esther Cushing were reporters. Many of the departments reported upon were identical to those of THE PEN, i.e., student functions, town news, club activities, etc. But a major addition—a reflection of the times—was the column "Unga Boys in Service," which ran monthly. This column provided addresses of all servicemen from the area, updating when appropriate, and offered tidbits of allowable information on their activities and well-being. "Unga Boys in Service" was a popular column and provided a unique service to those in the military as well as their family and friends anxious for news from sons and brothers. A more comprehensive review of the Shumagin area's contribution to the war effort is presented in a companion essay.

In late 1944, with the danger in the Western Aleutians diminishing, a relaxation in tension could be felt throughout the Shumagins. Military furloughs became more frequent and life appeared to be gradually returning to normal. With the arrival of Donald and Opal Lawvere, the Unga Territorial School was once again in a position to offer a full 12-year curriculum for the area's students. The Lawveres hailed from Indiana and had never before ventured beyond the Mississippi. Overwhelmed by seeing their first mountains, they were soon to be surrounded by the mountains of Delarof Harbor. Some 38 students greeted the Lawveres and Mrs. Petersen, who resumed her position as primary grades teacher. Thirteen of these students constituted the high school student body.

Mrs. Petersen and the students of Unga High School, 1943-44: Esther Cushing, Ruth Lauritzen, Mary Galovin, Aleck Cushing, and Evelyn Whittaker. Behind Ruth is Harvey Sharpe, who joined the student body in mid-term.

In addition to their school duties, the Lawveres were active in community affairs—Mrs. Lawvere in the Unga Women's Club and Mr. Lawvere in the Unga Community Church. Mr. Lawvere is particularly remembered for his sermons and the impassioned eulogy he delivered on the death of President Franklin D. Roosevelt. (TAP XI, 8, p. 2)   The highlight of the Lawvere tenure, however must be the guidance the school faculty offered in confronting the diphtheria epidemic. This is discussed in considerable detail in Part III, The Aftermath.

The Unga Women's Club

MOTTO
JUST THE BEST THAT YOU CAN DO IS
THE SERVICE ASKED OF YOU

ORGANIZED 1936
MEMBER OF THE ALASKA FEDERATION OF WOMEN'S CLUBS
UNGA, ALASKA

The town women organized the Unga Women's Club this fall. The officers elected were: Mrs. Edward F. Casey, president, Mrs. Lena Lauritzen, vice-president and Mrs. John Evets, secretary-treasurer. They met on Sept. 16th *[1936]* at the Unga Community Hall to sew articles for their Spring Bazaar.   (TAP III, 1, p. 6)

In the early 1930s, a number of groups were organized to offer extracurricular youth activities and to utilize adult skills for the betterment of the village. THE ALASKA PEN reports that during 1934 and 1935 several "Sewing Club" meetings were held. These included the Small Girls' Sewing Club, the Junior Girls' Sewing Club, and the Women's Sewing Club. In September of 1936, the Unga Improvement Club was organized with committees assigned to oversee the town's waterworks, its sidewalks, the dance hall, and the club house. At about the same time, a formidable group of ladies gathered at the home of Mrs. Viola Casey to consider combining the Women's Sewing Club and elements of the Unga Improvement Club into one organization. Thus was born the Unga Women's Club, which over the next 14 years provided invaluable guidance and services to the village. Their highest priority was to be the welfare of the citizens of Unga. As proclaimed in the Club's mission statement, their objective was "to promote fellowship and cooperation among its members, encourage interest in intellectual, civic and social problems, and to assist in civic improvement and community welfare."

As headlined in the brief announcement in the September 1936 issue of THE ALASKA PEN, the ladies of the Club elected Mrs. Casey to guide the group through its first year. Dues were established at 25 cents per meeting or one dollar a year. In one of its first orders of business, the Club agreed to seek membership in the Alaska Federation of Women's Clubs. The Club was welcomed into the Alaska Federation the following year and was charged annual dues of 10 cents per member. Since membership in the Alaska club automatically bestowed membership in the national, the Unga Women's Club became affiliated in its first year with the prestigious General Federation of Women's Clubs.

In its first official meeting, December 2, 1936, the Club's constitution and by-laws were adopted and the following members present signed as charter members: Misses Elna Bard, Florence Krone, Betty McCallum, and Clara Pearson; and Mmes. Laura Berntsen, Viola Casey, Isabella Evets, Nellie Krone, Anna T. Lauritzen, Lena Lauritzen, Genevieve Melseth, Frances Larsen, Tillie Pedersen, Jettie Petersen, Bertha Siemion, Harriet Williams, and Dolly Woberg.

Constitution and By-Laws

of the

UNGA WOMAN'S CLUB

———

Organized September, 1936

Joined the Alaska Federation of
Women's Clubs, 1937

Joined the General Federation of
Women's Clubs, 1937

Motto:
Just the best that you can do
Is the service asked of you.

Colors—Purple and Gold

Flower—Purple Violet

Three standing committees were organized: the Welfare Committee was designed to recognize and address personal needs and problems in the village; the Program Committee was charged with arranging programs for each meeting, and the Club House Committee's responsibility was the utilization and maintenance of the community club house. Ad hoc committees were to be created as needed.

In one of the first activities of the Club, the Welfare Committee encouraged families to plant vegetable gardens to supplement their diets with fresh produce. This led, in the fall of 1937, to a harvest ball. THE ALASKA PEN reports:

> Unga's first Harvest Ball was...held at the Community Hall the evening of September 18th [1937]. It marked the end of the Garden Project which was started in the spring to encourage the planting of gardens... Exhibits of produce at the hall made an attractive display and proved that gardens can be successfully raised in Unga...
>
> (TAP IV, 1, p. 2)

Prize ribbons were awarded for variety of vegetables raised, for the garden with the fewest weeds, and for the most attractive garden. In addition to garden produce, village handiwork was displayed and later auctioned. The proceeds—$270.75—were used "for the purchase of Christmas gifts for the children of Unga and also to help pay the indebtedness against the Public Dance Hall."

The Program Committee arranged interesting programs for each of their meetings and prepared a booklet each month to describe the programs. They might consist of timely talks, songs, or even skits. One program presented a minstrel show in which club members participated—this being long before the specter of political correctness was first raised!

The little building located across the sidewalk from Lauritzen's store served the community as a library, a Sunday school, a Girl Scout meeting room and the village club house. Its utilization and well-being was the responsibility of the Club House Committee. One of the first projects was building cabinets, cupboards, and shelves for storage and later for the display of the library's books and magazines. Since these projects were performed by volunteers, the only expense in keeping the building operational were oil for lighting and coal for heating. The Committee decided to ask each user group to donate $5.00 toward this expense. Sharing the cost in this manner made all users, including the children, responsible for their club house.

Not long after the Unga Women's Club attained membership in the regional and national clubs, the members embarked upon an ambitious program to persuade the Territorial Legislature to provide funds for several projects the ladies deemed critical to the well-being of the village. Their request, spearheaded by Mrs. Petersen, sought appropriations for a new school, a short-wave station, a breakwater, a telephone installation, and perhaps most important, the dispatch of medical personnel to the area. Although the former concerns received no immediate support from Juneau, the request for medical assistance apparently hit a responsive chord, and very shortly a public health nurse was on her way to Unga. THE ALASKA PEN reports:

> Word has been received through the Unga Women's Club that a public health nurse will arrive on the SS *Starr*. She will be here for two months and will give health instructions and programs.   (TAP IV, 3, p. 6)
>
> Mrs. Laura Elkins...arrived on the *Starr*. She was sent from the Public Health Office in Juneau. Her duty is to immunize against smallpox and diphtheria and also examine all the Unga school children...   (TAP IV, 4, p. 5)

According to a Club report, Nurse Elkins vaccinated 125 people against smallpox and immunized all children under 12 against diphtheria. The report further stated, "This service is a real help in isolated communities like Unga where, during the winter months, we have no wireless communication [and] the nearest doctor [is located] at Unalaska, some 300 miles away and only one boat a month [connects the two villages]."

As regards the other items on the Club's request to the Legislature, a new school was eventually built [in 1940], a privately-funded and operated short-wave station went on the air a few years later, but the dream of a breakwater to provide small-boat shelter was never realized. Thus, the long-term viability of the town was perhaps fatally compromised.

One eminently successful undertaking, discussed in detail in Part III of this book, was the organization of a public library. A Club report for 1937-38 announced:

> The major project of the Club this winter has been the organization of the Unga Community Library in accordance with the requirements of the Territorial Library Law. Five members of the Club were chosen to form the Board of Directors. An afghan crocheted by members of the Club was raffled to raise necessary funds for books and supplies. On February 3rd [1938], the library was officially opened with one hundred adults' and children's books ready for circulation. Librarians are members chosen from the Club who willingly contribute their services one afternoon each week—Thursday from 3 to 5 PM...

Not all civic activities of the Club were successful, however. An ambitious program to introduce both deciduous and coniferous trees to the island was undertaken in late 1938 to observe the sesquicentennial of the US Constitution. Cottonwood and spruce saplings were acquired along with detailed planting instructions. The trees were planted with appropriate ceremonies and in presumably good virgin soil along a path leading to the community dance hall in the center of town. The little trees were fitted with copper sesquicentennial tree markers and accorded considerable TLC. But within two years the trees were barely clinging to life. Anna T. Lauritzen, Chairman of the Welfare Committee, reported in May of 1940 that "The tree planting project shows very poor results. There is a wee, small life sign on one spruce tree. The rest are dead and dry." In May, 1941, Mrs. Lauritzen reported that "The tree planting project has proven a failure. All the trees that were planted are dead." So much for the TLC.

As the world drifted toward war, the national club mobilized a Department of International Relations to, among other things, "cultivate a bond of understanding and world friendship" and "to awaken a more intelligent and sympathetic interest in international affairs and world peace..." In this endeavor, the Unga Women's Club was particularly honored to have had Mrs. Petersen selected as Chairman of the Alaska branch of the Department. The Second World War engulfed the nation shortly thereafter, and many of the Club's activities were redirected toward support of servicemen and relief organizations both within and outside of Alaska. The Club actively supported the American Red Cross throughout the war by providing numerous knitted articles such as sweaters, helmets, socks, mufflers, and rifle mitts for the military. It sponsored USO activities for visiting military personnel that included, for example, 41 dances through 1941-42 that yielded $123.00 (rental of the dance hall at $3.00 a dance!) for the Club's treasury. Basket socials during this period were particularly lucrative. One such social in September of 1943 netted $788.80, which funded more social functions and provided moneys for ongoing projects such as cemetery maintenance, support of the local churches, the Children's Christmas Fund, and the Alaska Crippled Children's Association.

One continuing project that became quite popular during this period was the annual President's Ball and March of Dimes, in support of the work of the National Foundation for Infantile Paralysis. In endeavoring to elicit broad communituy support, the Club reached out and appointed Deputy US Marshal Allan L. Petersen to chair a special committee. One result of his efforts is the response the Club received from Basil O'Connor, President Franklin Roosevelt's confidante and President of the Foundation. His letter of thanks is shown below.

President Roosevelt counts dimes with Basil O'Connor, his ex-law partner and new chief of the National Foundation for Infantile Paralysis. The campaign, led by the President, calls upon the American people to send in their dimes, a veritable "March of Dimes," as comedian Eddie Cantor says.

The demobilization of Alaskan military installations in the aftermath of the war presented a unique opportunity for the Club to secure useful items for the village. Again, Mrs. Petersen stepped forward as corresponding secretary of the Club and began a concerted letter-writing campaign to seek support to acquire surplus equipment from Fort Randall at Cold Bay. Through the good offices of the *Alaska Weekly*, a Seattle publication that served as the unofficial mouthpiece of the Territory, and Lulu Fairbanks, its indomitable circulation manager, Alaska's lone official (but non-voting) member of Congress E. L. (Bob) Bartlett was contacted with a modest request: the Unga Territorial School wanted to acquire a 16mm movie projector and perhaps a generator to run it, some ping pong paddles and balls, a few baseball bats and balls, and a Quonset hut or two to put them in. Thus began a series of letters with the primary agency responsible for the disbursement of surplus equipment—

the US Department of Interior, Division of Territorial and Island Possessions. The upshot of the negotiations was that the government was disallowed from providing surplus equipment to "private organizations" (even Territorial schools?) unless these organizations were willing and able to purchase the articles for a "fair price" and that only after the entitled organizations had their pick. Needless to say, the effort became entangled in the Federal bureaucracy, and the hope for a few recreational items and a shelter for use of these items during the long winter was eventually abandoned. Shells of some of those Quonset huts still may be seen jutting out of the barren landscapes of many Aleutian outposts, but not a remnant was ever seen at Unga.

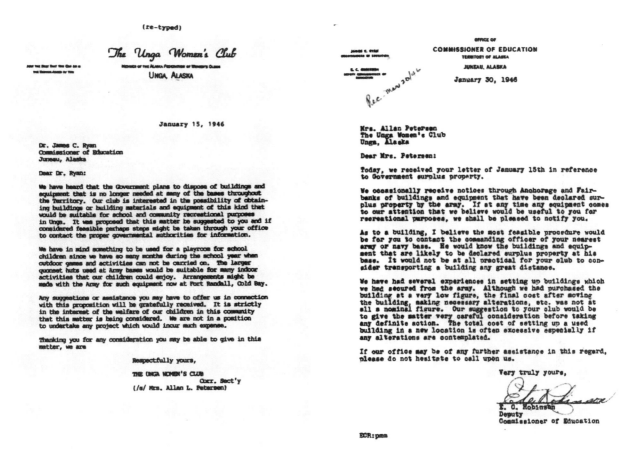

The Paper Trail That Led Nowhere: The Unga Women's Club's effort to acquire surplus military equipment at the end of WWII

(continued on following page)

THE ALASKA WEEKLY

1005 Western
2-11-46

Dear Mrs. Petersen:

I'm sending the enclosed letter airmail to Bob Bartlett in an effort to help you. I also suggest that you write at once to the Surplus Property Office, U.S. Dept. of the Interior, Office of the Secretary, Division of Territories and Island Possessions, Anchorage.

How I love the story of your Bird's Cafe...wish I might send up some fat for their little tummies ! We're having a lot of trouble getting butter out here...we just watch every scrap...funny how quickly we were turned from a nation of plenty to one of want...something wrong somewhere !

Your ALASKA PEN arrives and is always a pleasure...the youngsters are to be congratulated - but then, when they have a woman with your vision and energy, they cannot help it. I only hope that one of them will grow up to take your place in the community for progress and an always better living. God sent you to Unga for a purpose and you are not disappointing Him !

Much love to my Valentine,

Lulu

Congress of the United States
House of Representatives
Washington, D. C.

E. L. BARTLETT
Delegate from Alaska

February 13, 1946

Mrs. Allan Peterson,
Secretary,
Unga Women's Club,
Unga, Alaska.

Dear Mrs. Peterson:

Miss Lulu M. Fairbanks of the ALASKA WEEKLY has been kind enough to convey to me the interest of the Unga Women's Club in obtaining surplus equipment from the army base at Cold Bay.

Under the provisions of the Surplus Disposal Act and the regulations having to do with the Act, material in Alaska declared surplus is turned over to the Surplus Property Office of the Department of the Interior for disposal. The law does not permit the government to give away surplus equipment even to another government agency, but it might be that arrangements could be worked out so that the Club could obtain needed equipment at a moderate price. With that thought in mind I am sending copy of this letter on to Mr. John M. Barringer whose office is in Washington and who is in general charge of the Surplus Property Office in Alaska.

I hope something can be worked out so that the Club may obtain the equipment it desires.

With best wishes, I am

Sincerely yours,

E. L. Bartlett
Delegate

ELB/mgn

UNITED STATES
DEPARTMENT OF THE INTERIOR
OFFICE OF THE SECRETARY
DIVISION OF TERRITORIES AND ISLAND POSSESSIONS
ANCHORAGE, ALASKA

SURPLUS PROPERTY OFFICE

April 17, 1946

Mrs. Allan L. Petersen
The Unga Women's Club
Unga, Alaska

Dear Mrs. Petersen:

In reference to your letter of March 30, 1946, we regret to inform you that our office has not received any declaration of available surplus property at Cold Bay. However, from the information we have on hand, we are fairly certain that the items you have mentioned, with the possible exception of the light plant, will not be available.

At present, there is no light plant available, but as soon as one is declared we will notify you. In this regard, we are placing you on our mailing list.

Let us know if we can be of any further assistance to you.

Very truly yours,

Frank O. Brink
FRANK O. BRINK
Merchandising Division

UNITED STATES
DEPARTMENT OF THE INTERIOR
OFFICE OF THE SECRETARY
DIVISION OF TERRITORIES AND ISLAND POSSESSIONS
ANCHORAGE, ALASKA

May 29, 1946

SURPLUS PROPERTY OFFICE

The Unga Women's Club,
Unga, Alaska.

Attention: Mrs. Allan Petersen.

Dear Madam:

With reference to your letter of May 10, 1946, you are advised that because of the limited supply of 16 mm projectors, and demands by higher priority groups, such as Government agencies, none will be available to the public.

Regarding softball equipment, up to this point Army Special Services has declared none, but are contemplating declaring it in the near future.

There are no quonset huts, family washing machines or small refrigerators available for sale at this time. However, your name has been added to our mailing list, and in the event any of the above equipment becomes available for sale, you will be notified by means of a sales list.

We are enclosing herewith Fairbanks Sales List No. 16, which includes a number of light plants, and you are advised to contact Mr. Floyd Davis, Surplus Property Office, Fairbanks, Alaska, for further information regarding that.

If we can be of further service to you, please let us know.

Yours very truly,

Vernon Milliken,
Acting Chief of Merchandising Division.

FOR/lf

Enc.: Frbks. Sales List No. 16.

The failure of this admirable attempt to better the opportunities for a few school children was not only a bitter disappointment for Mrs. Petersen, who would shortly leave the Club and Unga after serving both for more than a decade, but represented in many ways the swan song of the Unga Women's Club. After 1946, the Club gradually declined as families moved to other villages. The end came with the following query in the October 1950 issue of THE ALASKA PEN:

> With news that the Women's Club has been disbanded brings us to the question, "why?"
>
> The Unga Women's Club has been kept up for years and has been especially noted for its generosity by giving money for the benefit of the children, the church, the Red Cross, Crippled Children and numerous other things. Club members were always ready to help in anything that was helpful toward the good of the community.
>
> Why is it then that such a helpful organization should break up?   (TAP XlV, 2, p. 5)

Why indeed! But the fact was that the Club could no longer sustain its mission with its shrinking membership. It was the sign of the times. Before the decade of the fifties came to an end, so did most of the businesses and activities that made the village a viable community.

The Unga Women's Club left a rich legacy of compassionate care and service to the village of Unga. Long after its demise, that legacy is perhaps best exemplified by the life of Genevieve Foster's daughter, Janice, who was born and raised in Unga where she was instilled with the attributes of service. She moved to Sand Point as a child, where she selflessly served her new community until her untimely death in 2005 at 56. Janice's service had earlier been recognized by a thankful community that proclaimed a day in December 2004 as Janice Shuravloff Day.

One final legacy—a living legacy—is prominent today at the Unga townsite: clusters of spruce trees dot the landscape with patches of green. These are not the trees planted by the Club: those trees withered and died. But the idea launched by the Club in 1938 to introduce trees to a totally barren landscape took root in the community and trees were planted in gardens, in the shelter of houses, and in the cemetery. Most of them somehow flourished and eventually dwarfed the houses that initially afforded them protection. They stand today in silent testimony to the indomitable spirit of the villagers of Unga and particularly to the women of the Club who were indeed formidable and who lived and practiced their motto, "The Best That You Can Do Is The Service Asked Of You." In memory, the Unga Women's Club could not be better honored.

—⊰●⊱—

Presidents of the Unga Women's Club. top row: Viola Casey (1936-37 and 1946-47), Jettie Petersen (1938-39), and Lena Lauritzen (1939-40 and 1944-46); bottom row: Nellie Krone (1940-41), Lena Hunt (1948-49), and Genevieve Foster (1941-? and 1949-50).

UNGA: METHODISM'S FRAGILE FOOTHOLD IN ALASKA

Unga Methodist Church

The year was 1886, a scant 19 years after Alaska's purchase and hardly 90 years after Imperial Russia established an outpost and chapel in the remote Shumagin Islands village. Unga was then a community of Russian-Aleut fishermen and hunters but was on the verge of exploitation by Euro-American fishermen and miners who sought the lucrative North Pacific cod and the gold that was discovered earlier in the decade. To service the growing population and to minister to the natives (the town population was reported to be 148 in 1890), the Women's Home Missionary Society of the Methodist Episcopal Church, in conjunction with Alaska's fledgling education department, sought to establish its first Alaska mission and school in Unga by dispatching the Rev. John H. Carr and his wife, Ethelda, to the village. The venture went awry, however, with the death of Mrs. Carr in 1887, and although the school continued after Rev. Carr's departure two to three years later, the mission was closed. Nevertheless, this spark of Methodism in Unga was sufficient to ignite a flame that spread westward to Unalaska and thence throughout the new Territory.

Although Unga lacked a resident Protestant minister or church for another 50 years, the seeds planted by the Carrs continued to bear fruit. Lay ministers from the village and medical missionaries and teachers dispatched to Unga preached the Gospel by word and deed, conducting Sunday School and church services for much of the early 20th century. The most prominent recipient of this religious environment was a young man born in Unga of Russian-English-Aleut heritage, raised in the Jesse Lee Home, a Methodist orphanage in Unalaska, who went on to become a bishop of the Methodist Church. The Rev. Peter Gordon Gould returned to Alaska in 1949 as Superintendent of the

Alaska Mission and was instrumental in organizing the Alaska Methodist University (now Alaska Pacific University) in Anchorage. Members of the extended Gould family live today in Sand Point and other nearby villages, in Anchorage, and throughout the Pacific Northwest. They can be justly proud of the contributions Rev. Gould made to Methodism, to the State of Alaska and particularly, to its youth.

The Methodists renewed their missionary interest in Unga by dispatching Dr. Walter Torbet, Superintendent of the Alaska Mission, to the village in the summer of 1935. He persuaded towns-people to organize a Methodist movement, the Epworth League, for the youth of the village. Meetings of the League were held in conjunction with the Unga Community Sunday School, which had long been shepherded by Mrs. Anna T. Lauritzen. Dr. Torbet returned to Unga in 1938, intent on establishing a "Marine Mission" and church in the village, and indicated that he was prepared to expend $12,000.00 to provide the facilities for such a venture. THE ALASKA PEN reports in its September, 1938 issue:

> On the sixteenth of September, Dr. Torbet and group arrived in Squaw Harbor on the *Nikanak*. They hired a boat from Squaw Harbor to bring them over here on the seventeenth. Those who came were: Dr. Torbet, Miss Leah Fanning and Rev. C. Clemons.
>
> Miss Leah Fanning was planning on staying here all winter to carry on the establishment of their work. But it was decided that since Mr. and Mrs. Welch were here she would go on to Ketchikan.
>
> Dr. Torbet plans on establishing a Marine Mission in Unga. This church building is to cost about $12,000.00. After the church is completed, Miss L. Fanning plans on coming back here to take over missionary work.　　　　　　　　(TAP V, 1, p. 2)

Reception of the Torbet party in Unga, September 1938. L - R: Dwain W. Norris, Anna T. Lauritzen, Jettie Petersen, Mrs. Norris, Lena Lauritzen, Laura Berntsen, Lena Hunt, Rev. and Mrs. R. J. Welch, Rev. C. Clemons, Leah Fanning, and Dr. Walter Torbet

In the meantime, missionaries of other denominations arrived to minister to the people: medical missionaries Evelyn Komedal, who lived in Unga as a child, Elna Bard, and Rev. and Mrs. R. J. Welch, who visited the village during the mid- to late-'30s. Following upon Dr. Torbet's 1938 visit, the Methodists sent Miss Hazel Paramore to Unga. She served the parish for a year or so and, along with Rev. Willard Mecklenberg, began the renovations of a former general store (the E. O. Wilson and later the E.

F. Casey store) into a parsonage and an adjoining saloon/pool hall/gymnasium into a church sanctuary. Rev. Mecklenberg preached the first sermon in the resurrected church on September 21, 1940, and a month later the first permanent pastor since Rev. Carr arrived to lead the Unga congregation. Rev. Oscar Olsen, who, along with his wife Kathryn and children, Ruth, Esther, and Robert, traveled from their home in New York to accept appointment to the Shumagin Islands Methodist Mission.

Miss Hazel Paramore

Rev. and Mrs. Oscar Olsen

The Olsen family was a welcomed addition to the church, the school, and the community at large. Oscar, with his thick Norwegian accent, fit in well with the largely Norwegian patriarchy of the village, and Kathryn's joviality lent a much appreciated levity to life in a town quite destitute of simple joys that they left far behind. One of the first things that Kathryn asked after wading onto the beach in Unga was, according to popular accounts, "Where's the bakery?" Of course, none existed. But she would soon be introduced to the parsonage's kitchen and its wood-burning stove and large oven. This writer (TL), an inveterate beachcomber at the tender age of eight, will always remember Mrs. Olsen's kitchen talents. The parsonage was perched at the very edge of a cliff that rose 20 or so feet from the beach. It seems that on one particular day, Mrs. Olsen's lemon meringue pie had turned out rather poorly and, to save the family from her culinary disaster, she tossed the concoction out the window overlooking the beach and directly onto the head of this passing beachcomber. And, as he remembers, the runny goo didn't taste at all bad.

The Olsens' sojourn in Unga was short but eventful. Rev. Olsen officiated at a number of weddings and funerals, in addition to his preaching duties in both Sand Point and Unga. Mrs. Olsen participated in local clubs and functions while the children attended Unga Territorial School. A weekly publication titled "Unga Beacon" was inaugurated by Rev. Olsen to publicize the work of the mission. The family left the parish at the end of the 1941-42 school year.

The Methodist Church was unable to provide a replacement pastor during the war years, but Sunday School and church services continued under the guidance of Mrs. Lauritzen and Mrs. Jettie Petersen. It wasn't until May of 1946 that a pastorate was re-established at Unga, with the dispatch of Rev. Constance Erickson to the islands. Miss Erickson had earlier served in remote locations. (See sidebar.) She was a dynamic preacher and an accomplished pianist, and she shared her musical knowledge with many of the village youth. This writer shared the piano bench with her on a number of occasions, belting out hymns on Sunday and Sousa marches and Hungarian dances at recitals. The Unga Methodist Church found a kindred soul in Miss Erickson, and her ministry and musical instruction were sorely missed when she departed in the spring of 1949.

CONSTANCE W. ERICKSON

Miss Constance Erickson, the pastor of the Unga Methodist Church, was born at Winthrop, Minnesota. When asked how old she is, she merely stated, "That's ancient history".

She was graduated from Winthrop High School and has also been graduated from the Rural Department of the Mankato, Minnesota State Teacher's College. Miss Erickson is a graduate of the National College at Kansas City, Missouri, with a Dss. She has had post-graduate work in New York University and Mankato.

While in Minnesota, she taught two years in the consolidated schools. She spent one year as Superintendent of an Italian Social Service Center in Newark, New Jersey, and also Director of Religious Education in Methodist churches in New York City, Minneapolis and Kansas City. She has also had pastorates at Spring Water and Jasper, Minnesota. Miss Erickson has been a promotional worker of the women's work in the Methodist Church for the states of Indiana and New York and the Mankato State Teacher's College. For five years, she has served as Superintendent and Pastor of the Eskimo Church and Social Service Center of Nome, Alaska. While at Nome, she was the pastor of the Federated Church.

In May 1946, at the Alaskan Methodist Conference, she was appointed the pastor of the Unga church for a three-year period.   (TAP XI, 2, p. 6)

*Miss Erickson's congregation,
Thanksgiving 1948*

The new decade was ushered in by Rev. Jim Heilbrun and his wife, Peggy. They were a popular young couple who inspired the village youths with their enthusiasm. But with the decline in Unga's poplation, the parish began earnestly looking beyond Unga for its ministry. This trend was continued with the arrival of Rev. Blackburn, who in 1953 transferred his operation to Sand Point, and the Unga church ceased to exist.

—————>•◦•<—————

The roof of the Russian Orthodox Church sits on the ground today, its walls having collapsed sometime in the late 1980s, its interior furnishings and religious artifacts scattered—who knows where. One of the three crosses that graced the roofline and peak of the cupola was reported to have served for a time as an altarpiece in a Lutheran church in the Seattle suburb of Shoreline, but its whereabouts today is unknown. The Methodist Church suffered a fate similar to its Orthodox cousin: unmaintained wooden structures deteriorate rapidly in the harsh saline environment of the Shumagins. Indeed, in the 30-odd years since the abandonment of the village, hardly a man-made structure remains standing. Even the tall stone monument that stood for 100 years over the grave of Ethelda Carr is reported to have collapsed. And thus had 200 years of Unga's religious history come to an end: as intoned by the scriptures, "earth to earth, ashes to ashes, dust to dust."

[Ed. Note: Much of the information presented in this essay, including the logo used to illustrate the piece, was taken from Have Gospel Tent Will Travel, an account of the first hundred years of Methodism in Alaska, written by Bea Shepard and Claudia Kelsey, and published by the Conference Council of Ministries, Alaska Missionary Conference of the United Methodist Church (1986) and from THE ALASKA PEN, where indicated.]

Dr. Walter Torbet and the Unga Community Sunday School, September 1938

CROSSINGS

Crossing the Bar
...Twilight and evening bell,
And after that the dark!
And may there be no sadness of farewell,
When I embark...

1940

PETER LARSEN

Mr. Peter Larsen passed away at his home during the afternoon of January 27th. Mr. Larsen, having been ill for a short time, lapsed into a coma on the evening of the 26th and passed away quietly and peacefully in his sleep.

Unga is going to miss Mr. Larsen, as he was one of the early settlers and was of much help in the development of this town. Mr. Larsen, born in Denmark in 1863, led a varied and full life, being in his early age a seaman, gold miner, big game hunting guide, fox rancher and captain of a purse seine boat.

Our sympathy goes out to his bereaved family in this time of their great loss. (TAP VI, 5, p. 5)

HOWARD TRUEBLOOD

Mr. Howard Trueblood, the school teacher at Sanak, Alaska, died at the school house January 26th, 1940.

Formerly he had taught school in the "States". Since coming to Alaska, he has been teaching at King Cove, Squaw Harbor and Sanak.

His former students and friends join together in mourning his loss.

Mr. Trueblood was the brother of Mrs. Graham, who taught school here at Unga.

(TAP VI, 6, p. 4)

FRED C. DRIFFIELD

September 25th marked the end of the eventful life of Judge Fred C. Driffield. He had been working for the Pacific American Fisheries at

Pete Larsen, big game hunter

Judge Driffield

Squaw Harbor, Alaska for many years. He went "outside" with the cannery crew this fall. He had been ill a short while this summer. He passed away in Bellingham, Washington. His many friends of the Shumagin Islands will miss him greatly.

(TAP VII, 1, p. 6)

PETER TORGERSON

Wednesday, October 16th, Peter Torgerson passed away at the Unga jail. Mr. Krone, the jail guard, made arrangements for the burial and the following day the services were held at the new church building. Rev. Oscar Olsen presided.

Mr. Torgerson was one of the real Alaskan pioneers and we are sure that his friends near Squaw Harbor will miss him. (TAP VII, 1, p. 3)

[Note: It is unlikely that Mr. Torgerson was incarcerated at the time of his death. Unga had no public facilities to board visitors, except for the spacious jail, which was often empty. Ed.]

DANIEL WILSON, JR.

On October 22nd, Daniel Wilson, Jr., passed away. He had been sick for quite some time. Mr. and Mrs. Wilson called in Mrs. Oscar Olsen *[a registered nurse]* and others who did all they could to help. Mr. Casey sent word *[by wireless]* to the doctor at Unalaska and received some good information.

In spite of all that was done, the baby passed away and we all sympathize with Mr. and Mrs. D. Wilson in their sorrow. (TAP VII, 2, p. 5)

SARAH HAAF

Mrs. Adolph Haaf, a late resident of Unga, passed away on November 27th. She had been sick for several weeks. All the town's people join in with Mr. Haaf and family in mourning the loss.

(TAP VII, 3, p. 3)

1941

FRANK SIEMION

The people of Unga were very shocked to hear of the death of Mr. Frank Siemion. Mr. Siemion had left his wife, Mrs. Bertha Siemion, and four children in Unga while he went to obtain work at Unalaska, where he passed away. The Penmakers and the people of Unga wish to express their deep sympathy for Mrs. Siemion and her family. (TAP VII, 6, p. 5)

Frank Siemion

PETER GILBERT

Mr. Peter Gilbert, a former resident of Unga, passed away quietly at his home in Squaw Harbor on April 1, 1941. Surviving is his widow, Mrs. Lena Gilbert, several small children, and several brothers and sisters, all of Squaw Harbor. Funeral services were conducted at Squaw Harbor by Rev. Oscar Olsen of the Shumagin Islands Methodist Mission. Interment was made in Squaw Harbor. May his rest be one of peace. (TAP VII, 7, p. 6)

JOHN HAMMER

The people of Unga were shocked to hear the sad news of the sudden death of John Hammer on September 18th. Mr. Hammer was born in Sweden in 1865, but had lived in this country a good share of his life. He was one of the old-timers in Unga, having come here over thirty years ago. In his younger days when codfishing was the main business here, he made his living in that trade. It has been just the last few years that he has quit fishing altogether, because of his advancing years. He had also done some trapping. He will be greatly missed by all the many friends he had in this part of Alaska.   (TAP VIII, 1, p. 1)

TOM SKULSTAD

The people of Unga and vicinity were shocked Friday, November 24th, by the news that the *Neptune* had burned at Sand Point Thursday evening and Tommy Skulstad had died in the fire.

The cause of the fire was not ascertained, but it is thought that a cigarette started the mattress upon which he was sleeping to burning. The smoke was probably the direct cause of death.

Mr. Skulstad was well known and universally liked in the Shumagins where he has lived for many years. He ran a fox farm on Simeonof Island.

The sympathy of the community goes out to his wife and four children. Mrs. Skulstad and the two younger children resided on Simeonof Island. The two older children, Karen and Thorwald, attend school in Unga.

(TAP VIII, 3, p. 1)

1943

CONRAD LAURITZEN

The people of Unga were stunned on September 27th when Conrad Lauritzen was accidentally drowned by being thrown from his skiff while attempting to start an outboard motor. "Conrad", as he was known to all, was one of the best known and best liked men in the entire Shumagin Island District. His friends can be numbered by his many acquaintances. He was always ready and willing to help and accommodate when needed. His passing is a real loss to our community and a deep regret to his many, many friends. Our sincerest sympathies are extended to his bereaved family.

Conrad Hoff Lauritzen was born in Tonsberg, Norway, August 30, 1900, and came to Unga with his parents in 1908, where he has lived ever since. He was the oldest son of Mr. and Mrs. Hjalmar Lauritzen, merchants and fish-packers of Unga. He and his father owned the M. S. *Elmer*, of which Conrad has been "skipper" for several years.

In 1924, he married Lena Nelson, niece of Andrew Grosvold who, before his death several years ago, was a prominent businessman of Sand Point, Alaska.

Friends: Tom Skulstad and Conrad Lauritzen

Conrad Lauritzen is survived by a lovely family: his wife and five children, Norman 18, Thelma 16, Ruth 13, Thorwald 11, Ann 7 and a step-son John Nelson, who is now in the Armed Forces. He is also survived by his mother and father, Mr. and Mrs. Hjalmar Lauritzen, two sisters, Mrs. Raymond Rodgers and Mrs. Jack Benson, all of Unga, and two brothers, Arthur, now in Seattle, and Thomas, who is serving in the Armed Forces.

Funeral services were held on September 30th in the Unga Community Church.   (PW I, 1, p. 4)

1944

LAURITZ PEDERSEN

Lauritz Pedersen, a resident of Unga for the past 30 years, passed away in his sleep the evening of February 28th. "Danish Pete", as he was known by his many friends, was born in Denmark in 1887. He received his naturalization papers on August 23, 1926 at Unga. Fishing and boating were followed by Mr. Pedersen since coming to Unga. He was employed as guard at the jail during the past year or so. The community of Unga will miss a good friend and loyal citizen in the passing of Lauritz Pedersen. (PW I, 6, p. 4)

Danish Pete and a string of ducks

ADOLPH RODGERS

The news of the tragic death of 1st Lt. Adolph Rodgers in an airplane accident in California on April 14th was received by all with deep regret. This is the first casualty among our boys in the service.

Lt. Rodgers was born in Unga, Alaska, on September 15, 1913, received his commercial pilot's license in 1939 and has been in the Army Reserve till 1941 when he enlisted into the Army. He was a test pilot at an Army airfield in California.

We of the Unga School extend our sincerest sympathy to Adolph's mother, Mrs. George Foster, and his sisters, Mrs. Andrew Gronholdt, Emily and Budilia Rodgers, and brother, Raymond Rodgers and also his many other relatives and friends.

Unga was proud of Lt. Rodgers and the silver star in our service flag will glow with pleasant memories of an Unga lad who gave all for his country. (PW I, 8, p. 3)

Adolph Rodgers and his grandmother Mary Larsen

1945

MARY LARSEN

In the September issue of THE ALASKA PEN it mentioned the death of Mary Larsen on August 5th.

Any person who has lived in Unga any length of time made her acquaintance and found her to be a very lovable individual. She served as midwife in the community for over forty years and was always ready to help in sickness and distress. She was a faithful supporter in all community work and was loved and respected by all. No task was too great or too small for her to add a willing hand. Her absence is much felt in the community.

Mary Larsen was born in Unga on December 23, 1876. She was the daughter of Mr. and Mrs. Isaac Hubley. Mr. Hubley was a sea otter hunter in the older days and his daughter has often entertained the younger folks by telling them of early life in Unga.

Mrs. Larsen had two sisters and two brothers. One brother, William Hubley, is living at Squaw Harbor at present.

Mary Larsen married Peter Larsen on May 29, 1893. She leaves behind ten children: Zenia Foster, Unga; Grace Brown, Petaluma, California; Alice Nutbeem, Seldovia, Alaska; James Larsen, Bellevue, Washington; Peter Larsen, Clara Oaks and Edmund Larsen, Bellingham, Washington; Betty McIntire, San Francisco; Norman Larsen, Unga; and Gladys Butler, Los Angeles.

Mrs. Larsen spent her later life visiting her children in the States and Alaska. (TAP X, 2, p. 7)

HILMA SJOBERG

Word has been received that Mrs. Gus Sjoberg died on September 19th in Seattle. She was the mother of Mrs. Edward F. Casey.

Mr. and Mrs. Sjoberg came to Unga in 1910 and later operated a store handling general merchandise. For the past ten years, the Sjobergs have made their home in Seattle, leaving the business in the hands of their son-in-law, Edward F. Casey. In the past year, Mr. and Mrs. Casey have been in Seattle in order to aid both Mr. and Mrs. Sjoberg, who have been in very poor health. At this time, Mr. Sjoberg's condition is quite critical.

Mrs. Sjoberg assisted her husband in the operation of their store while they were living in Unga.   (TAP X, 2, p. 7)

Mr. and Mrs. Gus Sjoberg

GUSTAV SJOBERG

A few days after the death of his wife, word was received here of the death of Gus E. Sjoberg in Seattle. Mr. Sjoberg came to Unga about 1900 as mate on a sailing codfish schooner. After spending several years in connection with the codfish industry, he became engaged in the merchandising business here. His last business association was with his son-in-law, Edward F. Casey.

He is survived by his daughter, Mrs. Edward F. Casey, (and granddaughter, Judy).

Robert Garlow is the present manager of the local firm of Sjoberg and Casey. (TAP X, 3, p. 4)

("CROSSINGS" conclude at the end of Part III: The Aftermath.)

PART III
THE AFTERMATH

Remains of the Methodist Church and Unga Territorial School, 2003

Principal Editor:
Edward Melseth

Co-editors:
Thor Lauritzen
Peggy Arness

INTRODUCTION

NINETEEN FORTY-FIVE WAS A PIVOTAL year in the history of Unga. As the school year began, World War II had just ended and the world—and Alaska—would be forever changed. How these changes affected the minds of Unga's younger generation can be appreciated by reading the editorials written by its high school students in the months and years following the war. It is these and similar essays, plus the day-to-day happenings in Unga and the larger community, that comprise THE ALASKA PEN, a monthly periodical written, printed, and published by the students of Unga High School, that provides the foundation upon which this historical account was built.

The war's end was only one in a series of happenings that had begun to reshape the village and would eventually result in Unga's decline as a viable community. Although the hope of a resurgence in gold mining was a perennial shining star, the 1930s saw no progress on that front, and the war years squelched any immediate interest in this non-strategic metal. Thus, the Apollo Mine at Unga languished through this decade, fell into disrepair, and was shortly abandoned. The '30s also saw a virtual end of the codfishing industry, which had sustained the Shumagin area and Unga in particular throughout the early decades of the 20th century, when small salteries were scattered along the shore of Delarof Harbor. By the 1950s, most of those stations had disappeared or had collapsed into piles of rubble. Farming and trapping of foxes, which had long provided a vital source of income during the lean and long winters, was another casualty of the war years, when frugality in women's fashions and a fledgling environmental movement effectively ended this occupation. The only livelihood remaining was the salmon fishing industry, which actually experienced a rebirth in the post-war years. Fish traps, once the bane of the independent fisherman, were being phased out in the late '50s, and fish processing changed from canning to predominantly freezing—a modernization that required less workers.

The shortage of jobs resulted, in the post-war years, in a gradual decline in the population of Unga, and the village regressed during that period to a largely bedroom community. Although the village infrastructure remained viable and in some respects improved during this period, there was no compelling reason why a family would choose to live in Unga when all the jobs were elsewhere. And the exodus began. The security of living in a safe community with local law enforcement suffered a devastating blow when the US Marshal's office and jail were closed in 1946. That same year, a potentially disastrous diphtheria epidemic emphasized the total lack of medical care in the community. In 1950, one of the only two retail outlets in town closed. The Unga Women's Club disbanded in 1951, the liquor store dried up in 1952, and the remaining retail outlet closed in 1953. The post office continued operating until 1957. The Unga High School, the only such institution west of Kodiak, was phased out in the early 1950s due to lack of a student body. This closure was followed by the abandonment of the entire school system in 1959. Unga's last permanent residents left in 1968. Thus, just 23 years after the end of the Second World War, the village of Unga ceased to exist.

This third and final chapter in the 20th century history of Unga—dubbed The Aftermath—will revisit the pages of THE ALASKA PEN from September 1945 until its demise in 1951 and will provide a glimpse into the years when, finally, the only inhabitant was a lonely horse roaming the footpaths and beaches, finding refuge in cellars and lean-tos. In the end, that solitary resident passed from the scene and only an eerie silence remains, punctuated by the wind whistling through the cracks of long-abandoned buildings.

HISTORICAL HIGHLIGHTS

❧ February 1946 ❧

(From time to time, THE ALASKA PEN has invited criticism and information from sources outside the school. The following editorial is one contribution that is an expression of a local citizen. Therefore, it is welcome, but does not necessarily express the policies of the school.)

———⟫•⟪———

POST-WAR PLANNING IN UNGA

Innumerable cities, towns and villages throughout the country have announced post-war plans, plans which are designed to better the respective localities in various ways.

Unga needs a post-war plan.

What should it consist of?

Look around: a hasty glance would reveal several conditions, the improvement of which would make Unga a more attractive place.

How about the main roadway? How many people complained that something should be done about it this past fall and winter? Why not do it?

How about the cemetery, the condition of which can be summed up in one word: disgraceful.

How about the dance hall? The one place suitable for social gathering in the village is a dilapidated eyesore badly in need of repair.

The above conditions are apparent to all; there is another condition not so apparent but more needful of attention and correction: the children's teeth and eyes. There is not a child in this village who does not need dental care. A cursory examination revealed that many also need eye correction.

You may ask, where will we get the money necessary to correct these situations. For many years the village has held benefits to raise funds for contributions to various organizations. Most of the money so raised has been sent out. However, there is still a considerable amount, over $1,000 remaining here, split into numerous funds.

Why not lump all the various funds into one, have it administered by a group consisting of the school principal as ex-officio chairman and three townspeople as members serving for three to six months on a revolving basis. This committee would make provisions for materials, labor and expenditures on the various projects. In other words, they would see to it that the work was done. In addition, this committee should have charge of all fund-raising activities.

You may again remark, "That's fine for some problems, but how about that of the children's teeth and eyes?"

Why not a clinic once or twice a year for several weeks? A few fund-raising affairs in the fall would provide an amount which would ensure the attendance of a reputable dentist for the clinic.

These are a few, by no means all, of the problems which, in my estimation must be given serious consideration by the residents of Unga if we are at all concerned with the future of the village and its inhabitants.

Signed, Robert Garlow
(TAP X, 6, p. 2)

❦ January 1946 ❧

CHURCH NEWS

Rev. Edward Knight, Alaska district superintendent of the Methodist Church, made an overnight stop in Unga on January 9th. He held servicers in the Methodist Church. His appropriate sermon was delivered to a large audience.

Rev. Knight had been making visits along the peninsula and had spent several weeks in Unalaska. He is now returning to Anchorage.

Services were held in the Greek Orthodox Church on January 7th, Christmas Day, and January 14th, New Years Day. Harry Kaiakokonok, one of the readers in the Perryville church, conducted the services.   (TAP X, 5, p. 4)

MASQUERADE BALL

In order to maintain the tradition of the Orthodox Church, the Unga school sponsored the annual Masquerade Ball at the dance hall on January 17th. An overflowing crowd attended the function.

Many clever costumes were worn by the maskers. Emily Endresen and her sister, Budilia Rodgers, won the prize as the best dressed couple. They were attired in clever patriotic costumes. Mrs. Endresen was dressed as Uncle Sam with red and white striped trousers and cut-away blue coat bedecked with many stars. She wore a tall top hat to match her costume. Her sister Budilia wore a similar costume with her skirt matching the coat of her escort.

For the best-dressed woman, the prize was awarded to Lena Hunt. She portrayed a south sea islander in her hula skirt and sun-tanned body. She was the attraction of the ball.

Raymond Rodgers won the prize as the best-dressed man by wearing a dark suit and a black face set off by a starchy white shirt.

Little Alice Cushing won the prize as the most comically dressed. Her hideous face was the main attraction of her costume.

An attractively-dressed Norwegian couple, old witches, clowns, pretty maidens, and a variety of other maskers all added to the gaiety of the occasion.

Allan Petersen, Alex Calugan and Charles Wood served as judges.

Snappy music was furnished by the Kaiakokonok brothers, Harry and Spike, from Perryville, on the accordion and guitar, Raymond Rodgers and Thomas Lauritzen on the saxophone and guitar, and Budilia Rodgers and Andrew Krone relieving the other players on the accordion.

A beautiful round plate glass mirror was raffled as a door prize. It was won by Budilia Rodgers.

Almost 250 ice cream cones were sold as refreshments.

The Women's Club donated the use of the hall to the school as their contribution to make the function a success.   (TAP X, 5, p. 4)

THE WEATHER

It was snowing some of the time today. There is snow on the mountains and a little on the ground. It has been very muddy and also rough.

Our coldest weather this year was seven above zero. At that time, the ground was covered with snow and there was ice in the bay.

Louise Berntsen, 5th Grade
(TAP X, 5, p. 5)

❦ February 1946 ❧

MORE ON THE WEATHER

You may have laughed at the weather Private Snafu had to endure but, considering Unga weather of the past few days, it wasn't too terribly exaggerated. Let's take, for example, the weather from Saturday evening to Wednesday. You probably remember that early Saturday evening it was raining. Preparing yourself for a siege of rain, you went to bed only to wake up a few hours later to find that the weather had changed to a howling blizzard. This blizzard raged through the night and continued through Sunday and part of Monday with a temperature two degrees below zero.

Finally getting out of breath, the wind halted for a spell on Monday evening and let the stars and moon shine awhile to brighten the spirits of those tired of the blizzards.

On Tuesday, we awakened to a multicolored sky that reflected all its splendor on a glistening blanket of snow. All day we witnessed the blinding sunlight, and the evening sky tried to outrival the brightness of the day by displaying all the brilliancy of the heavens.

An earthquake on Wednesday forenoon topped off all this changeable weather.

Now, wouldn't you like to have a pack like Private Snafu's, which contains all the necessary clothing for such Alaskan weather?"

Ruth Lauritzen, 11th Grade
(TAP X, 6, p. 4)

❧ March 1946 ❧

TOWN MEETING

The town meeting on March 11th proved to be a hot affair, not in vocal combat but due to the flue pipe becoming overheated and charring the wall. As the meeting progressed, the outside cold penetrated the wall and chilled the local citizens until they left, leaving the newly-elected committee holding the bag—$505.25—which is the balance in the dance hall fund.

Lena Lauritzen, president of the Unga Women's Club, took charge of the meeting by stating that the Women's Club was declining further management of the dance hall. She served as chairman until a new one, Robert Garlow, was elected representing the community.

The interested citizens present represented a large percentage of the local population. John Nelson, chairman, Raymond Rodgers and Thomas Lauritzen are the members of the newly-elected committee. Both Nelson and Lauritzen are capable of filling their positions well. Since they are returned veterans of the war, they have had

an opportunity to get first hand information from their travels.

Raymond Rodgers, as a skilled carpenter, is very capable of visualizing and directing the needed repair.

These men are working for the welfare of the community without pay. It is the duty of every Unga citizen to support them in their efforts and back them with worthwhile suggestions.

The Unga Women's Club is to be commended on their past efforts in managing the dance hall.

(TAP X, 7, p. 3)

UNGA HAS NEW RESIDENTS

Mr. and Mrs. Griska Grassamoff and son and daughter, Barney and Hilda, have moved into the Mary Larsen property from Simeonof Island where they have lived most of their lives.

(TAP X, 7, p. 4)

PAF HAS NEW SUPERINTENDENT

Ralph C. Rogers, who was assistant bookkeeper for the PAF cannery at Squaw Harbor last year, has been appointed the new superintendent for the cannery, according to a radiogram received here from Stanley G. Tarrant, who is the general superintendent of the PAF canneries in this section of Alaska.

Mr. Rogers replaces W. N. Williams, who has served as superintendent for the past two years.

Mr. Rogers has had considerable experience as superintendent of canneries in southeastern Alaska, but last year was his first experience in a westward cannery.

It is understood that Mr. Williams is retiring after many years of serving the PAF.

(TAP X, 7, p. 4)

❧ April 1946 ❧

THE DIPHTHERIA EPIDEMIC

[Note: Much of Volume X, Number 8 of THE ALASKA PEN was devoted to coverage of this epidemic that virtually paralyzed the village of Unga for two weeks in April of 1946. Articles pertaining to that tragic event are presented verbatim elsewhere in Part III. Ed.]

TIDAL WAVE !

April First was no April Fool's Day in Unga. About 4 o'clock in the morning, several sleepers were awakened by an earthquake. This was followed by a tidal wave which swept away two dories and the dock from the old fishing station across the bay. Debris of the dock was found on Agate Beach, a mile away. No trace of the dories was found.

A rock weighing several tons was moved from McCann's Point to no one knows where. A lot of sand and small rocks were churned in the inner bay and moved from one location to another. Thousands of butter and cockle clams were washed up on the beach below Lauritzen's dock.

There is a huge rock at the neck of the inner bay with a reef between it and the shore. The reef would bare every ten minutes while combers rolled in on the other side of the rock. This continued for several hours.

Combers four to five feet high were rolling in the bay until afternoon.

Radio reports caused considerable excitement as far east as Kodiak and Seward. The radio reported a 100-foot tidal wave was moving toward Kodiak and directed the people to take to the hills. It was reported that the people in Sand Point and Chignik spent a miserable night on the hills. The Coast Guard dispatched planes to isolated outposts to evacuate their personnel.

Twenty-six tremors were felt at Ikatan, which was hit hardest in Alaska. One man's home was washed off its foundation and was towed to False Pass a few miles away, where the man is living in it. The dishes were not jarred from their places in the cupboard.

Several homes were destroyed in Sanak.

The government has reported that the cause of these disturbances was a huge earthquake in the Pacific Deep. This also caused the disturbance in the Hawaiian Islands.

Evelyn Foster, 11th Grade
(TAP X, 8, p. 6)

[The earthquake felt by Evelyn and her neighbors occurred on the ocean floor off the southwest coast of Unimak Island, roughly 190 miles southwest of Unga. The quake generated a tsunami that obliterated the nearby Scotch Cap Light Station and killed the five Coast Guardsmen who manned the station. Scotch Cap Light, a reinforced concrete structure, was built in 1940, nearly 100 feet above sea level. The tsunami sped across the Pacific, slamming into the Hawaiian Islands, where over 100 people perished. Its effects were felt as far away as the west coast of South America. The cyclic tidal surges and recessions observed in Delarof Harbor were a mild response to the devastation suffered elsewhere. The people of Unga should have felt extremely fortunate that they and their village were spared. Ed.]

ONE SOLDIER'S STORY

Word has been received here concerning PFC Howard Oberg of Anchorage. He returned home recently to be with his mother, Mrs. Elizabeth Oberg, after seeing action in Europe with the U. S. paratroopers.

He was born in Unga and graduated from the Wasilla schools. In August of 1943, he volunteered for duty with the paratroopers and was sent overseas as a member of 513th paratroop infantry of the 17th airborne division.

During the Battle of the Bulge, he was sent into combat with other relief troops. For four days he fought his way into the town of Flamurge through a howling blizzard to capture a strategic ridge. When the battle ended, he was one of 33 men left alive out of the original 160 troops.

He was also in the Battle of the Rhine and spearheaded into Munster where the Yanks encountered some of the heaviest fighting of the war. There he fought against members of the Hitler Youth Army, made up of boys from 14 to 16 years of age. He was wounded during that action and sent to a hospital where he remained until after the war's end in Europe.

He recovered from his wounds and was enroute to the Pacific theater when V-J Day occurred. He was then returned to the States for discharge. (TAP X, 8, p. 7)

[Elizabeth (Eliza) Oberg was the daughter of Isaac Hubley, who came to Alaska shortly after the Civil War of which he was a veteran, and his wife Tatiana. Eliza was married to Elmer Oberg, a Norwegian immigrant fisherman, with whom she had five children, including Howard. Ed.]

WE'VE GOT MAIL!

On March 20th, the *Bittersweet* arrived bringing tons of mail, most of which was Christmas mail.

Mr. Lawvere dismissed school for the afternoon and went out to the boat in order to induce the skipper to show a movie. The movies shown were "Holiday Inn", "True to the Army" and a couple of short skits.

Besides the crew off the *Bittersweet*, some boys from a convoy in Squaw Harbor attended the dance in the evening. The high school girls prepared refreshments.

This is the first mail we have had since December 24th! *[Emphasis added.]*

(TAP X, 8, p. 7)

[A comprehensive review of the US mail situation over the years is offered in an essay elsewhere in Part III. Ed.]

❧ September 1946 ❧

FIRST WOMAN COMMISSIONER

Mrs. Kathryn Garlow, our present Commissioner, has the outstanding honor of being the first woman Commissioner ever to be appointed in the Unga Peninsula Recording District. This honor was bestowed upon her last August 2nd by the Hon. Judge Dimond, the Presiding Judge of the Third District Court and our former Representative from Alaska to the U. S. Congress. Since her appointment, one criminal case has been tried and one couple has been married in her court.

Prior to her appointment as commissioner, Mrs. Garlow had taught school in Sand Point and more immediately been a housewife for the former Commissioner, Mr. Robert Garlow, who combined business and pleasure on a visit to Los Angeles where his mother resides. Mr. Garlow is expected to return here Saturday, September 20th and when Mrs. Garlow was asked if she intended to relinquish the Commissioner's Office to him, she replied with a sigh, "Thank Goodness."

Meryl Hansen , 9th Grade
(TAP XI, 1, p. 9)

Dolly Foster, Kay and Vickie Garlow, and Ann Lauritzen in Squaw Harbor

---

THE *BOGDAN*

The *Bogdan* is a very common sight in Unga Bay. It may be of interest to know that this boat is about twenty years old and that it carries 15 tons of cargo when fully loaded. The *Bogdan* is owned by Andrew Foster, who bought it from the Alaska Pacific Packing Company about three years ago. It is about 39 feet in length and has a

70-80 horsepower Hall Scott engine. This boat is of great use to the people of Unga. It is utilized for many purposes such as bringing the school coal and lumber, carrying freight for the local stores and for passenger service.

Norman Brandal, 9th Grade
(TAP XI, 1, p. 10)

Mr. Casey says he should have sufficient power to supply all the people who want electricity. He had hoped to furnish the town with street lights, but this will have to wait on account of the shortage of supplies.

Arthur Hansen, 11th Grade.
(TAP XI, 2, p. 8)

❧ October 1946 ❧

UNGA'S ELECTRIFICATION

Mr. Casey's power plant, which is going to furnish the town with electricity, will be in operation about November 15th or sooner.

The engine is a 4400 Caterpillar Diesel Power Unit and with a General Electric 3-phase AC generator of the dual-voltage type. It will produce 110/220 volts at 60 cycles and its maximum is 20 kilowatts or 20,000 watts.

UNGA'S GENERAL ELECTION

October 8th marked the date for all Alaskans to go to the polls in deciding if they wished Alaska the 49th state of the Union.

In Unga, 40 people went to the Club House, which served as the polls, to vote for or against statehood, and also for Delegate to Congress, Territorial Treasurer, Commissioner of Labor, Senators and Representatives.

❧ October 1946 ❧

Editorial: ALASKA THE STEPCHILD

Alaska to many people seems simple. A simple flag, a simple life and a simple people. Though we may be considered "simple", we like the modern conveniences of life. But our economy is incomparable to that of other American citizens because Alaska is a stepchild to this great family of states.

Maybe if we weren't such a satisfied people with what we have and live on, we would find some ways of changing our lives. Only people do that, who have wants to satisfy.

Many are opposed to Alaska statehood, while others are not. We are opinionated according to our location. Some Alaskans live where they can work all the year round, while others work in seasons barely realizing enough to carry them through the winter. They feel that statehood would injure their incomes because of the taxes. Others feel that statehood would add more assets to Alaska than it would detract. Since we live in one of these seasonal, forgotten districts, our citizens seem to be influenced chiefly by the former group.

Some of the younger generation have already left for more lively places so that they could live a more exciting life, start more worthwhile careers. But these people do not seem to realize that if they would come home and practice their professions here it would make our "simple" country a better place to live and perhaps develop Alaska into a full-fledged child.

Virginia Brandal, 11th Grade
(TAP XI, 2, p. 2)

Mrs. Edward F. Casey, Mrs. Lena Hunt and Mrs. Lena Lauritzen were appointed as judges on the Election Board.

The majority of the people of Unga voted against statehood with a ratio of 23 to 17. *[Emphasis added.]*

The people seemed to favor the Democratic candidates by a large majority. One exception to this was, for Territorial Commissioner of Labor where Ross E. Kimball, Independent, received 32 votes—three more than Democrat Walter P. Sharpe.

Bob Bartlett won the people's favor overwhelmingly with a vote of 29 against Republican Almar J. Peterson's 9.

Oscar G. Olson, Democrat, led 31 votes to Republican Cash Coles' 7 for Territorial Treasurer.

Democrats Stanley J. McCutcheon and Victor Rivers won over their Republican opponents for Territorial Senators, receiving 32 and 26 votes, respectively.

The seven Territorial Representatives were all elected from the Democratic ranks and are as follows: Steve D. McCutcheon, 29 votes; William A. Egan, 27, Walter E. Huntley, 27; Glen Barnett, 25; Clarence Keating, 25; Arthur MacDonald, 24 and C. A. Pollard, 24.

Thorwald Lauritzen, 9th Grade
(TAP XI, 2, p. 8)

❧ November 1946 ❧

GOODBYE AGAIN TO CASEY'S DOCK

Mother Nature crept upon us a few days ago and gave us a day of bad weather. Sunday, November the 10th, the wind was wild and the sea was really roaring.

The waves of the sea rode roughshod over Mr. Casey's dock. It completely wrecked the dock which has withstood storms since 1938, when it was last wiped out. In the memory of the "old timers", the dock has been washed away four times.

The latest misfortune was caused by a high tide which was driven far up on the shore by a fifty mile blow from the southeast. Stones and debris were piled high up the bank and blocked the doors to Mr. Casey's warehouse. When the stom subsided, the dock was completely destroyed, with only the most distant end of steel girders still standing, which saved the winch from destruction.

This was an unfortunate blow at this time, as the relief ship is expected here soon with about 150 tons of freight for Mr. Casey.

(TAP XI, 3, p. 3)

Casey's Dock, before and after.

BERNTSEN FAMILY LEAVES

Last Tuesday the Coast Guard cutter *Clover* called into Unga Harbor to take Mrs. Laura Berntsen and her six children to Seward where the children will be entered into Jesse Lee Home.

Mrs. Berntsen has been the school janitor this year and we are sorry to see her leave, but have been fortunate to secure Mrs. Lena Hunt to take over the janitorial duties.

Needless to say, the school will miss the Berntsen children as they were all very active in their respective rooms. Bertha Jean had been the business manager of THE ALASKA PEN and Louise and Buddy have both had the honor of being flag monitors this year. Walter and Rosemary will also be missed in the primary room.

(TAP XI, 3, p. 7)

U. S. MARSHAL'S OFFICE CLOSES

Mr. Allan Petersen, Deputy U. S. Marshal of this district, received a wire closing the marshal's office in Unga and transferring him to Kenai, Alaska. Mr. Petersen has been in Unga for the past 12 years and will be greatly missed. Mrs. Petersen, primary teacher, is yet uncertain about her future plans.   (TAP XI, 3, p. 7)

PETERSEN-GUNDERSON WEDDING

On the day of October 31, 1946, Johnny Gunderson of Sanak and Caratina Petersen of Sand Point were joined in holy matrimony. Mr. Garlow, the Commissioner, performed the ceremony at his home. The couple departed after the ceremony for Sand Point. They plan to spend the winter at Sanak. Congratulations folks!

(TAP XI, 3, p. 10)

❧ December 1946 ❧

RELIEF SHIP ARRIVES

On November 27, 1946, the relief boat, which the U. S. Maritime Commissioner sent to Western Alaska to relieve the famine condition caused by the maritime strike arrived in Squaw Harbor. Its cargo was limited to necessary food provisions for Sand Point, Squaw Harbor and Unga.

A second relief ship, the *Wac 138*, arrived in Squaw Harbor Nov. 30th with coal, oil and mail.

The Bogdan and *Milfred* brought the much damaged provisions to Casey's and Lauritzen's stores in Unga. Then a couple of days later, the *Bogdan* brought over the coal and oil from Squaw Harbor.

Even though the freight was badly damaged and short in some instances, we are grateful for those that made possible the sending of these supplies.

(TAP XI, 4, p. 6)

FUR TRAPPING—1946

Albert Cushing and his son Aleck returned home December 4th after spending two weeks at the mainland. The *Milfred* came into Squaw Harbor December 13th with the Jacobsen family. This family has been at the mainland for six weeks. They are now on their boat, the *Vis*, gathering up trappers whom they took to the mainland.

Raymond Rodgers, Norman Larsen, Harry Hunt and Albert Krone came home Saturday, Dec. 14th. Messrs Rodgers, Larsen and Krone returned here previously for a few days to help unload the supplies of groceries and coal, which the relief ship brought to Squaw Harbor.

The Vis *at Unga.*

John Berntsen, Sr. also came home Dec. 14th. Many were glad to see him return, as much apprehension was felt regarding his safety, as the day he left a storm came up and he kept on going while the others turned back.

The *Vis* came in this week with Johnny Haaf, Fred Pomian, Norman Lauritzen, John Nelson and Johannes Olsen from the mainland.

Some of the trappers claim the season was poor so we wish you better luck next season, boys.

Mildred Hansen, 9th Grade
(TAP XI, 4, p. 5)

❧ January 1947 ❧

MR. CASEY'S NEW DOCK

On the afternoon of November 10th, a high sea came rolling in Unga Harbor. As the high sea rose, Casey's dock went down gradually. At 1:30, there were only steel girders standing.

Even before the storm had ceased, Mr. Casey had commenced plans for rebuilding the dock. The next day, there was a crew of seven at work although the usual crew was only three.

After many weeks of hard work, the men completed the dock on December 30th. We all hope it will stand up against storms that may come in the future.

The new dock is about 130 feet long and capable of holding about 10 tons. The dock's main use is for freight, coal, mail and landing passen-

The Bogdan *at Casey's New Dock*

gers. Besides its commercial value, it also has a noticeable social value.   (TAP XI, 5, p. 6)

STEPANOFF-SHANIGAN WEDDING

"Did you hyar them bells?" Another couple, Feona Stepanoff, age 17, and Freddie Shanigan, age 21, from Perryville, Alaska, were married the early part of January. This couple came to Unga on the *Vis* and were married by the US, Commissioner, Mr. Robert Garlow. After honeymooning here a couple days, they departed to Perryville where they will make their home.

(TAP XI, 5, p. 8)

MAIL BOAT *CLARINDA* BLOWS UP

Imagine waiting five years for a regularly-scheduled mail boat and then have the first one sent to the "Forgotten Westward" blow up!

(TAP XI, 5, p. 8)

[That is exactly what happened to the Clarinda *outward bound on her maiden voyage. Details of this ill-fated adventure are given in the mailboat essay elsewhere in Part III. Ed.]*

❧ February 1947 ❧

TOWN MEETING

A town meeting was called on February 21, 1947, at the club house. A majority of the families of Unga were present when Mr. Peters called the meeting to order.

A motion was made and carried that the townspeople elect men for a de facto council to handle the city affairs and centralize the various funds on hand.

Mr. Peters was elected as chairman, Mr. Nelson as secretary and Messrs Casey, Rodgers and Garlow as members of the council.

A motion was made by Mr. Nelson, chairman of the dance hall committee, to put the dance hall fund, which amounts to approximately $400.00, in the city fund for the betterment of the town, the town at the same time assuming responsibility for the upkeep of the dance hall. The motion was carried.

After much discussion, a motion was made and carried that the roads be fixed. It was stated that the last improvement was attempted in 1936. The council decided to go to work on this at once.

After the town meeting was adjourned, the newly-elected council held its first meeting.

(TAP XI, 7, p. 6)

❧ March 1947 ❧

WATERWORKS DISSOLVED

Members of the water district of Unga met at the home of Mr. Ed Casey to discuss the future of the waterworks.

The water district was originally created by selling memberships for $62.50 per person, which entitled the member to hook into the water main.

Since there was a great deal of confusion in their records, it was decided to clarify the issue once and for all.

During the meeting, many old dues were dropped because the people had moved away or it was so trivial that it was of no consequence. The ones who have not paid in full will be given a chance to work out their bills at $1.25 per hour when the tank lines need repairing.

It was further decided to dissolve the water district as a separate entity and become a part of the city administration. This means that the city council will acquire all the water department's headaches and liabilities and in turn will receive $500 in cash, which will be put in the general fund, and all other assets.   (TAP XI, 7, p. 6)

THE YOUTH SPEAK UP

Rumors! Rumors flying here, there and everywhere. At the present time, a certain one seems to catch the ear of all the teenagers of this certain locality. This rumor concerns stricter age limitations for admittance to the Unga Community

Dance Hall. To a certain extent, this is an excellent idea, but by setting an age limit it leaves only a few who can be admitted. If this should be done, some different place will likely be set up for the others for entertainment. Surely the older people don't expect them to sit at home and do nothing for pleasure! It would seem that this problem of proper age limit for attendance at the dance hall should be taken care of by parents and guardians.

Virginia Brandal, 11th Grade
(TAP XI, 7, p. 7)

Unga's Community Dance Hall.

THE *ALEUTIAN MAIL*!

Just think: another mail boat. Doesn't just those two words bring a little hope to you? This alleged boat is supposed to be on its way to these parts. If the dope we have is true, it should be in Sand Point tomorrow. Keep your fingers crossed and hope it doesn't blow up.   (TAP XI, 7, p. 9)

[The Aleutian Mail *did in fact show up the next day, March 15, 1947—intact! Ed.]*

TRAGEDY ON LITTLE KONIUJI

Upon their arrival at Simeonof Island to obtain some beef, the crew of the M. V. *Vis*, accompanied by Wm. Peters, were confronted with a gruesome experience.

The inhabitants of this once-prosperous fox ranch, Mr. Griska Grassamoff, his daughter Hilda and his two sons, Barney and Aleck, left Unga after the fishing season for their island home.

Barney, aged 39, and Aleck, aged 24, both army veterans of World War II, left Simeonof to go trapping on the adjacent island of Little Koniuji, 14 miles away, on Nov. 25th.

The men never returned home and they left no means of transportation to the island from their home.

The *Vis* arrived at Simeonof March 21st and, after finding Barney and Aleck missing, they immediately set off for Little Koniuji.

Upon arriving at the trappers' shack, they found the door wide open and the two boys lying in bed dead. The bodies were in such a condition from the exposure that they could not be taken to Simeonof Island, but were crudely buried. The last date marked on the calendar was November 28th (Thanksgiving Day).

How these boys met their death is unknown, but foul play is not suspected. They very likely could have frozen, as the days of the 28th and proceeding dates were very cold.

Surviving these boys are their father, Mr. Griska Grassamoff, his daughters Hilda, Margaret and Josephine, and two sons Andrew and Mike. The latter four are away from Unga.

Mr. Grassamoff and Hilda plan to make their home at Unga.

May we extend our deepest sympathy to the Grassamoff family.   (TAP XI, 8, p. 8)

❧ May 1947 ❧

MRS. PETERSEN LEAVES

Mrs. Petersen, who has taught in Unga for twelve years, is going to leave about May 10th, or as soon as possible, after school is out.

Mr. and Mrs. Petersen came to Unga in 1934. Mr. Petersen was U. S. Marshal in Unga for thirteen years and has just recently been transferred to Kenai, Alaska. Mrs. Petersen, after teaching twelve years in Unga, is going to join her husband in Kenai and expects to teach in the schools there.

Mr. and Mrs. Petersen have two children, who received most of their education in the local schools. Her son Jimmy, who is now attending college, is studying to be a forest ranger. Her daughter Peggy, the wife of James Arness, is visiting her father at Kenai at the present time.

Mr. and Mrs. Petersen in Unga

During the war years when teachers were unavailable in this part of Alaska, Mrs. Petersen was the principal in charge of the school. She was assisted by Mrs. Daniel Wilson one year (1942-43) and Peggy the following year.

We are very sorry that Mrs. Petersen is leaving us after teaching in Unga all these years. The townfolks and school children will greatly miss her. We all hope that the people of Kenai will appreciate Mrs. Petersen's work as we have during the past years.   (TAP XI, 9, p. 6)

❧ April 1947 ❧

...WHEN ONE TAKES ILL IN UNGA:

Unga witnessed a bit of excitement Monday night, April 14th, when word spread about town that Mrs. Lena Hunt, our school janitress, had been stricken with what appeared to be appendicitis.

Mr. William Peters was summoned to take Mrs. Hunt over to Sand Point since his boat, the *Hawk*, was the only boat available at that time.

Mr. Casey immediately got on the air and contacted King Cove, asking Mrs. Cohen to broadcast blind in hopes that someone would receive the message and get word to Mrs. Arthur Koskey, CAA operator, who is also a registered nurse, to meet the boat in Sand Point. Emil Gunderson luckily picked up the broadcast and informed Mrs. Koskey, who waited patiently at the dock for almost two hours.

Mrs. Hunt was taken to Mrs. Morris' house in Sand Point where she waited for a plane to take her to a hospital.

Mrs. Koskey, after relieving the patient as much as possible, faithfully stayed at her radio most of the entire night in order to contact a plane.

When the plane arrived early Tuesday morning, Mrs. Hunt was taken aboard and flown to Cold Bay. At Cold Bay, the doctor diagnosed the case as trouble caused by the gall bladder. She was flown from Cold Bay to Anchorage, since civilian hospital care is unavailable at Cold Bay.

The latest report is that she is feeling better but will be in the hospital about two or three weeks. We all wish her a speedy recovery.

(TAP XI, 9, p. 7)

[Mrs. Hunt returned home in September, hale and hearty once more. Ed.]

❧ September 1947 ❧

PETER CALUGAN RETURNS HOME

Peter Calugan, one of our Seniors this year, has just returned after being away since 1939.

At the time he left Unga, he had completed his Freshman year and then transferred to Eklutna, Alaska, where he completed his Sophomore year. During his schooling at Eklutna, he was taken ill and sent to a hospital.

His Junior course was taken by correspondence while at the Cushman Hospital at Tacoma, Washington. He spent about three and a half years there and it was from there that he returned to Unga. We are hoping that he will remain with us throughout the year and be graduated with the other three Seniors.   (TAP XII, 1, p. 4)

[Peter did indeed graduate from Unga High School, in 1948. He became a commercial fisherman, married, and raised a family in Sand Point. In later years, the family moved to Anchorage, where he died on December 17, 2003. Peter was 78 years old. Ed.]

OUR "OUTSIDE" GRADS

Evelyn Foster, Mary Galovin and Ruth Lauritzen were graduated from high school in the States this last spring. These girls had received all their education in the Unga school, including their Junior year, but went "outside" to complete their Senior year. Mary and Evelyn attended school in Bellingham, Washington, and Ruth went to school in Kirkland, Washington. Since these girls were members of our student body for so many years, we feel very close to them and wish them luck.

(TAP XII, 1, p. 4)

ANOTHER TOWN MEETING

A town meeting was held at the Club House on the 7th of September. The presiding officer, Mr. William Peters, chairman of the city council, first took up the problem of filling vacancies created by the resignation of Raymond Rodgers, who is now making his home in Seward, and Commissioner Robert Garlow who has moved to Squaw Harbor. Since the third member, John Nelson, is away receiving medical care, it became imperative to act at once.

Three candidates' names were submitted to fill the two vacancies: Olga Krone, Lena Lauritzen and John Berntsen, Sr. In a very close race, the later two were elected.

The next business pertained to the dance hall. There has been a great deal of complaint regarding rowdyism and open drinking in the hall, which has never been permitted. This proved to be a hot issue and many opinions were expressed. It was insinuated that the hall would be closed to public dances if the conditions persisted. Others suggested that those renting the hall put up a deposit to cover breakages and a further plan was suggested that those making the dance should pay an officer to police the dance. No final action was arrived at during the meeting.

Before the chairman could discuss the problem of the city waterworks, the crowd had drifted out.   (TAP XII, 1, p. 7)

UNGA'S ELECTRIFICATION-II

Mr. Casey's power plant, which is going to furnish the town with electricity, has been in operation for some time. However, due to the shortage of electrical supplies, he was unable to string his power lines.

This summer, Mr. French, who has a knack for doing the impossible, managed to procure supplies from the States.

Main Street electrification

Mr. Harry Foster has been busy the past week or so digging and dynamiting holes for the poles. The poles are now up and the power lines run from the power plant down through main street and then head north towards the school.

Mr. Casey is not sure yet as to the monthly rate but believes that the price may be under ten dollars for residents.   (TAP XII, 1, p. 8)

POST OFFICE BURGLARIZED

Sometime during the night of September 1st, Casey's store, which houses the Post Office, was entered and money was taken.

The burglar entered by the rear door where a hook and eye was pulled off an outer door and then a hasp was forced on the inner door.

Apparently the thief is no novice at this business. He very methodically tapped all the petty cash drawers and studiously avoided taking checks. Before leaving, he deliberately replaced the hasp on the rear door and left by the front entrance with $150 to $200 from the store and $24.07 taken from the petty cash drawer in the Post Office.

This is the third Post Office burglary that has been attempted this year: one at King Cove and the other at Sand Point. At the two latter places, the thief was unable to obtain any loot.
                                              (TAP XII, 1, p. 8)

NEW COLD STORAGE PLANT

The Aleutian Cold Storage Co., which recently took over the A. H. Mellick property at Sand Point, now has under construction at Sand Point a cold storage plant which is expected to be ready for operation next May. When completed, the plant will have a daily fish-freezing capacity of 100,000 lbs with storage for 3 1/2 million lbs. In addition, the plant will be equipped to store 2,500 tons of ice while freezing 50 tons daily.
                                              (TAP XII, 1, p. 10)

❧ October 1947 ❧

FUR TRAPPING—1947

Trapping on the mainland has become a topic of conversation since the first trappers left for the mainland on October 17th. The season does not officially open until December 1st, but the many chores that must be done before the cold weather sets in makes it necessary for the trappers to leave early.

The *Vis* took the first group of trappers, which was composed of Norman Lauritzen, Johannes Olsen and Fred Pomian, to their trapping grounds on the mainland. The *Southland* left on October 20th with Thomas Foster, John Foster, Harry Foster and Edward Gilbert to Pavlof Bay, where they will make needed repairs to their cabin before the opening of the season.

Within the next few weeks, there will probably be other trappers leaving. But it seems that each year there are less men leaving for the mainland to go trapping. One reason seems to be that the price of furs has gone down and there is not much profit on these trips.   (TAP XII, 2, p. 6)

ENDRESEN-GUNDERSON WEDDING

On the evening of October 14, 1947, Paul Gunderson, 26, of Nelson Lagoon, and Emma Endresen, 16, of King Cove, were joined in holy matrimony.

The Endresen-Gunderson wedding party

The wedding was held at the Methodist Church and the ceremony was performed by Miss Constance Erickson, pastor of the local church.

Arthur Johnson had the honor of being best man, Mrs. Susie Brandal, matron of honor, and Miss Nora Berntsen, bridesmaid.

After the ceremony, the guests were invited to Miss Erickson's home for a turkey dinner that was prepared by Mrs. Andy Endresen, siser-in-law of the bride.

Emma is well known here, as she often visited her dad, Mr. Ed Endresen, and her brothers, Andy and Arthur Endresen, who are local residents.

The groom has lived around here all his life except when he was in the army. He is the owner of the *Katie G* and follows the usual occupation of fishing and trapping.

After a short honeymoon, they will be at home to their friends at Port Moller.

(TAP XII, 2, p. 7)

FORMER TEACHERS VISIT

Mr. and Mrs. Brown, former teachers of Unga now teaching at Sand Point, were weekend visitors of Mr. and Mrs. Edward Casey.

The Browns taught here from 1929-1931 and there are undoubtedly many people who had them for their teachers.

In the 16 years since the Browns left Unga, they have taught in Kenai, Alaska, Tacoma and last year they taught in South Naknek, Alaska.

Georgia, the daughter of the Browns, is now married to Mr. Alexander Jacobsen and is now living at Kenai, with her husband and baby boy.

The Browns intended to make old acquaintances new again, but the weather became so bad that it was practically impossible for them to get around, but we are sure that they will be able to meet their old friends on another trip, which we hope will be very soon.   (TAP XII, 2, p. 10)

December 1947

WE HAVE CHRISTMAS TREES!

On the *Aleutian Mail's* last trip to the Westward, it had a load of Christmas trees which were sold for a couple of dollars to the people who wanted them.

The school and church received trees that were donated by Raymond Rodgers, who sent them from Seward and they were brought here by Captain Petrich of the *Aleutian Mail.* We appreciate Mr. Rodgers' kindness in remembering the school at this time of the year and we also wish to thank Captain Petrich for bringing the trees here.

(TAP XII, 4, p. 3)

FUR TRAPPING—1947

With furs, meat and fowl, the many trappers from Unga and vicinity returned recently from the mainland.

All had been quite peaceful and quiet in this little village for the past two months, but now again, with the return of a good many men and boys, a bit of excitement has arisen and things should liven up a bit.

The first trappers to leave this season were Norman Lauritzen, Johannes Olsen and Fred Pomian, and they returned on the *Vis* the 14th of December. John Jacobsen, owner of the *Vis*, picked up these men on his return from a short hunting trip made with his sons.

John Berntsen, Sr., who goes to his trapping grounds in his own dory, spent only about a month this year away from home.

Harry Foster, with his boat, the *Southland*, took a few days off from installing electricity in the homes of Unga to pick up his brothers, John and Thomas, and Eddie Gilbert.

Billy Gilbert of Squaw Harbor and his two sons, William and Bobbie, returned also from a spell of trapping on the Mainland.

Of course, along with the many furs that were trapped, most of these men came back with quite a bit of "fur" on their faces, too. For a time, we weren't just sure whether it was the same group of men who had left a short time ago, or whether there was a new crop of men who had come to Unga.

The men reported that they had a "fair" season. The animals trapped were red fox, wolves, for which there is a bounty of $30 apiece, mink, otter, weasels, wolverine and cross fox.

(TAP XII, 4, p. 8)

MOVIES?

The Dance Hall Committee has given its approval to Johnny Gundersen to use the local hall in which to show movies. At the present time, Mr. Gundersen is showing pictures at Sand Point every other night.

Mr. Edward Casey has stated that he intends to open a movie house here in Unga after the first of the year, depending upon the arrival of films.

The last movie house was conducted by Mr. Casey about seven years ago and was closed because the war prevented films from reaching Unga.

(TAP XII, 4, p. 9)

PIANO RECITAL

A piano recital was held Sunday evening, December 14th at 7 o'clock with a fair-sized crowd attending. The pupils taking part in the recital were: Ethel Cushing, Alice Cushing, Nellie Brandal, Ann Lauritzen, Martha Hunt and Thorwald Lauritzen. These students are all studying their music with Miss Erickson and some of them are 3-month students and others, 6-month students. The most difficult piece played was a Hungarian dance. A party followed with refreshments. (TAP XII, 4, p. 9)

CHRISTMAS DISASTER

King Cove, which is located about seventy-five miles west of Unga, was the scene of a great tragedy on Christmas Eve.

All of the facts are not available, but it was assumed that nine persons made an attempt to cross a treacherous lagoon in order to spend the

Christmas holiday with friends and relatives in King Cove. The supposition is that the dory with its occupants overturned in the swift current.

A list of the drowned persons follow: George Galashoff, Mrs. Ed Smith, Annie Nevzareff, Moses Nevzareff, Fannie Kochutin and children Harry, Julia and Martha.

Up to the time of publication, the bodies of all the victims with the exception of Moses Nevzareff and Harry Kochutin have been recovered.   (TAP XII, 5, p. 7)

❧ January 1948 ❧

LOCAL MEN DROWN

The night of January 14th proved fatal for Reynold Gilbert of Squaw Harbor, Benj. Brack of Seattle, John Gundersen, formerly of Sanak but living in Sand Point, and Kenneth Anderson, son of Mrs. Hilda Peters of Squaw Harbor.

Reynold Gilbert.

It is not known just what happened, but it is assumed that these four young men turned over in a small skiff with an outboard motor, while taking the first mate, Benj. Brack, from the mailboat to the Sand Point dock.

The wrecked skiff, minus the occupants, was found the following morning. The body of Reynold Gilbert was found the same day. As yet, the others have not been recovered.

We, the staff of THE ALASKA PEN, extend our deepest sympathy to the parents and relatives of these well-known and liked men.
(TAP XII, 5, p. 8)

[Reynold Gilbert had only recently taken a job on the mailboat, the Aleutian Mail, *as a deckhand. At the time of the disaster, the* Aleutian Mail *lay at anchor in Sand Point, immobilized after having run aground in Pavlof Bay the day before. See TAP XII, 5, p. 8 for additional details. Ed.]*

BERNTSEN-WILSON WEDDING

At seven o'clock in the evening of January 30, 1948, Aleck Wilson, Jr., and Laura Berntsen were joined in holy matrimony.

The wedding took place at the home of Mrs. William Peters, who is Laura's mother. The ceremony was performed by Miss Constance Erickson, pastor of the local Methodist Church. The best man was Mr. William Peters and the best woman was Mrs. Lena Hunt.

After the ceremony was over, all of the guests were invited to stay for coffee and cake.
(TAP XII, 5, p. 7)

PLENTY OF BEEF

On January 22nd, the *Vis*, owned by John Jacobsen, left for Simeonof Island to hunt cattle. George Grassamoff and a few other men went along.

It is understood generally that the island is abandoned and the cattle seem to be running wild without anyone caring for them. George Grassamoff probably has one of the best claims to the island because of his many years of faithful service on the island.

The men had to hike over the island to look for the cattle and then shoot and pack the beef to the beach, where it was freighted out to the boat.

The *Vis* returned after about a twelve-day trip. The fresh beef which they brought back was sold for fifty cents a pound and, according to all reports, was quite tender.

(TAP XII, 6, p. 7)

❧ February 1948 ❧

...AND ANOTHER MAILBOAT!

Captain Anderson and his barge, the *Lois Anderson*, brought some "long-awaited-for mail" from Seward.

The *Lois Anderson* is a power barge of about 110 feet in length with a beam of 42 feet. It has accommodations for only four or five passengers. With its twin motors, it has an average speed of about nine knots.

Captain Anderson, a very young man in shipping circles, has a master's and pilot's license, which enables him to pilot any size ship in any waters.

It is not known as to whether the *Lois Anderson* will have the contract permanently. At the present time, it is replacing the *Aleutian Mail*, which has gone to Seattle for general repairs of damage inflicted while going aground last month.

(TAP XII, 6, p. 7)

❧ March 1948 ❧

RODGERS-BRACKER WEDDING

Budilia Rodgers, a graduate of the 1946 graduating class of Unga High, was joined in holy matrimony March 1st to Jack Bracker, in Bellingham, Washington.

Since Budilia left school, she has been employed in Bellingham. Her husband is also employed in the same city at the cold storage plant.

Budilia expects to spend the summer with her mother, Mrs. George Foster, who resides here.

(TAP XII, 7, p. 4)

FOSTER-MOLINE WEDDING

Word was received that the wedding bells rang on March 10th for another former student of Unga High.

Evelyn Foster, daughter of Mr. and Mrs. Harry Foster, was married to Junior Moline, in Bellingham. This couple will leave on the *Baranof* Saturday for Anchorage, where they will visit Junior's sister. (TAP XII, 7, p. 4)

"HYGIENE" NURSE MARRIES

The people of Unga will undoubtedly be interested in an article from the February Department of Health Bulletin telling of the marriage of Miss Catherine Smulling and Angus Gair.

Miss Smulling will be remembered by most of the people in Unga for her untiring efforts as the Public Health Nurse on the *Hygiene* when it visited here in 1946. Her husband may also be remembered as the chief engineer of the same ship.

We are certain that many people in Unga join us in extending our congratulations and best wishes for happiness to Mr. and Mrs. Gair.

(TAP XII, 7, p. 4)

SAND POINT PRISONER

Johnny Chebetnoy of Sand Point was remanded to the local bastile by U. S. Commissioner Robert Garlow. He will be held here pending transportation to Anchorage where he must answer to charges of using a dangerous weapon upon Andrew Grosvold. The latter received injuries including a broken jaw, and was taken to Cold Bay Army Hospital for treatment.

(TAP XII, 7, p. 10)

[Was the "dangerous weapon" perhaps a fist?! Ed.]

NEW MAIL SERVICE?

A recent communication to the local Post Office has stated that the old mail contract has been cancelled. Effective March 1, 1948, the Reeve Aleutian Airways will carry the mail from Anchorage to Atka, discharging mail at Cold Bay, Dutch Harbor and Atka. The mail discharged at Cold Bay will be distributed by boat from Scotch Cap Lighthouse to Chignik by Messrs Uttecht and Gronholdt. The mail for the Akutan vicinity will be picked up at Unalaska and delivered by Verne Robinson.

According to the communication, this mail service will commence on March 15th, but the frequency of the service is yet unknown and is to be worked out at a later date. (TAP XII, 7, p. 10)

BOAT TROUBLES

The *Hawk*, owned by Wm. Peters of Unga, recently went on the rocks causing a hole to be torn in the bottom. While the *Bogdan* was towing the *Hawk* up the bay, the exhaust pipe from the latter punched a hole through the side of the *Bogdan*.

The Hawk *(left) tied up in Sand Point*

Later, the *Hawk* was sold to Edward Gilbert, who patched up the hole and the boat is again in running condition.

In the meantime, another one of our boats, the *Southland*, owned by Harry Foster, is laid up at Squaw Harbor with a broken clutch and the *Bogdan*, owned by Andrew Foster, is now tied up and having a new engine installed.

(TAP XII, 7, p. 10)

❦ April 1948 ❧

A PLANE SCARE

Several days of great anxiety were experienced by many Sand Point residents when a Safeway Airways plane out of Seward was flying three passengers from Kodiak via Port Heiden to Sand Point when it became long overdue.

Because of bad weather, no searching parties could be sent out. With the abatement of the weather, search planes from Cold Bay flew out to the region in which the overdue plane was last seen. After several hours of intensive search, the plane was finally located at Balboa Bay, more commonly known as "Left Hand Bay".

Two boats, the *Alasco* and the *Hawk*, were immediately dispatched to the scene. Upon their arrival, everyone was found safe and in good condition. The plane had been forced down because of bad weather.

The occupants of the plane were as follows: Mrs. Marina Carlson and infant, Pauline Osterback, Mr. Brooks and the pilot, Gentry Schuster.   (TAP XII, 8, p. 7)

OUR NEW MAILBOAT, THE *MOBY DICK*

The new mailboat, *Moby Dick*, owned by George Gronholdt and Mike Uttecht, has recently taken up the mail contract. She will deliver mail from Cold Bay west to Scotch Cap and east to Chignik. The Reeve Aleutian Airways will deliver mail to Cold Bay every ten days and pick up the outgoing mail.

The *Moby Dick* has a length of 65 feet and a 15-foot beam. Her cruising speed is 10 knots with a top speed of 12.5 knots. It is powered by a 165 horsepower Grey marine diesel engine. She carries 14 night passengers and 21 day passengers at the rate of fifteen cents per mile.

This boat will make three trips per month from April 1st to September 30th. After that, she will make two trips per month. (TAP XII, 8, p. 9)

CANNERY CREWS ARRIVE

The superintendent, Mr. Withrow, and a few other men for the Alaska Pacific Salmon Company arrived at Sand Point by way of Cold Bay. The tenders, *Beryl E* and the *Farallon* arrived about the last week of April, each 12 hours apart.

The superintendent, Ralph Rogers, and about twenty men for the Pacific American Fisheries at Squaw Harbor arrived on the S. S. *Denali*. The tender *Virginia E* arrived Monday, April 26th, and the *Empress* arrived Thursday night, April 29th. (TAP XII, 9, p. 7)

✤ May 1948 ✤
WORKERS LEAVE FOR THE CANNERIES

Soon after the cannery crews arrived in Squaw Harbor and Sand Point, the town of Unga became very quiet. This is due to the fact that most of the men of Unga have left for work. Those who have left for Squaw Harbor are: Alec Calugan, Andrew Krone, Martin Johansen, Norman Larsen, Alec Wilson, Albert Cushing, Alec Cushing, Ed Endresen, Harry Foster, Thomas Foster, Martin Gilbert and Johnny Nelson. Those who are working in Sand Point are: Albert Krone, Howard Berntsen, Henry Berntsen, John Foster, Jacob Johansen, Edward Gilbert, Arthur Endresen and Andrew Foster.

Some of the men are cannery workers while others are fishermen. The fishermen work on pile drivers getting the traps ready, and the web crews, or wire gangs, work on the traps until the fishing season actually begins. They also haul up their boats, caulk them, and some of them are repainted while others are repaired so they will be in top

shape for the fishing season. The cannery workers work in the beach gangs, or do general work about the cannery itself. (TAP XII, 9, p. 8)

FLOATING COURT IN UNGA

The Floating Court, U.S.C.G.C. *Northwind*, paid Unga a visit May 25, 1948, on its way westward. Personnel consisted of Judge Kehoe and his official party of the Third Division, Assistant District Attorney Moody, Social Security man Palaska and clerks of the US District Court. Also aboard were Mrs. Dorothy Novatney, Educational Supervisor for the Territory, Doctor Price and Dentist Bray.

The dentist, who set up his office in the Parsonage, was kept very busy during the visit. Approximately twenty persons gathered at the Parsonage to have teeth extracted. No repair work was done on the teeth as it would have taken more time than they could spend here.

The people of Unga seemed quite pleased that the Floating Court and those accompanying them could visit Unga and were happy to cooperate with them in their work with the village people. (No doubt, the children were glad to see the dentist leave with his tools!) The party arrived during the morning and continued on their way in the late afternoon.

It may be of interest to our readers to know that the US Coast Guard Cutter *Northwind* was used by Rear Admiral Richard E. Byrd in one of his Antarctic expeditions. (TAP XII, 9, p. 6)

✤ August 1948 ✤
BRANDAL-JOHANSEN WEDDING

Virginia Brandal, a former student of Unga High School, and Jacob Johansen left for Sand Point August 27th on the *Milfred* to be joined in wedlock. The best man and matron of honor were Mr. and Mrs. Martin Gilbert. They were married by U. S. Commissioner Robert Garlow. Immediately after the ceremony was over, they returned home in a dory. A wedding dance was held that night.

Mr. and Mrs. Jacob Johansen are now renting a home from Johnny Haaf, a local resident.

The student body of the High School wishes to extend hearty congratulations to the newlyweds and wish them happiness in their future married life.   (TAP XIII, 1, p. 7)

TRAGEDY STRIKES UNGA

Unga witnessed an unexpected tragedy August 22nd when Edward Wallin became suddenly insane. Mr. and Mrs. Edward Wallin and children and his brother, Johnny, were visiting friends in Unga when the tragedy occurred.

After attacking and attempting to choke several people, the victim broke into the local liquor store. Shortly after, he was seen running toward Casey's dock. From the dock, he leaped into the water. The body was recovered but an attempt which was made to revive him failed. The doctor from Squaw Harbor, after examining the body, stated that he died of a fractured skull. A large cut was discovered in the victim's head. It was suspected that he had a heavy fall during the first stage of his insanity and thus received the fracture. This is one of the very few tragedies ever to have happened in the community.

The funeral service was conducted by Alex Calugan in the Greek Orthodox Church, as our pastor, Miss Erickson, was attending the yearly Methodist Conference in Ketchikan. The body was laid to rest in the Russian Cemetery.

We wish to extend our deepest sympathy to Mrs. Wallin and the entire family in their bereavement.   (TAP XIII, 1, p. 8)

❦ Summer 1948 ❦

REVEREND GOULD PAYS A VISIT

Rev. P. Gordon Gould, who was born at Unga, visited here during the past summer. This was Rev. Gould's first visit to Unga in 41 years.

While in Unga, Rev. Gould visited with his brother, Mr. Isaac Gould of Squaw Harbor, Mrs. Fred Krone of Sand Point, and his half-sister, Mrs. Harry Foster.

Rev. Gould came here as a representative of the Division of Home Missions and Church Extension of the Methodist Church, which headquarters are in Philadelphia.

Rev. Gould came to Alaska "seeking the basic needs of the Territory and surveying the Church's needs and ways of meeting them".
                    (TAP XIII, 1, p. 9)

❦ September 1948 ❦

FORMER MARSHAL VISITS

Mr. Allan Petersen, former marshal of Unga, surprised his friends here by a very unexpected visit September 2nd. Mr. Petersen left Unga in 1946 to set up his office in Kenai, Alaska. Previously, he lived here for 12 years with his wife, Mrs. Petersen, son Jimmy and daughter Peggy. Mrs. Petersen was the primary teacher while she lived in Unga and took a leading part in the town functions and organizations.

Mr. Petersen was dispatched on official business to this area by Marshal Patterson, the head marshal of the Third District. He arrived on the mailboat *Moby Dick* after a trip by plane from Anchorage to Cold Bay. While in Unga, Mr. Petersen was guest of Mr. and Mrs. Casey, prominent Unga merchants. On the second day of his visit, the *Moby Dick* returned and he left for Cold Bay to continue his trip home.

Undoubtedly, Mr. Petersen enjoyed renewing acquaintances with his old friends and we were glad to see him again.   (TAP XIII, 1, p. 7)

❦ October 1948 ❦

HALIBUT FISHING

In May of this year, the Aleutian Cold Storage at Sand Point was completed and opened to take halibut. Many boats from Seattle, Southeastern Alaska, Kodiak and a few from Sand Point fished for the Aleutian Cold Storage.

The halibut was bought by the pound. The price was determined by the size of the halibut. The smaller halibut, having a better meat, brought more per pound than the larger. During the first part of the fishing season, the prices were low, but later on the fishermen demanded and received higher prices. Halibut fishing proved to be very good during May and until the latter part of June when the average delivery of fish began to decrease. Halibut fishing and the Cold Storage were closed July 11th.   (TAP XIII, 1, p. 5)

SALMON FISHING

The salmon fishing for the cannery had been very poor this year. The *Southland*, owned by Harry Foster, was high boat this year for the Pacific American Fisheries and the *Bogdan*, owned by Andrew Foster, was high boat for the Alaska Pacific Salmon Co.

A few of the local boats went fishing for the Aleutian Cold Storage at Sand Point. They took on ice at the Cold Storage for the freezing of salmon. During the middle of September, after about a month's fishing, the run of salmon decreased and the fishermen stopped fishing.
                    (TAP XIII, 1, p. 5)

"HYGIENE" ARRIVES IN UNGA

The floating clinic *Hygiene* arrived at Unga on October 11th. The *Hygiene* before [being] converted to a medical ship was a small army boat [similar in design to the ill-fated *FP-33* described in Part II]. This ship was sent out by the Territorial Department of Health to give medical aid to the villages along the Alaskan coast. Her headquarters are at Juneau and she makes her trips North annually. The medical staff is composed of a doctor, Hazel Blair; nurse, Mrs. Gair; bacteriologist, Miss Batcheldor; secretary, Mrs. Raatikainen, and fortunately, this year, a dentist, Mr. Crim.

During the summer, the *Hygiene* was at drydock in Seattle receiving repairs. Prior to her arrival at Unga, the *Hygiene* visited all the towns along the Peninsula and the Aleutian Islands. While in Unga, the people went aboard by means of dories for X-rays and blood tests. Those who needed immunizations received diphtheria shots and small pox vaccinations. About 25 people went aboard every day for four days.

On Tuesday, a tuberculin test was given and on Friday, the results were checked. A movie was shown Wednesday for the women and another was shown on Saturday for the men. Movies on health education were shown at the school for the pupils.

Many people received dental care aboard the *Hygiene*, either to have teeth extracted or filled.

We enjoyed seeing Mrs. Gair, formerly Miss Smulling, again and are looking forward to seeing the whole crew on their next trip here.
                    (TAP XIII, 2, p. 5)

B.C.G. SHOTS GIVEN

On October 22, Dr. Florence Marcus and Miss Ruth Grover arrived here on the *Moby Dick* to give immunization shots for tuberculosis. The only people that could take these shots were the ones whose tests, given by Dr. Blair, showed negative. Over half of the people in town could not take the shot. These B.C.G. shots are supposed to prevent your getting tuberculosis by building up a bodily resistance.
                    (TAP XIII, 2, p. 5)

TOWN MEETING

The Chairman of the Town Council, Mr. William Peters, called a meeting Friday, October 8th, for the purpose of discussing further development of the newly-constructed board walks and other town improvements. The meeting was held in the Club House, where twenty people assembled.

Before any discussions began, the minutes of the last meeting were read by Acting Secretary of the meeting, Mrs. Ed Casey, followed by the report of the Treasurer, Mr. Ed Casey. This report showed a balance of $1006.60 in the town Treasury.

As this was the first meeting of the year, an election of new officers was held. Thomas Lauritzen succeeded Mr. Peters as Chairman and Mrs. Lena Lauritzen became Secretary-Treasurer. Also on the Council are Messrs Peters, Alec Wilson and Albert Krone.

Several matters such as the continuation of board walks to all necessary points; repairing of the Community Dance Hall, and the construction of fences around the two cemeteries were open to discussion. A benefit dance is being planned for New Year's Eve as a means of raising more money to meet the coming expenses. It was decided that two town meetings should be held each year, namely, March 1st and October 1st. The Council members plan to meet more frequently. After the discussions were closed, the meeting adjourned.   (TAP XIII, 2, p. 6)

NEW BOARDWALKS IN UNGA

A large improvement has been made in Unga because of a boardwalk which has been laid along the entire length of the main walk. Several local men were hired to construct the walk. A great portion of the lumber for the walk was gener-

On the boardwalk: Edward Melseth and David Wilson

ously donated by Mr. Lauritzen. Other lumber was donated by Mr. Casey and tank staves were given to the town by Mr. Ralph Rogers, superintendent of the Pacific American Fisheries cannery at Squaw Harbor. The staves were obtained from tanks which formerly were used to store water and codfish. A rail was constructed along a short length of the walk where it runs close to a bluff. Now it will be safe to wander around in the night without falling over!

The construction of the walk was put aside for awhile because no decision had been made as to how far the walk would extend. At a town meeting which was held to discuss the the matter, it was decided that this walk should be connected with Albert Krone's walk. It was also decided that walks should be built in other needed parts of town.

Thanks for the nice job, men. At least we can't yell about mud, mud, mud anymore!

(TAP XIII, 2, p. 7)

UNGA'S GENERAL ELECTION

The General Election was held at the Unga Club House October 12th for the purpose of electing the Delegate to Congress, Attorney General, Auditor of Alaska, Highway Engineer, Territorial Senators and Representatives for the Territorial House of Representatives.

Mrs. Lena Hunt, Mrs. Lena Lauritzen and Thomas Lauritzen were appointed judges on the Election Board.

The people of the Unga Precinct, which includes Unga and Squaw Harbor, seemed to have favored the Democrats, as is shown by the following report given by the judges of the Election Board.

Bob Bartlett won the people's favor overwhelmingly with a vote of 38 against Republican R. H. Stock's 4, for Delegate to Congress.

J. Gerald Williams, Democrat, received 35 votes to Republican Almer J. Peterson's 7, for Attorney General.

Frank A. Boyle, Democrat, received 35 votes to Republican Albert E. Goetz's 7, for Auditor of Alaska.

Frank A. Metcalf won 35 votes to Republican Donald MacDonald's 6 votes, for Highway Engineer.

Democrats Walter E. Huntley and Steve McCutcheon won over their Republican opponents for the Territorial Senate, receiving 28 and 27 votes, respectively.

The seven Territorial Representatives who were chosen from the Democratic ranks are as follows: Clarence P. Keating, 35 votes; William A. Egan, 33; Stanley J. McCutcheon, 33; Chester C. Carlson, 32; Alfred A. Owen, Jr., 29; C. A. Pollard, 27; and Jack Conright, 27.

It may be of interest to note that J. Gerald Williams, who is running for Attorney General, was a former school teacher here at Unga, in 1936-37.

(TAP XIII, 2, p. 9)

❧ November 1948 ❧
FUR TRAPPING—1948

The *Southland* left for the mainland with five local men who plan to stay for a few weeks to do some trapping. The following men listed for trapping are: John Foster, Thomas Foster, Howard Berntsen, Henry Berntsen and John Berntsen, Sr. They plan to trap three weeks.

The *Vis* also left some time ago with Fred Pomian and Norman Lauritzen. They plan to be back home by the middle of December.

(TAP XIII, 3, p. 7)

[All trappers returned safely but "reported that they had a very poor season."] (TAP XIII, 4, p. 9)

[Since THE ALASKA PEN was not published during the 1949-50 school year, we have no record that fur trapping was conducted in the fall of 1949. The next and final entry regarding trapping occurred in THE ALASKA PEN's Harbor Highlights of October 1950, which stated that the Vis *took Johannes Olsen trapping on the 17th. (TAP XIV, 2, p. 6) It is very likely that this brief entry signalled the end of fur trapping, an occupation whose demise was the victim of changing times and fashions. Ed.]*

EARTHQUAKES

On November 3rd, Unga received four unexpected(!) earthquakes. There was a series of three during the evening and one later in the night. Several more, which were reported at different times, have occurred recently.

The cause of these disturbances is unknown but some people believe them to be volcanic disturbances in the Peninsular area. (TAP XIII, 3, p. 8)

❧ December 1948 ❧
A REAL TREE FOR CHRISTMAS

The Unga School was very fortunate this Christmas. They had the pleasure of gathering around a "real" Christmas tree at school. The tree was brought up to Sand Point on the Fish and Wildlife boat *Penguin*. We owe our sincere appreciation and thanks to Capt. Dan Drottning, the captain of the *Penguin*, for thinking of us in Unga.

This Christmas, the people here had to dig through their attics for an artificial tree or decorate a large house plant because of expensive air transportation on trees. (TAP XIII, 4, p. 4)

Christmas Boat: USFWS Penguin

❧ January 1949 ❧

RELIEF SUPPLIES ARRIVE

Southwestern Alaska finally was recognized as "still existing" when the Alaska Steamship Co.'s freighter *Palisana* arrived at Squaw Harbor. This was the first ship bringing freight and supplies since September.

The *Palisana* docked at the PAF cannery at Squaw Harbor on January 9th from the Westward, discharged freight for Unga, and proceeded to Sand Point. It was understood that the *Palisana* carried only the necessities of the various peninsular towns and no great amount of freight was received at any one place.

Although we of Unga suffered no acute food shortage during the maritime strikes, the incoming freight was welcomed with its needed supply of potatoes, butter, fresh fruits and vegetables, and other foodstuffs. (TAP XIII, 5, p. 6)

NEWS FROM CHIGNIK

Mr. and Mrs. George Osbekoff are the proud parents of a baby boy born on December 4th, and 11:30PM.

A dance was given for Miss Harriet Harris on her 17th birthday, December 9th. All who attended enjoyed her angel food cake!

The population of Chignik increased 13 on Dec.10th, when the Alvarados and Lydas returned from the States. Daniel Lyda and Joe Alvarado fished here in the summer.

A baby girl was born to Mr. and Mrs. Henry Sanguinetti, December 17th at 5:00PM. The six and one-half pound baby was named Laura Elaine.

The *Moby Dick* was delayed in Perryville with engine trouble and couldn't make the trip to Chignik this trip, December 20th. The *Reliance*, owned by Rudolph Carlson, took the outgoing mail to the *Moby Dick* at Perryville and picked up the Chignik mail.

Henry Valli, the proud owner of the Chignik Pool Hall, took a trip to Perryville to spend the Christmas season.

At approximately 5:00PM, December 24th, a baby girl was born to Mrs. Stella Wallin. She weighed seven and one-half pounds. The baby was named Carol Eve.

The Chignik School presented a Christmas program early in the evening of December 24th. After the program, a dance was held which lasted until the wee hours of the morning. The dance was enjoyed by all who attended.

Mr. John F. Wallin lost his outboard motor and skiff which broke loose from the beach and drifted out to sea, on December 26th.

The *Reliance* left with some men for a hunting trip December 27th and returned three days later all iced down.

A New Year's Eve dance was held on December 31st. A midnight lunch was served and then everybody participated in shooting the old year out. We hope 1949 will bring more happiness than did 1948. (TAP XIII, 5, p. 8)

[This tidbit of news from our peninsular neighbor was sent in by Mr. John F. Wallin, in response to an invitation from the staff of THE ALASKA PEN. Ed.]

❧ February 1949 ❧

MARTIN GILBERT RETURNS

Martin Gilbert returned home after approximately two months at Kodiak, where he went for medical attention. This is the second time Martin has been to Kodiak since his accident last fall. The first time he was there, he had his leg set and placed in a cast. After he returned home, where he stayed for a couple of weeks, he went up to Cold Bay to have the cast removed from his leg. While there, the doctor told him that his leg had to be broken over because it was not set properly. Martin came back home on the *Moby Dick* and was lucky enough to catch the *Penguin* going Kodiak way. When Martin got back to Kodiak, the doctor there advised him that his leg was healing nicely and removed the cast. Martin had to wait at Kodiak for transportation home. After several weeks stay, he went by boat to Chignik. From there, he returned home on the *Moby Dick*.

Martin is now able to be around. We all hope that he will have no more difficulty as a result of the unfortunate accident.   (TAP XIII, 6, p. 7)

UNION MEETING HELD

On February 12th, an AFL Union meeting was held at the town hall for all fishermen and cannery workers belonging to the AFL. The purpose of this meeting was to get things organized and to give the members an idea of what the union was like and what is expected of the members. Union books were also given to the members who joined.

After all business was finished, the meeting was adjourned.   (TAP XIII, 6, p.7)

JOHN NELSON RETURNS HOME

John Nelson, who had been in Sand Point caring for the Shumagin Trading Company store since the Garlows' departure for the States, returned home on the *Vis*. John also acted as U. S. Commissioner during the absence of Mr. Garlow. Reports would lead us to believe that Unga is preferable to Sand Point, in John's estimation.

(TAP XIII, 6, p. 8)

PENINSULAR NEWS

[In response to THE ALASKA PEN's call for news from our neighbors, the following dispatches were submitted by Albert Carlson of Sanak and Nora Osterback of Sand Point. Ed.]

SANAK

A new post office was established at the beginning of the new year at Pauloff Harbor, Sanak, Alaska, which makes it much more convenient for the residents of the village. The postmaster is Mr. Peter Nielsen.

Two children were born recently—one to Mr. and Mrs. John Holmberg, and the other to Mrs. Nielsen.

Mrs. Katy Olsen and daughter Lena of Caton's Island, Sanak, have been in Seattle since last fall. At present, they are working in Seattle but expect to come back to Alaska for the summer to work in the cannery at False Pass.

SAND POINT

At Christmas, a Christmas program was held at the school. "The Christmas Quiz Contest" was presented by the upper grades. The play was about teenagers in a quiz contest. Mr. Brown, the teacher, acted as master of ceremonies. The younger children gave "The Christmas Mix-up". Various poems were recited by Peter Ludvick, Margie and Isabel Morris and Marie Chebetnoy.

Athletic equipment, which was ordered by the school, arrived on the *Moby Dick*. The new equipment consisted of baseballs, baseball bats, volleyballs, footballs, boxing gloves, catcher's mitts and other outdoor equipment. The students are anxiously waiting for suitable weather so that they may be used.

The school days which were missed in September were all made up on February 11th, as a result of going to school on Saturdays.

The school pupils were busy making valentines for everyone. A valentines party was held on Saturday, February 12th.

The eighth graders, Nora Osterback and Ralph Bjornstad are studying pretty hard this year in preparation for the final Territorial examination to be given in May.   (TAP XIII, 6, p. 9)

❧ March 1949 ❧

THE *ELMER* LEAVES UNGA

After a long absence from the water, the M. S. *Elmer* again was seen in Delarof Harbor, to the surprise of many people here. The *Elmer*, previously owned by Norman Lauritzen, has been disabled for over two years. She was last used in 1946.

As she would require a great deal of reconditioning, the *Elmer* was sold to Andy Endresen

Elmer *in her heyday, late '30s*

of Sand Point, who is skilled in carpentry. He has been in Unga for several days during this month fixing the boat temporarily so that she could withstand the trip to Sand Point, where Andy plans to remodel her.

The *Elmer* was launched after the work was completed and was towed by the *Vis* to Squaw Harbor where the heavier portions of the Atlas Imperial Diesel, by which she was previously propelled, were removed onto the PAF cannery dock.

In the previous years, the *Elmer* served as a fishing boat with the minor work of transportation and freighting.

During her two and one-half years of idleness, the *Elmer* rested in Unga's "drydock" at the head of Delarof Harbor.

Elmer *in drydock, late '40s*

We are looking forward to seeing the *Elmer* again in operating condition in a few years.

(TAP XIII, 7, p. 6)

[The Elmer *never again returned to the sea. After being disgorged of her engine, she was towed to Sand Point, where further examinations revealed that she was beyond repair. She was eventually burned: a proper Viking funeral for a gallant vessel. Ed.]*

FREIGHTER *LUCIDOR* ARRIVES

The freight boat *Lucidor* arrived at Squaw Harbor on March 15th with freight for the nearby ports of the Shumagin Islands.

For Unga, Sjoberg & Casey and Lauritzen's, the two local stores, got in a supply of staples, fresh vegetables and meat. All the children of Unga seem to be enjoying the new supply of candy very much, as well as the fresh vegetables and other things.

It is said that the captain of the *Lucidor*, Chris Trondsen, is a fellow well-known to most of the local people of Unga. He used to be mate on the former mailboat *Starr* some years ago.

(TAP XIII, 7, p. 6)

UNGA TOWN MEETING

A town meeting was held at the Club House at 7:00PM March 14th. The meeting was called to order by Mrs. Lena Lauritzen, who is secretary.

An election was held to choose council members to fill the places left vacant by the deaths of William Peters and Thomas Lauritzen. John Nelson and Norman Larsen were the two new members elected. John Nelson was elected to the office of chairman.

They planned to have a spring cleanup week from the 21st to the 26th of March, weather permitting.

The present town council members are: Nelson, Larsen, Mrs. Lauritzen, Alec Wilson and Albert Krone.

The Treasurer reported a Balance on Hand of $190.51.   (TAP XIII, 7, p. 6)

FRESH BEEF

On February 25th, the *Vis*, owned by John Jacobsen, arrived in port to take Johannes Olsen and Norman Lauritzen for a beef hunting trip to Chernabura Island, one of the small islands of the Shumagin Islands group. Johannes was in charge of the beef and the sale of it after reaching Unga.

They were lucky enough to have fine weather all their trip so they made a quick return, arriving March 2nd.

The beef was brought into the village and sold to the residents who enjoyed it immensely.

(TAP XIII, 7, p. 7)

❧ April 1949 ❧

PLAY PRESENTED

From the impression made by the successful presentation of a three-act comedy, "Marriage by Midnight", it seems that there is a group of talented "actors and actresses" isolated on Unga Island, a long way from Hollywood! This might easily be the drawn conclusion after summing up the remarks that were heard after the play was presented.

"Marriage by Midnight" was presented by the Unga Players at the Unga Playhouse, Saturday evening, April 23rd.

Tickets were sold at the two local stores. Admission charges were: Adults: $1.00; Children: $.50.

The play started at 8:15PM and the curtains were drawn to a close at 10:00. The male lead was played by John H. Nelson and the female lead by Miss Elizabeth Anderson.

Following the play, a dance was given at the Dance Hall. Refreshments were served later at the nominal charge of 25¢ per person.

The receipts taken in from the show, including contributions, amounted to $103.50. $23.75 was taken in at the refreshment sale. The total amount of $127.25 went into the Unga Town Fund.

(TAP XIII, 8, p. 9)

UNGA PLAYERS
present:

"MARRIAGE BY MIDNIGHT"

E ACTS

DAY EVENING, APRIL 23

P. M.

RG

(rance)

.........THORWALD LAURITZEN
...........JOHN H. NELSON
....MISS ELIZABETH ANDERSON
.........NELS BRANDAL
.......MRS. LENA LAURITZEN
.......MRS. VIOLA CASEY
.........MISS MARTHA HUNT
.........EDWARD F. CASEY
.......ALEX. CALUGAN, SR.

"Billy," "Wanda," and "Kitty"

MORNING
AFTERNOON
ACT THREE-----(same)------EVENING

STAGE MANAGER.......
PUBLICITY MANAGER.....

STAGE SETTING EXECUTED

DANCING WILL FOLLOW I
BE SOLD AT THE

THE UNGA PLAYERS WISH
HAVE ASSIST

THE TOTAL F

Part of the cast. From left: John Nelson, Alex Calugan, Johannes Olsen, Beth Anderson,
Martha Hunt, Thorwald Lauritzen, and Lena Lauritzen.

❦ May 1949 ❦

S. S. *DENALI* ARRIVES

The S. S. *Denali* arrived at Squaw Harbor on May 8th with passengers, cannery workers and freight for Squaw Harbor. There was also freight for the two local stores here.

Mary and George Galovin, former Unga residents, arrived on the *Denali* to work at the Squaw Harbor cannery this summer.

Mr. and Mrs. Peter Gould also arrived on the *Denali* to visit his mother, Mrs. Isaac Gould of Squaw Harbor. This is his first visit home in several years. (TAP XIII, 8, p. 4)

[Since THE ALASKA PEN took a vacation from April-May 1949 to September 1950, no Historical Highlights are available for this period. However, the accompanying essays cover much of the year's memorable events. Ed.]

❦ September 1950 ❦

PORKY PANICS PEOPLE

What's happening in Unga? You peer through the windows and you know there's some excitement going on. You see scampering, screaming children running all about. Looks as if we have a new visitor here, but what sort of beast is it? It looks so terribly big and is acting somewhat crazy. Look at it racing up the hill, and people not far behind it with a rope in order to catch it! Goodness! I've never seen anything like it. It's wearing a black and white coat of fur. Oh! I just now remember. It's the Heilbruns' pig! It unexpectedly arrived from the Jesse Lee Home at Seward, on the M. S. *Garland*.

Mr. and Mrs. Heilbrun named her "Esmeralda". In order to find a place big enough for it to stay in, Martin Johansen, a local resident, offered his chicken house until they could find a place for it to stay.

But now since "Essy" has six more little pigs, she finds it a little crowded in the small chicken coop, so Mr. Heilbrun with the help of Mr. Shimer

built a larger yard out of town a ways for "Essy" and her family. (TAP XlV, 1, p. 3)

[The location of the new coop was at McCann's Point, a short walk up the bay. I remember it well. Ed.]

A NEW BOAT ON THE BAY: THE *ANNA T*

The name of the new purse seiner in Unga is the *Anna T*. The boat is owned by Norman Lauritzen. The *Anna T* was built in Seattle this last spring. A diesel motor powers the 40-foot craft, which Norman brought up to Unga with a three-man crew consisting of himself, Robert Olsen and Harold Pedersen. Because it is a dangerous trip coming across the Gulf, they followed a couple of tenders from Seattle. The *Anna T* and her young skipper appear to be well on the way to a successful career. (TAP XlV, 1, p. 3)

[The Anna T *was named in honor of Norman's grandmother, who spent most of her life in Unga and who died in 1947. Ed.]*

Norman Lauritzen and the Anna T

❦ October 1950 ❦

CUSHING-ANDERSON WEDDING

Alice Cushing and Harold Anderson were married October 25th at 7:00 PM in the Methodist Church. Handsome Hal comes from Chignik, where the couple is now living. Mr. Heilbrun led the ceremony. It was very beautiful, with candles and music—Mendelssohn's Wedding March.

Alice came down the aisle following Meryl Hansen, the bridesmaid. The bride wore a blue net gown with white finger-tipped veil. The cap of the veil was embroidered with flowers. She wore pearls of the same tint. These colors were attractive with Alice's reddish-blonde hair. I think the groom had a suit on.

After the ceremony, a reception took place at Rev. and Mrs. Heilbruns' house. Following the reception, a dance was held at the Unga Community Hall. It was exciting for everyone. A wedding doesn't come very often in Unga, especially to my sister.

Joan Cushing, 8th Grade
(TAP XlV, 2, p. 4)

HOLMBERG-ANDERSON WEDDING

Mr. Emil Anderson and Miss Nellie Holmberg of Sanak were united in marriage at Sand Point on October 14th by Mrs. Robert Garlow, U. S. Commissioner.

A wedding dance was held the same night with everyone reportedly having a good time.

The bride and groom plan to go to Sanak where they will make their home.

(TAP XlV, 2, p. 4)

UNGA TOWN MEETING

A town meeting was called to order recently in the local library by John H. Nelson, who had been head of the Town Council during the past year.

A fairly good crowd of solid citizens turned out, and immediately decided upon and voted for five council members who would most likely "buckle down" and start some action on civic affairs.

The civic leaders elected were Charles B. Wood, mayor, Mrs. Edward F. Casey, Secretary,

John Nelson, Treasurer, and William Torgramsen and John Berntsen, Sr.

In the ensuing meeting, many arguments ran pro and con.

The first thing decided upon was the repair and maintenance of the town dance hall which is badly in need of "fixing up".

A fence which should be constructed around the cemeteries was also discussed.

A good start toward improvements was made last week when a group of men got together and cleaned the tank and dug out the ditch line which supplies water for the town.

With practically all new members on the Town Council, it is hoped that there will be more action now and less talk.   (TAP XlV, 2, p. 5)

GOODBYE, ESMERALDA!

Our best friend, Esmeralda, saw her last days Saturday, Oct. 21, 1950. We all miss her now that she is gone, for when we walk by her pen we heard her grunting. Now it is just an empty rutted-up pen.

The fate of "Essy"? Hams and bacon smoked by Fred the Whaler, sausages prepared by ace sausage maker Heilbrun, and pork chops made by just "Essy". Think of old "Essy" when you eat her, how she chased Norman Larsen up the hill when she arrived, how her pen was the goal of our after-school walks, and how she gave her most soul-stirring porcine look just before the end.

(TAP XlV, 2, p. 6)

❧ November 1950 ❧
NEWS FROM BELKOFSKI

[The following news items were submitted to THE ALASKA PEN in response to the staff's call for input from local communities. The village of Belkofski lies to the west of Unga, on the mainland. This news was sent in by Grace W. Fowler, Belkofski's school teacher. Ed.]

Born: to Mr. and Mrs. John Dushkin on September 20, 1950, a boy, Macar; to Mr. and Mrs.

Alex A. Dushkin on September 20, 1950, a girl, Lou Ann; to Miss Maggie Kochutin on September 24, 1950, a girl, Susan Marie.

Mrs. John Dushkin passed away September 7, 1950.

Some of the villagers went goose hunting last month and all had excellent luck. We were presented with five nice ones, three of which we salted away for future special occasions. The other two were consumed quickly enough to make our stomachs squeamish. They are also still catching lots of nice fresh-water silver trout.

The mailboat *Pomare* arrived at 4:00AM November 4th and couldn't rouse anyone. Therefore, they launched their power boat and knocked at the door of two very sleepy and surprised people with sixteen bags of very welcome mail. There is no postmaster here now, and the teachers must receive and distribute mail for the villagers.

A Hallowe'en school dance was held October 28th and everyone present had a grand time. I think the most fun was had by the pupils watching the teacher and her husband try to "jitterbug".

TAP Editor's note: Mr. and Mrs. Fowler are the new teachers for the Alaska Native Service school at Belkofski. Mrs. Fowler is from New York and Mr. Fowler is from Oklahoma. They are a very jolly couple and should make many friends at Belkofski. We know they are working hard, from what we hear. Mr. Fowler is sending a SOS for cigarettes since there is none at Belkofski.
(TAP XlV, 3, p. 4)

M. V. *HEALTH* VISITS UNGA

Monday morning at 12:00AM, the Public Health barge, M. V. *Health* dropped anchor in Unga Bay. The *Health* came here from Belkofski.

The medical staff of the *Health* barge were ashore and ready for business almost as soon as the anchor sounded. Unga's leading citizen, Leroy A. Heilbrun, had his dory out to the boat as soon as he heard there were two beautiful ladies to come ashore.

Dr. Blair, who is in charge of the medical program of the *Health*, began to arrange for examinations with the help of Charlie Wood, the Chairman of our Town Council.

Monday afternoon, Dr. Blair called for some of the people she wanted to see again after the last visit of the *Hygiene*. At 4:00PM, Miss Bagley began giving TB tests. She explained that this test does not show who has TB. The test shows who should take BCG vaccine.

On Wednesday, they gave this BCG vaccine to those who needed it. Sunday morning, the *Health* returned from Sand Point to finish up the work they hadn't finished on account of bad weather.
(TAP XlV, 3, p. 6)

"ARE WE PINCUSHIONS"?

Since the health boat came in, everyone is beginning to think they are pincushions. They are all getting vaccinations for several sicknesses. Some of them were afraid, so they had to catch and lead them down to the boat. Most of the people were happy to go out to the health barge while others were crying because they didn't want to go.

Jerry Gilbert must have given Nurse Bagley the best idea of how Unga people feel about being pincushions. Jerry had been pricked thirty times to give him the BCG tuberculin vaccine. When the nurse finished the painful puncture, Jerry politely said, "Thank you".
(TAP XlV, 3, p. 6)

❦ January 1951 ❦
TWO LITTLE PIGGIES WENT TO MARKET

Saturday morning, January 27th at five o'clock, anyone who was getting home late saw two bloody butchers set out for McCann's Point to destroy the Primary Room's special pets. A little while later, two shots rang out and the deed had been done. Unga's pig population was reduced by two members.

Actually, the Primary Room did not mind so very much, and we are glad to know that Heilbruns and Johansens are going to get a few tasty pork dinners for all their hard work in raising those squealers.

There is just one request we have and that is that Sharon Torgramsen wants Nick to save the part that does the squealing for her. There also are a few eighth graders who might like to have some other parts saved for the ghouls' party next Hallowe'en.   (TAP XlV, 5, p. 3)

THE *GARLAND* IS BACK!

The mail proposition is something that does not seem to be working so well around here lately. The *Pomare* resigned and the old mailboat *Garland* is now taking up the contract for carrying the mail.

We hope that the *Garland* won't hit as many rocks as the other mailboat did. We also hope that this mailboat will last for a while longer...
(TAP XlV, 5, p. 3)

THE LOSS OF THE *BOGDAN*

In the January 1951 issue of THE ALASKA PEN, the following cryptic entry appeared in the Historical Highlights of the paper:

Jan. 20...Very windy day. *Bogdan*, owned by Andrew Foster, dragged out of the bay and presumably sank out in the heavy sea.
(TAP XlV, 5, p. 8)

The Bogdan *was one of the most popular boats on the Harbor, ferrying freight and passengers among the islands, delivering trappers to and from the Mainland, and most important, serving as a fishing boat for Mr. Foster. The* Bogdan *often spent the cruel winter months on the water when most other boats were hauled out for safety. This fact, in the end, may have sealed the fate of the vessel.*

I was a lad of seven and watched in horror as my step-dad's boat began dragging anchor that snowy day in

January. A gale was blowing out of the northwest and swept the Bogdan *from its anchorage in the outer harbor. We all watched helplessly as she disappeared in the raging sea. She was never seen again. Edward Melseth, Ed.*

CALUGAN-RUPERT WEDDING

Miss Pauline Calugan, daughter of Alex Calugan, Sr., who lives here in Unga, was recently married to Norman Rupert of Oregon.

Many who know Pauline will remember that she attended school here as a little girl.

Our congratulations go to Mr. and Mrs. Rupert, who now reside in Klamath Falls, Oregon.
(TAP XlV, 5, p. 8)

❧ February 1951 ❧
THE LAST SHOTS, HOORAY!

On February 2nd, the last of the series of inoculations for tetanus, typhoid and whooping cough was completed. This series of inoculations was begun by the staff of the M. V. *Health* late in November. The series was completed by Mrs. Torgramsen. We all appreciate Mrs. Torgramsen's skill and generosity in offering to provide this service for the children of Unga. She made it possible to get this project done safely and with the least possible trouble.

Mr. Shimer's contribution to the program was a purple and green face. This face was put on the ceiling for children to look at while they were being inoculated.

So, if any children injure themselves, particularly nail injuries in the foot, we can be glad they have tetanus immunization to prevent what we usually call "lock jaw". Thanks to the M. V. *Health*; thanks to Mrs. Torgramsen.

(TAP XlV, 6, p. 5)

BOXING AND WRESTLING

The Recreation Committee has been planning things for Friday evenings for the people of Unga. For the last week in February, they put on a boxing and wrestling match.

The boxers were the Melseth brothers, Frankie and Eddy. Frank won that bout. Sammy Brandal and Martin Gilbert mixed it up then, and Sam had the match. Next came Fred Hunt versus Jack Cushing. Jack won that battle. The last scrappers were Norman Larsen and Jerry Gilbert. The winner was Jerry. There were two three-minute rounds with a prize for each winner.

Then came the sad part of the evening: the wrestling match. Jim Heilbrun and Martin Johansen had the first round of their three-round match. While they rested, Peg Heilbrun and Flossie Brandal wrestled. Due to injury in the second round when Jim sprained his back, the wrestling matches were cancelled. Jim is getting better now. The rest of the evening went very well.

Norman Larsen, 8th Grade
(TAP XIV, 6, p. 5)

OUR RESPONSE TO A "NEWSWEEK" ARTICLE

Under the title "Arctic Sharecroppers", Newsweek Magazine printed a report of the very bad living conditions of the people of this area and especially the native Aleut people. The general idea of the article was that the natives out here are in bad shape, not helping themselves nor getting help, either. They are unemployed, poor and not getting proper diets. The Newsweek article said that these people don't eat well because they have given up their native foods.

This is all true, as far as we know. It is pretty true of other Aleut towns, too. But, it is not true that they get no help. They are being told to eat half-forgotten native foods. The native foods are cheaper and they are often better than expensive canned foods.

Native foods seem odd to outsiders at first, but the Alaska Health and Native Service doctors have found that native foods are often best.

Here is one example of many native foods described in a pamphlet called "Food Resources of Alaska":

"Tipnuk" is prepared by burying fish (salmon, for example) without cleaning, in a shallow pit covered with dirt. It is allowed to putrify or partly rot before being eaten as is.

This is probably like the fish used by the Japanese, which contributes large amounts of Vitamin K to their diet. (Vitamin K is important to have, since it helps the blood to form a "scab" over cuts. People may bleed to death without it.)

Kelp or sea weed: There is a type of brown kelp which can be obtained here at low water and is a valuable diet supplement for the iodine it contains. This particular kelp is found growing attached to rocks. Only about a foot of it nearest the rock is used, and it can be eaten raw.

If you would like to send in other good local foods, THE PEN will be glad to print them. *[...and to which we might add, "bon appetit"! Ed.]*
(TAP XIV, 6, p. 7)

[Unfortunately, readers were unable to submit their favorite recipes for bidarkis, sea eggs, cuttle fish, or seagull eggs, to name a few, since Volume XIV, Issue No. 6 was the last and final issue of THE ALASKA PEN. Gourmets need not despair, however. Fifty years later the Unga Tribal Council published a cookbook titled, A Taste of Tradition to Treasures of Tomorrow that contains a vast collection of gastronomic treats that would satisfy the most discerning of palates. Copies of the book may be purchased from the Council at P.O. Box 508, Sand Point, Alaska 99661. Ed.]

THE DIPHTHERIA EPIDEMIC

THE ALASKA PEN, Volume X, Number 8

TO THE PEOPLE OF UNGA

No one can be given the credit for the killing of our recent diphtheria epidemic. Such catastrophe can only be stopped by the cooperation of all. Never before have the people of Unga joined their efforts in overcoming an obstacle as they have in the past few days. Every person is to be commended on his promptness in reporting to the clinic set up at the school building. Even those who live up the bay, as well as the townspeople, braved the unpleasant weather to call at the stated hour.

Those who had sickness at home were helpful in carrying out the doctors' orders. Everyone showed a spirit of cooperation.

When the school pupils were informed of the likely epidemic, they immediately returned to their homes and refrained from visiting their neighbors.

Letters of thanks and appreciation have been mailed to Lt. Francis A. Torrey, Ft. Randall, who was the first doctor to come to Unga and administered treatment on some that otherwise might have proved fatal. Letters were also mailed to Lt. Cdr. Batts, Lt. (j.g.) Margie Gammel, NC, James A. Strehle, PhM 1/c, NAS Dispensary, Kodiak, Cpt. Frank G. Robertson, Ft. Richardson, Miss Vivian Stahl and Mrs. Doris Reherd, Red Cross nurses, Anchorage. Letters were also mailed to their commanding officers.

The radio operators contributed their part in defeating the epidemic by keeping incessant vigilance at their posts. Letters commending them have been mailed to Mrs. Kenneth L. Cohen, King Cove, Charles Franz, Nelson Lagoon, Arthur Koskey, the CAA at Sand Point, and Robert Garlow, Unga.

The Pacific American Fisheries and the Alaska Pacific Salmon Company were mailed letters thanking them for the assistance of the skippers and crews of the *Katmai*, *Glenwood*, *Howkan*, *Beryl E*, and *Pacific Pride*.

Many people of Unga also deserve a hearty thanks for their efforts and assistance.

So, to the cooperation of all in behalf of the school and myself, I, as principal of the Unga Territorial School, wish to express a most hearty thank you.

Donald V. Lawvere

THREE DEATHS IN UNGA

Mrs. Griska Grassamoff died Sunday, April 7th at 9:30am. Myrtle Berntsen died at 8:30pm on Tuesday April 9th. Gerald Berntsen passed away two hours after a tracheotomy had been performed.

Mrs. Grassamoff became ill in Saturday evening with a throat ailment and died the next morning. The Grassamoff family recently moved to Unga from Simeonof Island where they have lived the greatest part of their lives.

Surviving besides the husband are Barney and Hilda at home, Alex in the service, Margaret in Seattle, Fannie and Mike in Anchorage and Andrew in Seward.

Myrtle Berntsen, six, and Gerald Berntsen, four, were the daughter and son of Mr. and Mrs. Louis Berntsen. Surviving besides the parents are Bertha Jean, Louis Jr., Louise, Walter, Rosemary and Trudy.

Myrtle spent some time last fall on the island with the Grassamoff family and Mrs. Grassamoff became quite fond of her. It is an unusual coincidence that they should die on the same day.

DOUBLE FUNERAL HELD

A double funeral was held in the Greek Orthodox Church for Mrs. Grassamoff and Myrtle Berntsen. Harry Kaiakokonok, second priest from Perryville, conducted the services on Tuesday at 12 o'clock. They were buried in a double grave.

Gerald Berntsen was buried the evening of the next day beside his sister.

DIFFICULT TRAVELS

Soon after the second death on Sunday, April 7, and the symptoms of these that were ill were studied, Robert Garlow, the local wireless operator, dispatched messages for assistance. By 2:30am the next morning contacts were made and word received that a doctor from Ft. Randall was eager to get to Unga in the shortest time possible.

Since there is no landing strip in Unga, the only possible means of travel was by boat. Several hours were lost since the *Katmai* had to travel from King Cove to Cold Bay, a distance of 50 miles..., then pick up the doctor and proceed toward Unga. The *Howkan* left Squaw Harbor to meet the *Katmai* and bring the doctor to Unga. Lt. Francis A. Torrey arrived at 1:50am Tuesday morning and immediately proceeded to the homes of the ill. After examining them, he immediately injected antitoxin.

Later in the day, Lt. Torrey examined a smear under the microscope and pronounced the epidemic diphtheria. The doctor visited every person in town and injected toxoid alum precipitate.

On Monday word came via radio that a plane carrying medical aid was coming from Kodiak. Due to weather conditions the PBY was forced to turn back only a few minutes out of Sand Point. The personnel were then flown to Anchorage and joined by another doctor and two nurses. It was necessary for the C-45 to return to its base because the Radar system developed a defect. Finally on Tuesday a plane landed them at Cold Bay at 11:30pm.

A false report stated that a boat was standing by to carry them to Unga. When no boat was alongside the dock, it was necessary for another cannery tender to again go from King Cove to Cold Bay and pick up the corps of doctors and nurses. This time the *Glenwood* went to their assistance. Early Wednesday morning the party headed for Unga.

The PAF tender Glenwood *was one of several "mercy ships" that came to the aid of Unga in its time of need.*

MEDICAL AID DELAYED

Late Tuesday evening the *Howkan* dispatched a wireless message calling Unga. It was accidently picked up by a party listening in. The local operator, Robert Garlow, was notified and contact was made with the *Howkan*. Mr. Garlow was informed that a young man, who had been visiting in Unga for the past few days, was seriously ill with diphtheria symptoms in Squaw Harbor. The patient had also visited several homes prior to his illness.

The doctor was notified and called to the radio. The *Howkan* by this time had traveled the seven miles from Squaw Harbor to Unga and was entering the Unga harbor. After the doctor learned of the symptoms, he immediately grabbed some supplies, boarded the *Howkan* and started on their journey until a runner brought information that Hilda Grassamoff's condition was much worse. The doctor returned to shore, administered medicine then proceeded to Squaw Harbor, Lt. Torrey returned to Unga immediately after treating the patient.

The *Howkan*, a PAF tender, immediately left to meet the *Glenwood* and return with the corps of medical aid.

Since Lt. Torrey is the only medical officer at Ft. Randall, he was called to his post upon the arrival of the other doctors and the nurses.

The *Howkan* took Lt. Torrey to Sand Point and he continued his journey on the *Pacific Pride*, an APS tender.

OPERATION PERFORMED

Gerald Berntsen was one of the patients who was in the most critical condition. The doctor reported his tongue and throat swollen. At 4pm Tuesday, April 9, Gerald's condition became acute and his throat became blocked. The doctor immediately performed a tracheotomy. Lt. Torrey was assisted by the four year old patient's mother Mrs. Laura Berntsen who administered the anesthetic. Dr. Torrey called for additional assistance. Mr. and Mrs. Allan L. Petersen, with whom the doctor was staying while in Unga, came to the doctor's assistance. Gerald died two hours later.

PLANE DROPS SUPPLIES

A land base plane, C-45, flew over Unga on Tuesday afternoon, April 9 and dropped some medical supplies. Many people were watching the plane as it swooped low over the village. When the plane circled a second time, a yellow parachute was released and down floated the supplies. It was taken to the radio operator and confirmation of its being received was given.

SQUAW HARBOR INOCULATED

The corps of medical workers stopped at Squaw Harbor on Wednesday, April 10 and treated the one patient and inoculated the entire community.

Lt. Cdr. Batts was given full charge of affairs. He immediately declared the village of Unga in a state of quarantine and prohibited anyone from leaving or entering the village. Dr. Batts was assisted by Lt.(jg) Margie Gammel NC, James A. Strehle PhM l/c, from the Navy Base at Kodiak.

Cpt. Frank G. Robertson from Ft. Richardson near Anchorage, Mrs. Doris Reherd and Miss Vivian Stahl, Red Cross Nurses working out of Anchorage, were also a part of the medical corps that served during the diphtheria epidemic.

The medical corps that came to Unga's rescue: Lt. (jg) Margie Gammel, Lt. Cdr. Batts, Doris Reherd, Vivian Stahl, PhM 1/c James Strehle, and Capt. Frank Robertson

Dr. Batts and Dr. Robertson are from St. Louis, Miss Gammel is from Orange, California, and Mr. Strehle, Dayton.

CLINIC ESTABLISHED

A clinic was set up at the school building on Thursday, April 11. Every person in Unga, except those who were ill, called at the clinic and received injections of antitoxin. Dr. Batts took charge of the clinic while Dr. Robertson made house calls.

Dr. Batts was assisted by the nurses, Mrs. Reherd and Miss Stahl, and by the pharmacist's mate, James Strehle.

Lt. Gammel accompanied Cpt. Robertson while making house calls.

On Friday everyone at the clinic had his pulse and temperature checked. Those who had any symptoms of diphtheria were immediately sent home to go to bed. On Saturday, Sunday and Monday, routine checkup were made on those who visited the clinic.

TEN PRONOUNCED DIPHTHERIA

Besides the three deaths there were ten pronounced cases of diphtheria in Unga and one in Squaw Harbor. Hilda Grassamoff, Bertha Jean, Trudy and Rosemary Berntsen were the more critical cases. Buddy, Walter and Louise Berntsen and Flossie Brandal had less serious cases of diphtheria and Richard Berntsen and Alice Cushing each had a mild case of the disease.

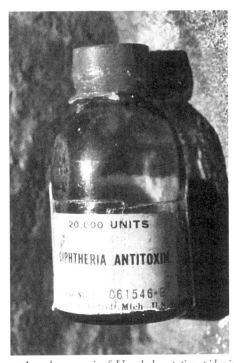

A somber souvenir of Unga's devastating epidemic

OTHER DIAGNOSIS

While people were passing through the clinic, the doctor made notations on individual cards. This information revealed that six people need tonsillectomies and 81 people need dental care.

Donald V. Lawvere the school principal, has submitted this information to the Board of Health in his report. He has requested that the Board of Health inaugurate a program of vaccinations and inoculations as well as other medical attention in these isolated communities.

NUMBER TREATED

There was a total of 115 people who received medical attention in Unga. Two left to go to work at the early part of the epidemic, after they received inoculations. The medical authorities treated 113 people daily at the school building and in their homes. There was a total of 2,567,500 units of antitoxin given in Unga. No report was received concerning the number treated at Squaw Harbor.

WIRELESS OPERATORS BUSY

In order to keep communications open, it was necessary for the wireless operators to maintain constant schedules. In order for communications to go through, a network had to be established whereby if one operator failed to pick up a broadcast another was on the job to receive it.

In order to have efficient communication during the diphtheria epidemic a radio network was set up that involved all cannery tenders that had transmitters and receivers, the CAA at Sand Point, the operators at Ft. Randall, Charles Franz at Nelson Lagoon, Mrs. Kenneth L. Cohen at King Cove, and Robert Garlow at Unga.

These operators were standing by every hour of the day and night in order that communications would not fail to go through.

CANNERY TENDERS

The cannery tenders arrived from Bellingham and Seattle in the past few days. The day and night service of the skippers and crews was a major factor in halting the diphtheria epidemic. Prior to their arrival, few seaworthy boats were available. If they would have been a week or two later in their arrival, the people of Unga would have been helpless. The *Howkan*, *Glenwood* and *Katmai* are tenders for Pacific American Fisheries, Inc. The *Beryl E* and the *Pacific Pride* are tenders for Alaska Pacific Salmon Co.

LOCAL ASSISTANCE

The community of Unga owes a debt of gratitude to the many people who completed small tasks and errands during the recent epidemic.

Mrs. Harry Foster laundered nurses uniforms, Mrs. Lena Hunt and Mrs. Lena Lauritzen baked bread and pastries.

John Nelson and John Foster furnished boat transportation in the bay, and Allan L. Petersen served as guide for the doctors and nurses who made house calls.

Board and lodging for the three nurses was furnished by Mrs. Robert Garlow, a doctor and corpsman by Mrs. Allan Petersen and two doctors by Mrs. Donald Lawvere.

PING PONG PLAYERS

While the medical aid was in Unga, Dr. Roberts and Margie Gammel displayed skillful ping pong playing in their spare moments.

REOPENING OF SCHOOL

School will reopen Monday morning April 22 after being closed for two weeks.

THE HYGIENE

On the 8th day of September, the Public Health boat, the *Hygiene*, came into the outer harbor of Unga and after hooting its horn several times, Howard Berntsen responded in a dory and brought the crew ashore. Soon after landing, Dr. Krusich, the medical doctor in charge, made known her plan to have the entire town folk taken to the boat for X-rays. Since the distance was so great, and not being too sure what Mother Nature might conjure for us in the way of weather, Howard and Kenneth Foster, being quite familiar with the harbor, volunteered their knowledge and ability to pilot the *Hygiene* into the inner harbor. To these two boys, along with Alexander Calugan, Jr. and a few other public spirited men, the people of Unga are indebted for their safe and comfortable trip to and from the boat.

Besides the X-rays that were given aboard the boat, thorough physical examinations were given the adults of the town who were in need of special attention, and to every child in the community. Diphtheria shots and smallpox vaccinations were also given on a large scale.

We are sure that the people here in Unga join us in expressing their appreciation to the boys who were in charge of the dories and to the owners of the dories, who made it possible for us to receive this invaluable examination and medical care that was so generously and efficiently given by the members of the *Hygiene*.

Mildred and Art Hansen
(TAP XI, 1, p. 6)

Verbatim excerpts from 14-year-old Thorwald Lauritzen's diary, September 1946:

September 8:
Wet + very foggy day. Medical ship *Hygiene* came here today. All medical people are women—a doctor, an X-ray taker + a nurse + a stenographer—all women.

September 9:
Very beautiful day. Everyone went out on the *Hygiene* for a chest X-ray. We had a movie of health this evening pertaining to tuberculosis. No school today.

September 10:
Favorable day—very hot sun. Everyone except adults got an examination. All town people got shots for diphtheria + smallpox + the little ones got shots for whooping cough. All was done at school. Mildred and I worked as secretaries for the nurse.

September 11:
Quite a breeze all day. We started school again. *Hygiene* left today to continue journey. Received results of X-ray proved this family all normal.

The crew of the M. V. Hygiene *in Unga (September 1946)*

The hard-working medicos of the health ship *Hygiene* were not without their lighter moments thanks to the hospitality of the people of Unga. From the time they first came ashore, through their introductions at church Sunday night down to the last minute before the boat departed, they were entertained either in groups or individually, not only once, but several times, at the Caseys'. The Garlows, the Frenches, the Petersens' and at Miss Erickson's. At the latter's home, hot coffee and food seemed always to be waiting—after church Sunday night—after the movies Monday night—and again Tuesday night. When not dining, or reminiscing, souvenirs of Alaska or pictures of Unga were exhibited to the guests.

The climax came after a hard, laborious day, when, Monday night, after the movies which were shown at the high school, Mrs. Lena Lauritzen graciously announced that a dance was to be given in honor of the personnel of the *Hygiene*. The usual nice crowd turned out and a jovial spirit was manifest throughout the evening, ending in a broom dance where everyone danced with everyone else. In the wee small hours of the morning, when some of the more serious-minded of the crew insisted on returning to the boat, the crew reluctantly left, but spared no words in expressing a great amount of gratitude and appreciation of the hospitality and friendliness of the people of Unga.

(TAP XI, 1, p. 6)

Our PEN reporters told of the *Hygiene* and how the town appreciated all the work and care the staff brought to Unga. Here is a portion of an article included in the book *Alaska's Search for a Killer*, written by Susan Meredith of the *Hygiene*'s tour of Alaska coastline towns from 1946-48:

Monday, Sept. 9 to Wednesday, Sept. 11. Unga was only six miles as the crow flies across the mountains of Shumagin Island, but an hour's cruise by water. Larry, worried by the shallow harbor, anchored two miles from the town. Rain and wind made the prospect of the long ride in a small open boat unappealing.

Two dories came racing through the rough water to greet us. To our relief they guided Larry through the reefs so he could safely anchor the *Hygiene* within a half mile of shore. Our small rowboat was inadequate in communities without docks.

The 40 tidy homes with curtained windows gave Unga the appearance of a Cape Cod town. The village had two stores, two churches, a community hall, a liquor store and chickens. A concrete building held the only high school west of Kodiak.

The Hygiene *riding at anchor*
(Delarof Harbor, Unga)

Though isolated from the world, this small community had won national recognition for its Red Cross and war bond drives. A Women's Club kept the women busy and informed. A Girl Scout program, although adapted to local conditions, taught the girls about life in the "lower states." Two young women from the village were cadet nurses in training.

The men of Unga ferried groups of 10 to 20 people from the beach to our clinics. Ruthie greeted each boatload and sent the families down to the clinic for the routine tests and exams. The X-rays of Unga's population surprisingly revealed only one active, far-advanced case of tuberculosis. We taught her and her family home-isolation techniques, how to keep her dishes, bedding and everything she used separate from the others, and to empathize the need for bed rest.

We had arrived at Unga on Sunday afternoon, and the minister invited all of us to Sunday evening church services. Almost everyone went, including Rex and Gus who said, "It isn't every day you get to listen to a lady preacher, especially a good looking one."

Monday evening we went in to show our health films and to see the town. As we walked down the street, housewives along the way invited us in for coffee and dessert. The village planned a dance in our honor for the following night. We were a bit mystified when they directed us to a large old codfish processing tank. A lively fiddle and guitar provided the music and the bottom of the codfish tank made an excellent dance floor. Even Dr. Krusich joined in the fun and proved to be an excellent dancer. All ages from children to grandparents, took part in the jitterbugging along with waltzes and schottisches. I went along to watch but was pleasantly surprised when I was asked to dance every dance. This was most unusual for me. People did not usually ask me to dance because of my limp. Here, they accepted me the way I was, what a wonderful feeling!

The next day as we prepared to leave, the thoughtful housewives of Unga sent out sacks of homemade candy, smoked fish and fresh vegetables. Naturally warm and gregarious, the wives and mothers in this town were particularly happy to meet with new and different women who were interested in their situation and wanted to help them improve local conditions.

Sand Point and King Cove were typical cannery towns, and they lacked the community spirit we had experienced at Unga.

(Susan Meredith with Kitty Gair and Elaine Schwinge, *Alaska's Searching For a Killer—A Seafaring Medical Adventure: 1946 to 1948*, Alaska Public Health Nursing History Association, 1998, by permission of the author.)

SCHOOL NEWS
Unga Territorial School
1945 - 1959

When I first went to school I thought it was hard to count and the teacher had to help me and after school I went out to slide and I had a race down the hill with Jackie and we pulled our sleds up the hill agen after we got up the hill we went down and tried to turn a corner and turned over we rapt on the dor and Mama let us into the house we had to sweep ourselves off they were playing crib Mama told me to impte the slobucit and I minded her she askd me why I had curly hair.

Freddie Hunt, Second Grade Spelling Class
(TAP XIII, 7, p. 4)

Freddie and his pals: Judy Casey, Freddie, Raymond (Puggy) Rodgers, and Bobbie Berntsen

In the summer of 1945, Unga's new school was no longer new. Its roof leaked like a sieve and its wind-generated power plant had long since failed. While his wife, Opal, vacationed in Indiana, Principal Donald Lawvere spent the summer directing the renovation of the building and overseeing the installation of a more conventional power plant. This writer remembers that period quite clearly: my first full-time job (I was 13) consisted of hoisting buckets of hot fluid tar to the rooftop and sweeping the black, smelly, sticky goo over the surface of the gently-sloping roof. I was a "gofer" for the job foreman, Andrew Brandal.

The summer of 1945 was a particularly active one for the community as well. (TAP X, 1, p. 4) The Second World War had ended in August and some semblance of normalcy was returning to the village. Its young men were being released from military service; folks were travelling once again. Unga was entering the post-war period full of optimism for the future and Alaskans were beginning to talk of statehood. This was a heady time for the students of Unga Territorial School and they expressed their opinions and concerns in an October 1945 editorial in THE ALASKA PEN which said, in part:

> ...the one thing that should be first and foremost in every Alaskan's mind is the question 'what will statehood mean for our children, will it provide a better school system for our children?'
> The greatest asset—far greater than minerals, fish, fur, or forests—is the child. In discussing the statehood proposal, the welfare of the children needs [to be] the most important consideration.   (TAP X, 2, p. 2)

It would be another 14 years before this dream was realized—a period that also spelled the final phase of the Unga Territorial School. This third essay in the series "School News" covers that period, as reported in THE ALASKA PEN and, after its demise, by reminiscences of teachers and students who lived these years. TL.

Thirty-nine students enrolled in Unga Territorial School for the 1945-46 school year. Thirty-three were returning students and six constituted the entering first grade class. The twelve primary grade students were welcomed by Mrs. Allan Petersen, in a ceremony she had repeated for the previous 11 years. Mrs. Donald (Opal) Lawvere greeted 16 students in grades 5 through 8, and Donald V. Lawvere,

in his second year as high school teacher and Principal, welcomed the 11 students of grades 10 through 12. Since there were no students in the ninth grade, Mr. Lawvere relieved his wife of the eighth grade—the six students of which were warmly welcomed into the vaunted halls of the Unga High School. THE ALASKA PEN reports that "the high school students are pleased to have the 8th-graders in their group since it affords a bigger number for social activities." (TAP X, 1, p. 3) Call this establishing priorities!

Donald V. and Opal Lawvere and Mrs. Allan Petersen

A complete breakdown of the Unga Territorial School student body for the beginning of the postwar period—the period we have dubbed "The Aftermath"—is given below:

First Grade:	Christine Brandal, Jackie Cushing, Mary Jean Haaf, Mary Larsen, Myrtle Berntsen, and Raymond Rodgers, Jr.
Second Grade:	(none)
Third Grade:	Flossie Brandal, Glen Brandal, Norman Larsen, Jr., and Walter Berntsen.
Fourth Grade:	Joan Cushing and Russell Foster.
Fifth Grade:	Nellie Brandal, Louise Berntsen, Louis Berntsen, Jr., and Ann Lauritzen.
Sixth Grade:	Martha Hunt, Bruce Foster, and Nels Brandal.
Seventh Grade:	Alice Cushing, Carolyn Haaf, and Nora Berntsen.
Eighth Grade:	Norman Brandal, Ray Galovin, Thorwald Lauritzen, Meryl Hansen, Mildred Hansen, and Bertha Jean Berntsen.
Ninth Grade:	(none)
Tenth Grade:	Ethel Cushing, Howard Berntsen, Arthur Hansen, Kenneth Foster, and Virginia Brandal.
Eleventh Grade:	Esther Cushing, Ruth Lauritzen, Mary Galovin, and Evelyn Foster.
Twelfth Grade:	Budilia Rodgers and Emily Endresen.

The 1945-46 school year began normally and without incident. Severe weather, a normal winter happening, was thankfully contained outside the refurbished building. Students in the Primary Room watched a variety of seeds germinate and grow, in spite of the long hours of darkness. Those in the Intermediate Room and the expanded high school enjoyed their social activities. The calm was shattered, however, when the diphtheria epidemic swept across the village in early April. But, thanks to the combined efforts of the townspeople, the school faculty and the medical teams that were quickly dispatched to Unga, a tragedy was averted. Although several students were diagnosed with the disease, the school lost only one: first grader Myrtle Berntsen. THE ALASKA PEN dedicated its April

1946 issue almost exclusively to the epidemic (TAP X, 8). An abbreviated version is presented else-where in Part III.

School was interrupted for just over a week during the peak of the epidemic, and when classes resumed, preparations were well underway for the graduation ceremonies that would cap the school year. Graduating from high school were sisters Budilia Rodgers and Emily Endresen, who, except for their freshman and sophomore years, received their entire undergraduate education in Unga. They

Budilia B. Rodgers

Emily M. Endersen

were joined in graduation by the six eighth graders who had earlier been accepted into the ranks of the Unga High School.

The diphtheria epidemic was a defining event for the school, and for Mr. Lawvere, in his final year at Unga, his response to the emergency would represent perhaps his finest hour. Donald and Opal Lawvere left Unga in May for assignment elsewhere in Alaska, and the 1945-46 school year passed into history.

A pair of new teachers—Harold and Lillian French, who hailed most recently from California—introduced the 1946-47 school year. They joined Mrs. Petersen, who was beginning her thirteenth and final year at Unga. Enrollment for the term began at 37 and included three student transfers from Squaw Harbor. These additions filled some of the vacancies created by students moving "outside." Prominent among the latter were three of last year's junior class—Mary Galovin, Evelyn Foster, and Ruth Lauritzen—who entered high schools in Washington State as seniors. This exodus left the present senior class with one student and Esther Cushing gamely carried the high school banner for the year, graduating the following May. Esther also served as the year's editor-in-chief of THE ALASKA PEN.

The school year began with the visit of the MV *Hygiene*—the Alaska Public Health vessel—during which all students received physical examinations and inoculations against diphtheria and smallpox. It ended with the graduation, on the 9th of May, of the eighth grade and senior classes. THE ALASKA PEN reported:

> The five graduates this year consisted of one high school senior, Esther Cushing, and four eighth grade girls, Nora Berntsen, Alice Cushing, Carolyn Haaf and Martha Hunt.

All these girls are truly local products, having been born in Unga or immediate vicinity, and all have received their education in the local schools. In spite of the fact that their travel has been very much localized, they seem to have acquired a most amazing understanding of the outside world.

We are particularly proud of our graduating Senior as she is the first one in her family to have completed the high school even though six have gone before her. Esther has shown remarkable perseverence in acquiring her education and has surmounted many obstacles such as finding herself without a high school to attend after being graduated from the 8th grade. She has been editor-in-chief for THE ALASKA PEN for this last year and until recently has had the responsibility of all the typing for THE PEN. She has been a fine leader in the high school and exudes her personality to its best advantage. We are hoping that she will attend college as we are sure that she will be a great success and a credit to Unga.

We are sure the eighth grade graduates will be an asset to our high school and will also take an active part in the social life of our community.   (TAP XI, 9, p. 4)

The 1946-47 school year also marked the end of Mrs. Allan Petersen's tenure at Unga Territorial School. The departure of Mrs. Petersen represented a milestone in the history of the school and the village. Since arriving in Unga in 1934, she had served the school for an unbroken term of 13 years, longer by far than any other teacher in the history of the Unga school. Because she taught the primary grades through much of the '30s and intermediate grades during the war years, for many of Unga's students, Mrs. Petersen was the only teacher they had ever known. Her departure created a void not only in the school but one in the community that proved difficult if not impossible to fill. The several volunteer activities that she shepherded through the '30s and '40s, including the Community Library, the Women's Club, the Girl Scouts, and Sunday School, were particularly affected by her departure, but her legacy endures in the many lives she touched during the years she and her family called Unga their home.

Esther Cushing and her schoolmates. From left: Virginia Brandal, Evelyn Foster, Ruth Lauritzen, Ann Lauritzen, Esther, Budilia Rodgers, Ethel Cushing, Alice Cushing (front), Mildred Hansen, and Martha Hunt.

September 1947: AN EDITORIAL

Just look at the beautiful hot sunshine beaming in through the doors and windows! Who said Alaska sunshine came down in drops? For awhile we almost believed it ourselves, but at last we have real Alaska sunshine.

Is it because school has started again that the sunshine has returned? That long summer of rain and fog, day upon day, when the tops of the mountains were so immersed in fog that they appeared suspended from the clouds, no longer hides the beauty of our bedecked mountains. The water of Unga Bay is now smooth as glass when only a short time ago it appeared like boiling water as it was churned up by the constant falling rain. With this radiant sunlight shining on the hills of brown and yellowish looking grass, which was once green and sweet smelling, we realize autumn is here again, and along with autumn, school days.

The sound of running feet and pleasant and contented voices recalls one's reasoning to its normal channel and we realize that happiness makes sunshine and those of us that are fortunate enough to be a part of school are really happy. Thus, much of the sunshine appearing outside is but a reflection from our own souls.

Jennie Johansen
(TAP XII, 1, p. 2)

The September 1947 issue of THE ALASKA PEN reports on a significant highlight for the previous year's eighth grade class:

UNGA SCORES AGAIN

In the recent standard eighth grade examination given for those graduating into high school in Alaska, the Unga school made an enviable record by having 75 percent of its graduates place in the upper 10 percent of those taking the examination.

Martha Hunt of Unga scored the highest grade in the Territory with 229 points. The average score for the Territory was 145, and our only student not in the upper ten percent scored higher than the Territorial average.

This examination was composed of ten separate tests and the Unga average was higher than the Territorial average in nine of the ten tests.

Below is a quotation from a letter received from Dr. Dorothy Novatney, Education Supervisor:

"I am glad to report the following pupils as being in the top 10 percent of the 66 taking this examination:

Martha E. Hunt	Unga
Evelyn Sandvik	Naknek
Donald Dairs	Vank Island
Carolyn Haaf	Unga
Dick Craig	Dutch Harbor
Nora J. Berntsen	Unga"

(TAP XI, 1, p. 3)

Miss Elizabeth Anderson, of Arlington, Colorado, joined Mr. and Mrs. French for the 1947-48 school year. Miss Anderson, in her first year of teaching, replaced Mrs. Petersen as primary grades teacher. Fourteen students greeted her on the first day of school. They were joined by 13 intermediate room classmates and eight high schoolers. Volume XII, No. 1 of THE ALASKA PEN "hit the presses" on September 25, 1947, with seniors Kenneth Foster and Virginia Brandal serving as co-editors. Kenneth assumed the sole editorship in November with the departure of Virginia in mid-term. The remaining seniors were Ethel Cushing and Peter Calugan, the latter having returned to Unga after an eight-year absence. The junior and sophomore classes contained only one student each. The sophomore class was particularly devastated by the departure of four students. Bertha Berntsen and Meryl and Mildred Hansen (along with their brother Arthur, a junior) transferred to Seward High School, and Norman Brandal dropped out of school in order to help support his family. The sole sophomore and junior students were Thorwald Lauritzen and Jennie Johansen, respectively. Their underclassmen were Nora Berntsen and Alice Cushing. Martha Hunt would join them later in the term.

Harold and Lillian French

HIGH SCHOOL GRADUATES - 1948

Ethel Cushing   *Kenneth Foster*   *Peter Calugan*

Another school year has drawn to a close bringing with it three high school graduates—the largest graduating class Unga High School has ever had. Ethel Cushing, Kenneth Foster and Peter Calugan were the fortunate ones to attain the goal of acquiring a high school education this year. This is the sixth graduating class from our high school and the total number of graduates now amounts to twelve.

Kenneth Foster should be especially proud of this honor since he is the first in his family to be graduated from high school—there being six preceding him.

Peter Calugan is also the first in his family to complete high school. He also should be especially proud of attaining this goal since he has had to acquire a good share of his high school education by correspondence while he was in the hospital in Tacoma, Washington.

Ethel Cushing is the second one in her family to be graduated, her sister Esther preceding her by one year. Ethel tells us that she might take post-graduate work next year if she doesn't go on to college, and it is to her honor if she is striving to get more education.

Kenneth and Peter are also interested in going on to college. Peter has first chance at the scholarship award offered by the University of Alaska. In case that he does not take this award, Kenneth and Ethel will have second and third choice of taking the advantages offered by this scholarship.   (TAP XII, 9, p. 3)

⋙⋘

In the waning days of the 1948 summer, students of the Unga Territorial School were awarded, quite unexpectedly, with several more weeks of vacation. The reason: no teachers! That was the good news. The bad news was that the missed school days would be made up later in the school year. As THE ALASKA PEN reports:

The opening of school was delayed two weeks this year due to the late arrival of our teachers, Mr. and Mrs. Philip W. Tate and Miss Elizabeth Anderson. They came on the Fish and Wildlife Service's boat, *Penguin*, which was delayed in Seattle and enroute up, made several unplanned stops which took more time than was otherwise expected. The *Penguin* docked at Sand Point September 15th and the teachers arrived in Unga on the *Southland*, skippered by Harry Foster, September 16th. Monday, September 20th, school was opened with a total enrollment of 30 pupils. The Primary Room has a present enrollment of 13, the Intermediate, 11, and the High School, 6.

We plan to regain the two weeks we missed by going to school on Saturdays after the first of January.   (TAP XIII, 1, p. 3)

The Tates—Philip, Carrie, and daughter, Toni—hailed from Idaho and Nebraska and came with impressive credentials. Mr. Tate graduated from the University of Idaho and Mrs. Tate from the University of California at Berkeley. Experienced Alaskans, they had previously taught at outposts stretching from King Island in the Bering Sea to the Kuskokwim River town of Kwethluk.

Beth Anderson returned to her primary classroom that included, among the 13 students, a first grade consisting of five girls. Whether she considered herself lucky, or otherwise, was not revealed in THE PEN. This, however, was her last year at Unga. Mrs. Tate's 11 intermediate room students and Mr. Tate's seven high schoolers (Martha Hunt joined her tenth-grade co-eds later in the term) included only one senior: Jennie Johansen. Jennie and her brother, Alvin, lived and attended school in Squaw Harbor until the summer of 1946, when the family moved to Unga. Jennie enrolled in Unga High School as the sole sophomore; Alvin joined Joan Cushing and Russell Foster in the fifth grade. Issue No. 8 of THE ALASKA PEN Volume XIII reported on Jennie's graduation, the thirteenth and, as it turned out, the last graduate of Unga High School. Sharing graduation honors with Jennie were three eighth grade graduates, Nels Brandal, Ann Lauritzen, and Bruce Foster.

Mr. and Mrs. Tate returned in late summer of 1949 for their second and final year at Unga, welcoming 32 students, six of which constituted the dwindling high school. There were no potential graduates, this writer having transferred to Seward High School. Nevertheless, despite the small number of students and the fact that the

Jennie Johansen

school faculty consisted only of the Tates, those high school students remaining were given ample opportunity to pursue their studies. In fact, as Martha Hunt Fletcher recalls, some of her subjects were offered as correspondence courses. Martha, the school's perennial honor student, went on to complete her junior year, then transferred with her lifelong friend and neighbor, Ann Lauritzen, to schools in Colorado and Washington, respectively. Because of the shortage of students, THE ALASKA PEN was not published during the 1949-50 school year. Reporting activities as well as news, thus, was dependent largely upon reminiscences of those who, like Martha, were students at the time and have now, some 50-plus years later, joined the ranks of senior citizens.

A plucky attempt was made to resurrect THE ALASKA PEN the following year. Nora Berntsen served as editor-in-chief of the first issues of Volume XIV and Peter Calugan, one of the school's 1946 graduates, returned to edit the final issues, but on February 28, 1951 the venerable student publication passed unceremoniously into history. In a parting shot, THE PEN reported on issues as divergent as Flossie Brandal's "Story on Alcohol" and a critique of a *Newsweek* article on Aleut nutrition mis-titled "Arctic Sharecroppers" and an update of a current event, "Battle of Korea" authored by Russell Foster.

From 1950 to 1959, enrollment in the Unga school varied between 19 and 29 students. The Alaska Department of Education archives report on as many as 13 teachers assigned to the school. The archives' demography of these final years are tabulated below:

Year	Teacher	Number of Students
1950-51	Mr. & Mrs. Robert Shimer	28
1951-52	Margaret Heilbrun	19
1952-53	Mr. & Mrs. Jacob Eisenstein	21
1953-54	Roberta Hill	20
1954-55	Malven R. Gaither	19
1955-56	Evert Tigner	25
1956-57	Mr. & Mrs. Jerold O'Rear	29
1957-58	Mr. & Mrs. Wilson Eckles	29
1958-59	Charles Heier	24
1959-60	Wilberta McGlashan	9

The Pacific American Fisheries salmon cannery at Squaw Harbor in the mid 1930s. The original Squaw Harbor school shown in the inset can be seen in the upper left-hand corner of the large photograph.

In the fall of 1959, with the enrollment down to nine students, Wilberta McGlashan closed the school ten days into the session and moved books, equipment, and students to a vacant Pacific American Fisheries building on the Squaw Harbor waterfront. The site was just below the original school building that had been vacated 14 years earlier and was no longer habitable. Among the artifacts that found a new home in Squaw Harbor was the collection of ALASKA PENs dating back to 1934 that had been gathered together during the latter years of the Unga High School. It was a precious archive that detailed the life and impending death of Unga. Unfortunately, the entire collection was lost in a fire that swept the building in the late 1960s. THE ALASKA PEN lives on, however, in the archives of the Alaska State Library in Juneau—the result of a cooperative effort in 2004 to complete the partial collection that was donated to the library by THE PEN's first editor and graduate, Elizabeth Rodgers Gronholdt. At this writing, the collection is three issues shy of a complete run, and is available on microfilm at most public libraries, or on request.

REMEMBERING UNGA: 1953 - 1954

The following reminiscences of Roberta Hill Allen are excerpted from her contribution to "I Remember Unga," an out-of-print account of a reunion of former residents of Unga held at Westport, Washington, in August of 1993. As Roberta Hill, she conducted school in the vacated Methodist Church personage because of maintenance problems with the Unga Territorial School building. After the parsonage was accidentally destroyed by fire, school was held in the adjacent church. Enrollment for the school year stood at 20, covering grades one through eight.

I left my home in Lewiston, New York, in August 1953. I arrived in Seattle and waited for passage aboard M. V. *Garland*. When I purchased my ticket to Unga, Alaska, the office man asked if I knew where I was going. He asked me if I had a grub stake and other supplies. He proceeded to ask where I was going to live and many other questions like, "Do you know anyone there?" When my answers were all negative, he just shook his head. He did help me by taking me to a wholesaler who helped me get a grocery order for nine months.

There were six other teachers on the same trip going to other villages beyond Seward and westward. We had a great trip, stopping at all the villages. It took 12 days to get to Unga.

We arrived in late afternoon. Lena Hunt (the school custodian) met me and took me to the parsonage. It was to be my home and school house. We made the large living room the classroom, and I lived in the rest of the down-stairs. This was my first teaching position....

The Unga Methodist Parsonage and Church

The parsonage burned in March... The house burned very quickly but...[townfolks] were able to save all our school supplies. School took up at the church. Desks were set up and the blackboard was in place. Drapes were placed across the pulpit and that was my bedroom. I took my meals at Lena Hunt's home, which I enjoyed very much.

I found out teaching is my job. I enjoyed observing all the activities and progress the children were able to make. They had a lot of learning experiences. I did too.

Lena took me to Sand Point and Squaw Harbor visiting with friends. Dolly Foster came to get me to spend the weekend several times at Squaw Harbor. Remembering now, I must have had a busy time: going up to the head of the bay with Lena to visit her dad. Taking hikes with the children. We hiked to Squaw Harbor—it got too late and Harry Foster had to take us home by boat.

My home was like a rec hall for the kids. We played games, had crafts, cooked fudge, baked cookies and had lots of fun. Sounds like I was just one of the kids! When weather was too cold or windy and the furnace wouldn't work good, I'd give homework and send them home.

I was in Unga for one school year and made friend-ships that have lasted... I went on to Ikatan and taught two years. I taught two more years at Bettles, Alaska (north of Fairbanks). I married and settled in Kent, Washington. I have taught school 27 years here. Now I have retired.

Alaska is very special to me. I have made one trip back via highway and two by air.

                                        Roberta Hill Allen   *Roberta Hill*

REMEMBERING UNGA: 1955 - 1956

The following is by Evert Tigner, who taught in Unga in 1955-56. I remember him as a strict disciplinarian, a probable reflection of his then-recent tour of duty in the US military. Mr. Tigner lives and writes in California and Texas. Several of his novels are currently in print.

Evert Tigner

I will always remember my first year of teaching school in Unga, Alaska. It began several decades ago when I read about the need for teachers in Alaska, and I had just been released from military service in Japan and Korea.

I have always had a desire for adventure so I applied for a teaching position. Of course, my parents were not pleased since they wanted me to remain in our small community in Oklahoma and teach there.

I was accepted by the Commissioner of Education and assigned to the Unga Territorial School. I had difficulty locating Unga on the map, but finally located it on the long peninsula of Alaska in the group of Shumagin Islands.

I was shocked when I arrived from the long boat ride from Seward. Unga was extremely remote and awesome with few trees and wood sidewalks. Some of the houses and buildings were interesting, and my apartment in the school was comfortable with a nice view of Unga bay.

All supplies and goods had to be shipped to the island by boats. Our boat came once a month with the mail and food. It was an exciting time for everyone. I was anxious for letters from family and friends.

Mr. Tigner's students, 1955-56.

Teaching was interesting. I taught all grades from first through eighth. There were twenty-four students, and it required organization to cover all subjects. I recall art period because every student drew a boat or a dory. Sometimes I required them to draw a house or something else, but they preferred boats which was natural for them.

Students were quiet and exhibited self-discipline. They did not share their thoughts or opinions with me, so different from students today.

Unga Island and its people grew on me. Each month became more important. Lena Hunt, the school agent, often invited me to share dinner at her home. She also baked delicious bread which she shared with me. There were few other people who I visited and enjoyed knowing, including Lena's father who lived at the end of the bay where he had been involved in an extinct gold mine. When the weather was agreeable, we would hike up to his nice cottage. Her father had come from Hamburg, Germany.

I am glad I had the opportunity to live and teach school for a year on Unga Island. I was sorry to hear that all residents had left Unga. It was a unique place, but I know that changes are usually necessary. I will hold good thoughts for all the people who lived on Unga Island.

Evert Tigner

Evert Tigner on the dock in Unga

THE UNGA COMMUNITY LIBRARY

Books are the key to wisdom's treasure,
Books are gates to lands of pleasure;
Books are paths that upward lead,
Books are friends; come let us read.

Anon
(TAP IV, 5, p. 5)

On the edge of a rocky cliff overlooking Delarof Harbor sits a small one-room clapboard building. The little house fronts on what was once the main boardwalk that ran from Sjoberg & Casey's store, past the marshal's residence, Lauritzen's store, the Methodist Church and ending at the cove dubbed, in later years, Susie's End. The back of the house faces the bay and affords a commanding view of the entire southern expanse of the harbor. Over the years, this structure had served as a community meeting room, a club house, a Sunday School venue, a morgue, and after Unga's demise, a squatter's residence. But its primary function during the thirties, forties, and fifties was to provide a home for the Unga Community Library.

THE ALASKA PEN, in its January 1938 issue, reports:

The Unga Community Library is the most recent institution of community improvement organized in our town. It is a major project sponsored by the Unga Women's Club and has been organized to comply with the requirements of the Territorial Library Act...

Articles of Incorporation and By-laws for the...library were drawn up on October 28, 1937 by members of an elected library board...[consisting of] Mrs. E. F. Casey, President; Mrs. Harold Pedersen, Vice-president; Mrs. Allan Petersen, Secretary; Mrs. Conrad Lauritzen, Treasurer; Anna Cushing, Library Assistant.

The library will be maintained in the Community Club House, and will be open Thursday afternoons from 3 to 5PM...

Mrs. Walter Borgen was appointed librarian and Mrs. Raymond Rodgers, Anna Cushing and Anna Wilson her assistants.

The first order of books which included 100 volumes for children and adults has been received. The library shelves are being built by the High School Manual Training Class under the supervision of Mr. [D. W.] Norris. The materials were purchased with library funds...

The Library Board solicits the cooperation and support of every resident of Unga in this new community institution. We are confident untold benefit, pleasure and inspiration will be gleaned from the books of the library. Visit the library often. It is organized to serve you. (TAP IV, 5, p. 4)

The library opened its doors for the first time on the third of February, 1938, and in the intervening years its inventory grew from the initial 100 volumes to more than 1500. Although some of the books were donated, the majority were purchased new, and one remembers preparing the crisp new volumes for distribution. This included removal of the dust jackets, lacquering the cloth covers, painting library codes on the spines, carefully breaking in the bindings and gluing in card pockets and due-date slips. The library also subscribed to numerous magazines for both youth and adult readers. Funds for the operation of the library, including monies for the purchase of books and subscriptions, were provided by annual grants from the Territory of Alaska in amounts "not to exceed one hundred and fifty dollars in any one year." (TAP IV, 5, p. 5) Operating expenses were supplemented by one-dollar annual memberships, proceeds from fund raisers such as raffles and bazaars, and by private contributions.

By October of 1941, the library boasted an inventory of 800 books, and to better accommodate users, the library opening was changed to 2:30-4:00 P.M. on Saturdays. Adult membership continued at $1.00 per year, but children's cards were sold for $.50. Clearly, the library had filled a need and its success was measured by its continued growth. But, along with growth and popularity came the inevitable problems in the handling of books by borrowers. THE ALASKA PEN reports that:

...During the recent checking and cleaning of...books, surprising evidence of carelessness...was very noticeable...[requiring] hours of tedious work...patching and cleaning...

From now on a closer check will be made of all books and magazines when returned. We see no excuse for finding pages marked with soiled hands, chocolate candy, jam and orange juice. Neither should the corners of the pages be turned down for bookmarks or the books used for ash trays. Books can become our best friends...let's treat them as such. (TAP VIII, 2, p. 2)

Despite these and similar problems that are endemic to libraries everywhere, and particularly the haphazard mail service during the war years, the Unga Community Library continued to serve as a beacon to villagers craving the enjoyment of reading. In November 1943, the library boasted an inventory of 1138 books and 25 magazine subscriptions. This inventory increased to 1500 books and 30 magazines by 1948.

This editor (EM) has fond recollections of the little library he visited often during its waning years:

The Unga Community Library, established in 1937 by the Unga Women's Club, was stocked with books and magazines for readers of all ages. The library was run by volunteers from the village and served the community at scheduled times during the week, the principal opening being from 1 to 4P.M. on Saturday.

Annual membership fees of $2.00 for adults and $.50 for children entitled the member to borrow books for one week, the only exception being members who lived out of town. They were allowed to keep books and magazines for two weeks because of the distance they had to travel to visit the library. Fees were charged for late or damaged books, the money collected going toward additional book purchases and supplies.

In addition to housing the library, the little building served as a community clubhouse for the Women's Club, the Girl Scouts, the Sunday School, and on occasion, even a morgue. During the war years, the building was a gathering spot for servicemen. It was truly a multi-purpose facility.

As a student in the late 1950s, I spent many happy hours in the library, lighting fires in the woodstove, checking books in and out, talking with visitors, and listening in on the local gossip.

Spending Saturday afternoon at the library was something I eagerly looked forward to. I particularly remember standing in line waiting for the doors to open, hoping to get first pick of the new comic books (we called them "funny books") or the latest issue of *Jack and Jill*.

Saturday afternoon at the library was a time to visit with friends and relatives—a time to catch up on all the latest happenings in and around Unga. As a little boy, I remember eavesdropping on the women, gathered behind the magazine racks, whispering the latest news. One particularly newsy lady generally held the others' attention with her stories, punctuated now and then with a hearty laugh and an admonition, "Just between you and me." THE ALASKA PEN may have been our monthly newspaper, but the library served us weekly. EM

As the village population declined, so too did library services. Still, it continued to provide books to the dwindling community well into the '60s. When the Russell Foster family moved to Squaw Harbor in 1966, the library's doors were closed for the last time and an institution that served the community for almost 30 years became a part of history.

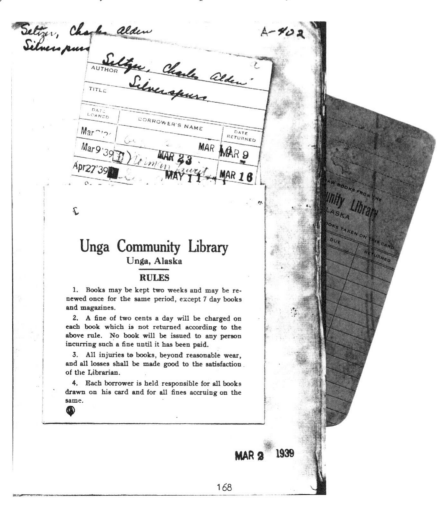

A SHORT EXPOSITION ON THE LITTLE WORD "PEUGH"

I was out fishing with Daddy on the *Alice*. I saw bear's tracks and squirrel holes in the bank. We went to the *Beryl E* and I pewed out fish. Sometimes I got cookies and cake from the cook. Once the *Beryl E* was half loaded.   Norman
(TAP XI, 1, p. 5)

    This innocuous little "vacation story" by 4th grader Norman Larsen led to the following challenge by Mr. Edward F. Casey, proprietor of Sjoberg & Casey's, Unga's premier general store and outfitters:

"PEUGH"

    The word "pew" as used in THE ALASKA PEN prompted Mr. Casey to offer $2.00 prize to the first H. S. student who could find its proper spelling.

    After diligently searching during all spare time, some decided to return to school in the evening to continue the search for the puzzling word. Norman Brandal was rewarded for his efforts when he discovered the word "Peugh" and Mr. Casey gladly awarded him the $2.00 prize.

(TAP XI, 2, p. 5)

To peugh or not to peugh.
That seems to be the question on the minds of these intrepid fishermen preparing to dress cod on the dock at Pirate Cove, early 20th century

Misspelling "peugh" was the rule in the fishing industry and even in official publications pertaining thereto. The definitive monograph on codfishing in the Shumagin Islands, "Pacific Cod Fisheries" (Bureau of Fisheries Document No. 830), contains the following descriptive phrase regarding the transfer of fish from the dory to the shore station dock:

> ...the fish are then pewed onto this stage, whence one of the crew pews them over the rail onto the deck, where another man pews them into the hold. This method is very expensive, as it requires a large number of men, is quite slow, and also injures the fish through the excessive number of times that the pew is driven into them.

Norman Brandal's uncovering of the true spelling of this essential tool of the cod fisherman was more of a revelation than a simple discovery. One might reasonably assume that he located the word by simply looking "pew" up in the then-current library edition of *Webster's Collegiate Distionary*, which was available at school. "Peugh" would have been listed directly above pew. But the latest edition of *Webster's* shows no such word, nor, for that matter, does the Internet's search engine Google. A small local (Southwest Washington) fish hatchery periodical, however, revealed what Norman had obviously learned:

> The handiest single tool...would be the long wooden pole with a single sharp meal spike attached to the end, that the hatchery guys use to toss the fish around. It's called a **FISH PEUGH** [Ed. emphasis]. It looks like a spear, but the metal spike has a slight bend to it. A pitchfork is a crude but serviceable replacement. Other than that, some gloves, rain gear, rubber boots, a short gaff hook or two, and a freshly sharpened machete are pretty much all you need.
>
> (Bill Bartmettler, "More Adventures in Nutrient Enhancement," Drops of Water, April 2003, Vol. 4, No. 2.)

We will never know the source of Norman's revelation (Norman died in late 2003), but of two things we are certain: his quest was rewarded with enough money to purchase a bag of candy at his benefactor's store and neither he nor his high school companions ever forgot the true spelling of the word "peugh."

Some years ago I found a peugh on the beach at Westport and have found it to be an ideal slug impaler! And, after having waded through this rather lengthy exposition of a very simple word, the one word that no doubt expresses the reader's sentiments is: **PHEW**!

BRIEF HISTORY OF THE APOLLO MINE

THE ALASKA PEN, Volume XI, Issue 6, Page 7

Men have been born, married and have died. Countries have grown, become powerful, and declined in a few years to nothing. Such is the repetition of the history of man. The Apollo Mine was born from a stake, flourished, and eventually declined to a memory. The only thing that remains the same, and will continue to be so, is the great and wonderful works of nature. The Apollo Mountain may someday, a few hundred thousand years from now, crumble to dust, but it still towers majestically like an aged sentinel over the mine that bears its name. The picturesque mine creek may have been worn away considerably in the long years of heavy rains and winter freezes but trout still pack the banks of the ever winding road to the sea.

The hospital still stands, a ghostlike skeleton, among the high alders at one part of the mine, as does the once fine home of the Superintendent.

Abandoned machinery, long ago stilled, is scattered everywhere. The mill itself stands, but with an air of weariness. Tunnels are caving in and shafts are filled with water to the water level. Por-

tions of the railroad tracks are still intact but the locomotive has long since run off the tracks and now stands upright on a slanting hill. Large piles and lines of bricks are remnants of the large ovens in which concentrates were treated.

The pipeline winds around hills to the dam but is being constantly covered with the good earth and will soon be a part of that ground. Just as a man's body decays and mixes with the soil, so do the many other things mix in "….Ashes to Ashes, Dust to Dust…." A lonely cemetery stands among the high hills southeast and a short distance from the mine. The crosses are rotting and are falling into decay from the many decades of ever changing typical weather of the Alaska Peninsula.

The cyanide plant is gone, except for a few posts marking its foundation. The many pieces of machinery, reminiscent of greater glory, are lying silent and will remain so until some foreign force acts upon them.

Soil wastes are continually filling up the breakwater and the outer delta of the mine creek where there is said to be much gold concentrates and wastes that have been washed down in the mining years.

This bright period in Unga's past history brought about by the Apollo Gold Mine started about the year 1884 when a prospector, by the name of King, found a conspicuous looking metal at the head of Delarof Harbor. With his practical knowledge of gold and mining, he at once set out and staked claims which were to be the future site of the Apollo Mine.

The Alaska Commercial Company bought shares in the prospect and as a result, they gained control of the mine and held it from that time down to the present day.

The first superintendent of the Apollo Mine was Mr. Mayne who had the task of building a mine from nothing. Mr. Brown succeeded him as superintendent from 1887 to 1906. In the latter year, Brown took a trip to the States and Mr. Fletcher took over from 1906 to 1909. Brown came back from the States in 1911 with a lease on the Apollo Mine and he held it until his death in 1939.

The ledge of Apollo runs North and South. At one particular place, there is a breakoff and the ledge disappears against a blank wall. Consequently, the gold also disappears and for years specialists have been trying to follow the lost ledge. Diamond drills also have been used in an effort to find how or where the metals stopped but in spite of all efforts the problem was never solved.

The main shaft above the mill is 750 feet deep. It was shut down in 1906 and a concrete bulkhead was built to hold the water back for the purpose of securing the machinery within.

Another shaft reaches a depth of 400 feet. There are several branching cross cuts of a few thousand feet in length.

In 1905, the Apollo Mine was given credit for having the longest double-tracked mining tunnel in Alaska.

Four hundred feet was the greatest depth at which gold was found. The most valuable gold was found from 100 feet sub-surface to the surface ground.

Apollo was operated on the basis of a free milling mine. The mill housed the 60 stamp battery which was used to crush the ore. A stamp is a heavy steel or iron pestle, raised by a cam keyed on a horizontal revolving shaft and let fall by its own weight. The stamps are arranged in groups of five having a mortar box in common.

When the ore is crushed to the required size the amalgam treatment is needed. The discharge of the mortar passes over copper plates. These plates are treated with quicksilver and dressed so that the gold amalgam formed on the plates will catch more gold. A very high percentage of the gold is recovered in this method.

The Apollo Mill, late 1930s

The mine treated its own concentrates on the chlorination walks but due to the slow and hard shipping of coke necessary for treating the concentrates this process was given up. Hence the concentrates were shipped out for treating before the cyanide method was established.

Freighting facilities were none too easy. The Apollo Mine set out a private mooring off Cross Island to be used by schooners as these ships could not venture much closer into the bay. Two lighters and a gas converted steam launch, the *Apollo*, hauled the freight from the ships to the Apollo Dock. The freight was then loaded onto the railroad cars pulled by a Shay locomotive, which ran between the mine and the dock. Concentrates, tailings, etc. were also hauled down by means of the locomotive. The bullion was shipped out by the regular mail boat. A mule also was used for minor haulings but was continually running away and became quite useless.

The chief means of producing power was water. The water was supplied from a dam which was built across the creek which flows by the mine. Water was brought down through large pipes which in turn was fed to the large water wheels. Hence, water again showed and offered its capabilities. But everything has its disadvantages and such was the case at Apollo. In winter, the dam

The Shay locomotive, Apollo, late 1930s

would freeze so coal was used to furnish steam power for the long winter.

By 1905, a total of $7,000,000 of good grade gold was recovered from the Apollo Mine.

The real mining stopped in 1906. After this date, pillars were removed from the tunnels.

In the year 1914, a cyanide plant was built as an effort to treat their own concentrates. The cyanide process works on the order that diluted cyanide solutions will dissolve the precious metals from their ores when finely crushed. The cyanide process proved beneficial at the Apollo Mine because more gold was recovered by this process. The gold occurred in such fine particles that extraction of only 70% to 73% had been obtained by amalgamation.

The cyanide plant did fairly well in the beginning. They worked 200 tons of concentrates daily and a roller mill was employed to work the tailings.

The cyanide process was very beneficial till the First World War was felt in this part of the country. The cyanide was at that time obtained from Scotland. The pre-war price of cyanide was 35 cents a pound but it jumped to a wartime price of $3.50 a pound. The recovery from tailings amounted to $3.00 a ton, and obviously, it didn't pay to operate the plant.

At one time, there was a total of 400 men employed at Apollo. Seven families besides the superintendent's family had their homes built at the mine site.

A doctor, nurse, and a very nice hospital offered their aid to the miners.

A telephone line connected Apollo with the judge at Unga as Apollo had no official men other than their own guards.

Saloons, to be sure, would have to follow the men and consequently two were built at Apollo.

Robbery was uncommon but it happened a couple times. In Mayne's time of superintendency, a brick of gold worth $60,000 was stolen and very "cleverly" hidden under some scrap iron in the mill. After a long search, gold attracting magnets disclosed the lost brick of gold. The thieves were also identified.

At another time one of the saloons was robbed. The thief confessed that he stole the money but it could not be found. He was hung out on the dock boom and the rope was cut throwing him into the water below. He was told to leave Apollo the first chance and never return. The thief

The dam, late 1940s

The cyanide plant as it appeared in 1915. Note the Apollo dock.

Remains of the cyanide plant, ca. 1948

The Apollo Hospital

left. Many years later the money was found and disclosed by a couple men from Unga in an old abandoned shack at Apollo.

These facts are but a brief summary of the gold mine Apollo. Someday, perhaps in the near future, it will become more than a dream. Perhaps when other mines of Alaska are worked out, Unga Island will be pointed to as a pos-

sible source of wealth. All evidence indicates that this mine was high graded, that is, only the high grade ore was taken and the low grade ore was left untouched.

With the price of gold twice what it was in the Apollo days and with newer methods devised for saving more gold this mine will live again. Undoubtedly these gold and silver lodes on Unga

Island have only been scratched. Was that what Frank Brown knew when after 20 years of superintendency he saw fit to lease the mine after it had closed down? He did not live to see his one great ambition materialize—the reestablishment of the Apollo Mine. He did, however, by actions, renew our hopes in the future of the once well known and prosperous gold mine, Apollo. He was not a dreamer, he was a practical man, and undoubtedly there are many men like Frank Brown who are only waiting to be told of the

Fred Pomian

Frank Brown

great expectations and future to be found on Unga Island.

Note—Thorwald Lauritzen, the author of Apollo Mine, wishes to express his appreciation to Fred Pomian for his contribution of facts for this article. Mr. Pomian has been associated with the mine in various capacities since 1904.

MAILBOAT!

An exciting event occurs each time the mailboat enters this haven of "mail-hungry people". The young and the old scurry to and fro asking about and watching for the usual signs—a beam of light or the sound of the whistle, which sounds much like that of a streamline train entering a railroad depot.

As the boat enters the harbor, a dory starts chugging out with the passengers and mail, unmindful of the heavy seas which roll in quite frequently during the winter months.

The people, in the meantime, mill about wondering if their C.O.D. has arrived, and hoping that they get that certain letter or package.

With the boat's departure and the arrival of the dory ashore again, the children, big and small, rush to the beach and carry the sacks of mail to the Post Office with the hopes that their new skates or shoes ordered from Sears & Roebuck will be waiting for them when they get home from school the following day.

After the mail is distributed, everyone waits patiently for the next trip of the mailboat from Seward and the familiar voice of Captain Petrich on the radio calling KCB at Unga.

(TAP XII, 3, p. 7)

One of the major complaints about living "out the Westward," an area that stretches along the southwest Alaska coast from Seward to Unalaska and beyond, has been the infrequent and often haphazard transport of the US Mail. Dependent as it was on the movement of ships among the various villages, the schedule for mail delivery and pickup was always qualified by the phrase, "weather permitting." And for good reason: this thousand-mile route traversed a coastline pounded in summer as well as winter by some of the most vicious storms on the planet.

Servicing the Westward began shortly after Alaska's purchase from Russia in 1867, but for the first decade, the identity of the vessels comprising this essential lifeline is unclear. In 1880, however, a most remarkable ship began an equally remarkable voyage—one that stretched virtually uninterrupted for the next 38 years. The ship was the *Dora*, a small, ungainly vessel that, except for her tall slender funnel amidships, retained the lines of a schooner: rakish twin masts each supporting a boom, a stubby bowsprit, and a squat superstructure surrounding the funnel, low enough in profile so as not to interfere with the fore-and-aft sail on the foremast. For, although the *Dora* was technically a steamship, she was rigged to operate as a schooner as well.

S. S. Dora *(J.E. Thwaites photo)*

In the years that the *Dora* sailed Alaskan waters, she participated in the Pribilof Islands fur seal trade, the rush for gold at Nome, in the Klondike and at Apollo on Unga Island, the burgeoning codfishing industry, and other enterprises that were instrumental in the development of Southwestern Alaska. But her crowning achievement was her contract with the US Postal Service to deliver the mail, and this she performed without fail until her retirement in 1918. The fact that she fulfilled her contract year after year was extraordinary. That she succeeded in navigating what many consider the most challenging sea routes in the North Pacific without serious mishap was simply remarkable. Ironically, her luck ran out on her first venture out of Seattle after her retirement as a mailboat: she foundered off the coast of British Columbia in 1919 and was judged a total loss.

A no less impressive vessel eventually replaced the *Dora* in 1921 and continued her reputation for dependable service until 1939. Like the *Dora*, the S. S. *Starr* was built to withstand the rigors of North Pacific waters. She was built to be a halibut schooner, with a high bow for ocean travel, a midship well to stow the catch, a center-aft cabin, and a low stern for easy access to and from the water. Except for the limited passenger facilities, the *Starr* was well suited for the Westward Run. This handicap was shortly corrected by elevating the aft deck to a height corresponding to the sheer of the foredeck. The additional space allowed for more accommodations for passengers and crew but gave the ship the profile of a floating bathtub, but what a bathtub she turned out to be. She ran her route with a dependability that was unmatched in the annals of the Westward Run. But for an annual detour to Seattle for refurbishing and a maritime strike in the fall and winter of 1936 that shut down West Coast ports, the *Starr* delivered the goods and provided the only regular passenger service between Seward and the villages of the Aleutian Chain every month throughout the year.

The S. S. *Curacao* relieved the *Starr* during her 1935 and 1936 checkups. The *Curacao*, an Alaska Steamship Company coastal steamer of 1548 gross tons, was the largest vessel to have served the Westward Run to that time. She was sold by the company in 1939, and enroute to her new homeport, she exploded and sank off Grays Harbor, Washington. During the maritime strike, the Westward Run was serviced sporadically by government vessels such as the *Boxer* that happened by, and by the

Blue Fox, a local vessel that ferried mail among the far-flung islands of the Shumagin group. The *Blue Fox* herself was wrecked some months later, thus lending further credence to the treachery of seafaring in this part of the world. But the *Starr* continued to lead a charmed life. After resuming her regular route in February 1937, she continued the run until mid-1938. Her last voyage as a mail carrier occurred between April and September, and she departed without fanfare. THE ALASKA PEN reported simply that on April 19th "...the S. S. *Starr* arrived [from the Westward]. Those leaving were Mr. Culbertson and Mrs. Zenia Rodgers. Mr. George Neilsen arrived." (TAP IV, 8 & 9, p. 5) When THE PEN resumed publication in September, a new mailboat, the M. S. *Fern* had taken over the run. Thus ended the reign of the venerable *Starr*. She survived the stormy North Pacific to be sold in 1940 for scrap. Better that she would have been put to sea to brave the elements for one last time than endure the indignity of the wrecker's bar.

The *Fern*, a former US Coast Guard Buoy Tender, carried the mails without interruption until October 1940, when she was replaced by the S. S. *Lakina* and in January 1941 by the S. S. *Cordova*. Both latter ships were coastwise steamers of The Alaska Line, with displacements in excess of 2000 gross tons. They were by far the largest vessels to have served the Westward as official US mail carriers, their size being both an advantage (in freight and passenger accommodations) and a hindrance in that their size severely restricted their ability to approach villages like Unga that offered no docking facilities or close-in anchorages. As a result, Unga was often scratched from the ships' itinerary due to inclement weather, or when weather permitted, the ships cautiously lay a mile or more offshore, reqiring smaller vessels to ferry mail, freight, and passengers to shore. THE ALASKA PEN, in its January 1941 issue, vents the villagers' displeasure in the service:

WE DON'T LIKE IT

The news of the recent appropriation of funds by our Congress for the betterment of the mail and freight service for all of Westward Alaska brought much joy to the people here at Unga. Many letters have been written and our Delegate to Congress, the Honorable Anthony J. Dimond, fought hard and long to get the much needed improvement.

However, time has shown our hopes to be short lived. The carrier is the new steamship *Cordova* and apparently a ship of the proper size for this run. We say apparently inasmuch as the ship has yet to anchor in Unga Harbor. The S. S. *Lakina*, which is a "sister" ship and which took over the first two runs of this mail trip while the *Cordova* was in Seattle for overhaul, did enter the Unga Harbor and we enjoyed, all too briefly, excellent service.

Since the *Cordova* has been on the run, our mail service has gone from poor to much worse. Out of eight calls that were scheduled for Unga, only four were made. Three times recently we had to rely on the kindness of local people to go to Squaw Harbor and bring over the mail which had been put off there by the "mailboat" and yesterday the steamer did not call for the eastbound mail. Much of the mail is reported as being important official mail which by being delayed will cause irregularities in the duties of the local government officials.

The reason for not stopping in Unga Harbor and rightly fulfilling the mail contract is unknown to us. We only hope that if it is the fault of the company that owns the ship, a change will be made; if of the ship, or if of the captain or of the crew, a change will be made.

We only know that we want, and believe that we of Unga are entitled to, some regular, courteous and proficient mail service. It is disheartening to mail a letter and feel that it may go out this month or it may not go out until the next. (TAP VII, 4, p. 5)

Mail service continued intermittently through the winter and spring of 1941 despite the protests. The *Cordova* was retired from the Postal Service in November. She was subsequently requisitioned by the US Government and, in the early months of World War II, was assigned to evacuate inhabitants from Dutch Harbor. She was returned to Alaska Steam at war's end and was sold in 1947. The *Lakina* resumed the scheduled run, but not for long. In January 1942, THE ALASKA PEN reported:

MAIL!

Unga's Christmas mail seems to be coming in dribbles. Two installments have arrived so far and we hope for the rest soon.

On January 21st, we received one batch through the courtesy of Captain Trondsen and the S. S. "Lakina". Three days later, Mr. Casey heard there was mail for Unga in Sand Point. He hired Harry Sharpe and the crew of the M. S. "Pansy" to go over and find out. They found an army boat there with ten sacks of mail for us.

With the coming of war, the old phrase, "The mail must get through", seems to have been forgotten.   (TAP VIII, 5, p. 1)

Service was suspended shortly after World War II began, and the Westward seemed indeed forgotten by the US Postal Service for the duration of the war. When mail did arrive, it more often than not came via private fishing vessels from Squaw Harbor or Sand Point or occasionally from visiting military craft. Needless to say, the mail service or lack thereof elicited a roller coaster of emotions: great expectations, great joy, great frustration, disappointment, and finally, resignation.

The January 1945 PEN reported that "In December [1944], the Post Office and school had a complete sell-out of War Savings Stamps. A period of 54 days passed before a boat arrived with mail and a new supply of stamps."(TAP IX, 5, p. 6) The war's ending in August of 1945 saw no immediate improvement in the mail situation. In March 1946, the following editorial appeared in the PEN:

MAIL

I suppose the main topic of all conversation here for the past few weeks has been when and if mail will arrive. The mail service has always been a problem in Unga, but I can't remember when we have ever gone as long as two months without a bit of mail.

Oh! for the blessed day when we shall see a boatload of mail reach Unga Harbor. We would probably think it is Christmas again when we open all those expected Christmas cards. I wish we could at least learn if our mail is now stored in Davy Jones' locker or not.

It seems silly when we think about how we used to growl about mail service when mail was delivered two times a month or at least once per month. It also seems hard to believe we have gone almost three months without mail, but it's true. The last mail that has reached Unga arrived on December 24th and not a bit since. It might not sound so bad when you say it fast, but if you have to wait that long for it—Oh, boy!

I suppose we should hunt up all those letters we have saved and paste them in a scrapbook as a thing of the past. Here you can occasionally look at them and remember what it was like to see your name as addressee of a letter.

Uncle Sam, if you want to hear no more complaints, you had better get "hep" and speed up this seagull express.

It would not be nearly so bad if we did not know that boats have gone to the Westward loaded with TONS of mail for us and all our neighbors.

Our plea is, "Skipper, please return with your cargo."

Ruth Lauritzen, 11th Grade
(TAP X, 7, p. 2)

But then there was always hope: "Rumor has it that a mailboat will make two round trips a month from Kodiak to Adak starting in 1947." (TAP XI, 4, p. 6) For once, the rumor proved true. The only problem was that the new mailboat blew up before she reached Unga!

THE FIRST—AND—LAST VOYAGE OF THE MAILBOAT *CLARINDA*

Imagine waiting five years for a regularly scheduled mailboat and then have the first one sent to the "forgotten Westward" blow up!

During the war, the regular mail service to this area was discontinued and the military boats did a fair job of delivering the mails going their direction. Since hostilities have ceased, the Westward again was forgotten and has had to depend upon the graciousness of any boat or plane to carry the mail. At times, as long as three months would elapse between mail deliveries, so it was with great anticipation that word was received that a mail contract had been awarded, beginning January 1, 1947, and would be carried by the *Clarinda*.

The *Clarinda*, a boat apparently of an early vintage, about 110 feet long with a 14-foot beam, capable of carrying 14 passengers and 70 tons of mail and freight, encountered trouble soon after it left Seward on its first mail run. To add to its already slow speed, it was further handicapped by a postal inspector who consumed additional time at his official duties.

Upon arriving at Squaw Harbor, it was noticeably leaking oil and the engines seemed to be adding to the trouble already encountered along the way. In order to fix the engines, it was decided to pull into the dock at Sand Point. With much difficulty, the *Clarinda* arrived at Mellick's dock Sunday night, January 12th, and about 8 o'clock that night an explosion took place aboard the ship which was visible in the sky for miles around. All the crew and passengers escaped injury with the exception of one crew member who was burned. The ship immediately caught fire and partly destroyed Mellick's dock before a line was finally put on the *Clarinda* and it was towed out to deep water where it sank carrying to the bottom all mail, parcel post, freight, and reputedly a large military payroll. A few sacks have since washed up on the beach and it is believed that they will be sent to the Seattle post office to be salvaged.

Fortunately, Unga had already received its mail, as Mr. Casey had chartered Andrew Foster's boat to meet the mailboat at Squaw Harbor to bring back needed supplies and at the same time our mail was brought over.

E. L. Bartlett
Delegate from Alaska

Congress of the United States
House of Representatives
Washington, D. C.

July 10, 1946

Dear Friend:

It gives me great pleasure to inform you that preparations are being made to resume delivery of mail by steamship to Alaska Peninsula and Aleutian Island points. I know the people of these districts have suffered much inconvenience and undergone some hardships by reason of discontinuation of the service during the war period. Since coming to Washington I have conferred at frequent intervals with Post Office officials and have urged reestablishment of this service not only because it is essential in the delivery of mail, but also because steamship service all along the Peninsula and to the Islands is so necessary in the delivery of freight and passengers. The great difficulty has been that it appeared unlikely that interested parties would offer bids and I sincerely hope that this difficulty will be overcome in the present call for bids. I am informed there is every reasonable prospect that bids will be offered.

Proposals will be received by the Superintendent of the Railway Mail Service at Seattle until 4 PM August 31 for carrying the mail from October 1, 1946, to September 30, 1947, over the following route:

From Seward, Alaska, by Seldovia, Kodiak, Kanatak (n.o.) (one way), Chignik (n.o.), Perryville (n.o.), Sand Point, Squaw Harbor (n.o.), Unga, Belkofsky, King Cove, Cold Bay (n.o.), False Pass, Sanak, Scotch Cap LH (n.o.) (one way), Sarichef LH (n.o.) (one way), Akutan, Unalaska, Makushin (n.o.) (one way), Kashega (n.o.) (one way), Chernofsky (n.o.) (one way), and Nikolski (n.o.) (one way), to Atka (n.o.), returning by Unalaska, Akutan, Sanak, False Pass, Cold Bay (n.o.) King Cove, Belkofsky, Unga, Squaw Harbor (n.o.), Sand Point, Perryville (n.o.), Kodiak and Seldovia to Seward, equal to 1,440 miles and back, once a month; and from Seward by Seldovia, Kodiak, Kanatak, (n.o.) (one way), Chignik (n.o.), Perryville (n.o.), Sand Point, Squaw Harbor (n.o.), Unga Belkofsky, King Cove, Cold Bay (n.o.), False Pass, Sanak, Scotch Cap LH (n.o.) (one way), Sarichef LH (n.o.) (one way) and Akutan to Unalaska, returning to Akutan, Sanak, False Pass, Cold Bay (n.o.), King Cove, Belkofsky, Unga, Squaw Harbor (n.o.), Sand Point, Perryville (n.o.), Chignik (n.o.), Kodiak and Seldovia to Seward, equal to 1034.5 miles and back, once a month; all other ports at which contractor's vessels may call to be supplied, carrying all mail offered by a schedule satisfactory to the Department to leave Seward on the trip to Atka (n.o.) on or about the first day of each month and to leave Seward on the trip to Unalaska on or about the 20th day of each month; the contractor to provide service between the boat and each post office or other port of call and to furnish and use in the service a safe and seaworthy vessel of sufficient size to provide adequate space for mail, passengers and freight of a type satisfactory to the Postmaster General, and, if and when required by the Department to furnish suitable facilities for postal clerk service, including board, lodging and transportation; also a room, when postal clerk is assigned to the vessel, properly fitted up for a sleeping apartment with adequate sanitary heating and lighting arrangements for the exclusive use of the postal clerk and also a room properly fitted up for the assorting and safekeeping of the mail.

With very best wishes, I am

Sincerely yours,

E L Bartlett

E. L. Bartlett
Delegate

A plane was expected to arrive at Sand Point this week to take the crew out. The captain of the *Clarinda* has assured the government that he intends to carry out the mail contract and that he has a new boat about ready to take over the mail run.

(TAP XI, 5, p. 8)

The *Clarinda's* ill-fated debut was followed by the first regular mail service to Unga since 1942. The *Aleutian Mail*, a converted military mine sweeper, made her first run in March 1947. THE ALASKA PEN reports:

MAILBOAT IN SERVICE: THE *ALEUTIAN MAIL*

The *Aleutian Mail* has started its trip carrying mail to all the villages from Seward to the islands out west. The boat is about 138 feet long and will carry 20 first class passengers. The boat can carry 300 gross tons of freight.

The captain of the *Aleutian Mail* is Jesse Petrich. His first boat to take the mail run, the *Clarinda*, blew up at Sand Point on the evening of January 12th.

On the first run with the *Aleutian Mail*, the crew of the ship have been selling various articles such as meat, eggs, cigarettes, vegetables and so forth. The price of meat was about one dollar and twenty cents per pound, a carton of cigarettes, two dollars and eggs about one dollar per dozen.				(TAP XI, 8, p. 6)

THE *ALEUTIAN MAIL*: AN UPDATE

Mr. Petrich, the Captain of the mailboat, *Aleutian Mail*, seems to be making speedy trips on the Westward Run. According to his contract, he is required to make a long and a short trip each month. So far, he has made two round trips this month and one trip last month.

One of the high school students who took the *Aleutian Mail* from here to Kodiak reports that the rate charged one way from Unga to Kodiak was $44.00. She also stated that the rate charged from here to Seward was $74.00 and to Sand Point, $4.00.

The Aleutiam Mail *at Unga*

The big objection that Unga has, in spite of the fact that we are most happy to receive mail, is that the captain of the mailboat refuses to bring the mail in to Unga Harbor on any little excuse, saying the weather is too bad, or the waves too high—a statement a bit hard to understand to the locals since there are numerous fishing boats and dories that are always in and out of the bay, all of these boats being much smaller than the *Aleutian Mail*. At least twice since the beginning of the Run with the *Aleutian Mail*, Unga has been passed up.   (TAP XI, 9, p. 7)

The saga of the *Aleutian Mail* was something of a bad luck tale—one that began with the sinking of the *Clarinda*, the vessel she replaced. The *Aleutian Mail* was small and perhaps not ideally suited for this demanding route, but she served Unga fairly well during the remainder of 1947, having bypassed the village only a few times when the captain judged that weather conditions prevented safe anchorage for the transfer of mail, passengers, and freight. The vessel's luck began running out, however, in December when an attempt to land the mail at Cape Sarichef on Unimak Island in the Outer Aleutians resulted in the drowning of crew member Louis Loof of Sanak Island (TAP XII, 4, p. 4). The following month, the *Aleutian Mail* ran aground in Pavlof Bay and had to be towed to Sand Point for repairs. Two nights later, in a tragic chain of events, four crew members were drowned (see Historical Highlights for January 1948). She was subsequently taken out of service, towed to Seattle, and never returned to the Westward Run.

Taking over for the *Aleutian Mail* was a most unlikely vessel: the power barge *Lois Anderson*. Her captain, Jack Anderson, considered the February 1948 transit a trial run but, as THE ALASKA PEN reported in April, "...after one trip, [he] decided they were not interested in it." (TAP XII, 8, p. 9)

(For the historically curious, this writer "discovered" the *Lois Anderson*, quite by chance, tied up at the dock at the Port of Willapa Harbor, Raymond, Washington, in 2006, still fit and seaworthy after 58 years sailing the seas of the Pacific Northwest!)

The Lois Anderson *at Raymond, Washington (2005)*

After this abbreviated contract, a completely new mail service was about to begin and it was destined to push the Westward finally and abruptly into the 20th century. It was called AIRMAIL! The ambitious plan called for mail to be air shipped to Cold Bay and Unalaska from whence local vessels would be chartered to deliver it to the various villages. The air carrier inaugurating this service was the fledgling Reeve Aleutian Airways and the mailboat serving the Eastern Aleutians from Scotch Cap to Chignik was the *Moby Dick*. THE ALASKA PEN describes the new vessel:

THE *MOBY DICK*

The new mailboat *Moby Dick*, owned by George Gronholdt and Mike Uttecht, has recently taken up the mail contract. She will deliver mail from Cold Bay west to Scotch Cap and east to Chignik. The Reeve Aleutian Airways will deliver mail to Cold Bay every ten days and pick up the outgoing mail.

The *Moby Dick* has a length of 65 feet and a 15-foot beam. Her cruising speed is 10 knots with a top speed of 12.5 knots. She is powered by a 165 horsepower Grey Marine diesel engine. She carries 14 night passengers and 21 day passengers at the rate of fifteen cents per mile.

This boat will make three trips per month from April first to September 30th. After that, she will make two trips per month. (TAP XII, 8, p. 9)

The Moby Dick *at Unga*

But the precipitous leap into modernity was a bit more than many villagers had anticipated, and it took little time for them to vent their frustrations. In the following PEN article, their concerns are outlined:

AIRMAIL A HANDICAP?

...This [airmail] is all well and good as far as mail is concerned, but the mail boat gave a greater service than just carrying mail...they afforded passage and communication between the various towns on the Peninsula and in the islands. Since they connected with Seward, one could always take passage on the mailboat in going out for medical care or to the States. Likewise, goods and provisions could be shipped in at regular water prices. Under the present set-up, there will be no way for passengers to leave this area, or ship freight and produce into this area unless they resort to using the mailboats as far as Unalaska and Cold Bay and then resort to the highly exorbitant rates of air freight or parcel post by Reeve planes to Anchorage. In other words, the whole mail contract, as it stands today, does not benefit the people who live in the islands and Peninsula, but is strictly a monopoly on passenger service and freight service to this area since the Alaska Steamship Lines seldom come into this area and all those that do make these ports are freight boats and carry no passengers.

Ordinarily, before a contract is awarded concerning a group of people, they are consulted in regard to the most suitable methods to be used or allowed to register protest, or make bids on such contracts. As nearly as could be determined, none of these things were done in this territory. The contract appears to be rather un-American in nature, and contrary to the welfare of the locality concerned. It will have a definite effect on keeping people from moving into the islands or Peninsula communities because of the exorbitant cost involved.

Our schools will be greatly affected, as it will be practically impossible for these communities to obtain good, first class teachers unless a differential is made in salary to compensate for the difference between the exorbitant air rates and the original boat rate. It must be remembered that Territorial teachers must pay their own transportation.

Therefore, it behooves each and everyone living in these Aleutian-area communities to register a protest with all federal and territorial officials regarding the matter. If the present contract continues, the price of food will soar to greater heights; it will be impossible to send our sick out to obtain medical treatment, and this is a big item since there are no doctors in these communities; and last, but not least, the very backbone of democracy—our schools—will suffer.   (TAP XII, 8, p. 9)

Whether or not the concerns expressed in the PEN articles were instrumental in steering the governmental bureaucracy back to the Westward Run, the fact remains that in late April of 1949 the M. V. *Garland* sailed from Seward with a contract to provide mail, freight, and passenger service to 18 villages, sretching from Seldovia on the Kenai Peninsula to Nikolski on Umnak Island, a route of some 1200 miles. The *Moby Dick* continued to serve the Eastern Aleutian communities from Cold Bay, thus providing villagers with the option of air service to and from Anchorage and the

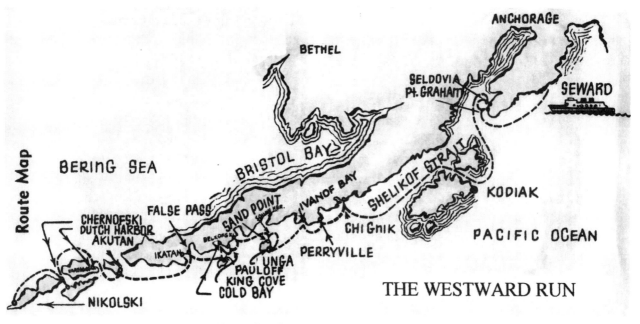

From a flier advertising the M. V. Expansion

"Outside." Mailboat service from Seward continued through the 1950s with the *Garland* and her sister ships, the *Pomare* and the *Expansion*. All three ships earned their stripes as army freight and passenger (later designated FS) vessels in the late war's Aleutian Theater. As such, they "knew" the lay of the land and served the villages well. The *Garland* covered the Run into the early 1950s with but

FOR ROMANTIC ADVENTURE
Sail to the
ALEUTIAN ISLANDS
"Land of the Smoky Sea"

Aboard the
Aleutian Mail Boat
M/V EXPANSION

Sail informally to that distant and historic land. Visit isolated villages and meet the friendly peoples that come aboard to buy and trade in the ship's stores

* **See majestic steaming Volcanoes.**
* **Witness the drama of life at Sea.**
* **See roaring sea lions, precious sea otter.**
* **Visit Dutch Harbor, scene of the First bombing of American soil.**
* **See enormous sheep ranches on Umnak Island.**
* **Get first-hand glimpses of fabulous King Crab and Salmon fishing and canning in the Shumagins.**

For the traveler with a yearning for real Alaskan Adventure off the beaten path, we offer accommodations for 12 passengers Vessel leaves Seward shortly after the first of each month on this 15-day trip to the Aleutian Islands, making 35 stops en route. Vessel may be seen at Seward the last 10 days of each month.

For reservations, write:
Capt. N. P. Thomsen, U.S. Coast Guard (Ret.)

Master M/V EXPANSION—P.O. Box 537, Seward
or Phone Main 374, Seward, Alaska

Sailing Schedule

Departs from Seward, Alaska
Shortly after First of each month

Round Trip Fare—$258.00 plus 10% tax

Stops two to six hours in each port

Not a Luxury Cruise.
Slacks and a Warm Jacket or Coat Recommended

Ports	Distance	Average Running Time
Seward		
Seldovia	141.2	13 hr.
Port Graham	15.4	1 hr. 25 min.
Kodiak	107	10 hr.
Chignik	242	23 hr.
Perryville	61.7	5 hr. 50 min.
Ivanoff Bay	22	2 hr.
Unga	61.7	5 hr. 50 min.
Squaw Harbor	8.5	45 min.
Sand Point	8.2	42 min.
King Cove	80.5	7 hr. 25 min.
Cold Bay	22.4	2 hr. 4 min.
Pauloff Harbor	51.1	4 hr. 48 min.
Ikatan	30.2	3 hr.
False Pass	7.1	42 min.
Akutan	124.7	12 hr. 10 min.
Unalaska	45.7	4 hr. 9 min.
Chernofski	62.7	6 hr.
Nikolski	80.6	7 hr. 35 min.

Nikolski is the last village on the mail run. Chernofski and Kashega have only one mail call. Kashega for a long time had only one resident where as now there are two. Chernofski has two families and a few sheep herders, but no lacking in company since there are approximately 4500 sheep

one interruption: she tangled with some rocks on her September 1950 run westward and was forced to retreat to Seattle for repairs. The *Pomare* took over the run from November to January, when the *Garland* returned to duty. Sometime after the last PEN was issued (February 1951), the *Garland* was herself replaced by the *Expansion*, which continued the service until it was finally terminated in the early 1960s.

And thus ended the saga of the Aleutian Run mailboat—a history of daring, devotion, tragedy, and triumph unmatched in the annals of North Pacific seafaring.

SELECTED BIOGRAPHIES

No historical account of the latter days of Unga would be complete without mentioning, however briefly, the colorful lives (and deaths) of some of Unga's prominent but largely unheralded citizens. These people were, in the truest sense, pioneers, who often led lonely lives, full of the dangers of living in a harsh and isolated wilderness. Most of them would have passed into oblivion were it not for people such as Lena Yarnell Reeve, whose unpublished 1933 memoir listed numerous self-described "old timers" who came to the Shumagin Islands long before the period covered by this present effort. As documented by Mrs. Reeve, many of these "pioneers" were known better by their nicknames than their surnames. They were Hungry Charlie and Pistol Pete and Portugee Joe and Captain No Danger. There was a Russian Town Charlie, an Old Man Topsy, a Whiskey Bill, and one who was called simply "Lazy." Surely, each had a rich story to tell, but the lives they lived were summed up in a few precious lines. Latter-day "pioneers" fared somewhat better, thanks largely to the students of the Unga High School, whose first-hand accounts of interviews were published in THE ALASKA PEN. Here, then, are a few biographies of "old timers" who graced Unga's more recent history.

"LOFOTEN"

Everyone knows "Lofoten", but how many really know the man, Edward Hjalmar Larsen? A short interview by the author of this article revealed that Mr. Larsen is a man of wide experience, who has known many sorrows, encountered many difficulties, and has many times been misunderstood because of his strong accent. In spite of all these burdens and handicaps, Mr. Larsen, for a man of his age, still remains a pillar of strength, and possesses an unusually keen mind.

Edward Larsen was born in Pensacola, Florida, March 19, 1876—the son of John Larsen, who was born in Norway and later came to the United States and fought in the Union Army during the Civil War. His mother was Anna Johnson, born in Finland of Swedish parents.

At the age of two, Edward returned with his parents to Norway to a little village near Hammerfest. One year later, his mother passed away and when he was only five years of age his father was lost at sea. During most of these early years, Edward was forced to shift for himself and eventually became a fisherman off the Lofoten

Ed (Lofoten) Larsen

Islands near Norway and in afteryears, his conversation regarding these islands caused people to call him "Lofoten".

At the age of 19, Edward Larsen returned to Pensacola, where he became a diver and repairer of ships. During this period, he met his future bride, Anna Petersen, and to them were born three children—one boy and two girls. But his happiness was short-lived. The 1906 hurricane in Pensacola, with a wind velocity of 125 miles per hour and which lasted about six hours, left many thousand dead in its wake. Among them were Mrs. Larsen and the three children, of whom no trace was ever found. Mr. Larsen received injuries which were to prevent him from ever diving again.

In order to start his life anew, he migrated to San Pedro, California in 1907 and remained there until 1912, during which time he carried on a cleaning and pressing business. He came to Alaska in 1913, making his first stop at Pirate Cove, where he entered the codfishing industry. Later, he worked for Hjalmar Lauritzen and Ed Pearson in the golden days of Unga's codfishing. About 1926, he followed salmon fishing in Port Moller and Herendeen Bay and in 1942 he returned to Unga where he has since lived in semi-retirement. Mr. Larsen is always ready and willing to serve the community in any way possible and at the present time is the community's shoemaker. He is active in social affairs and is said by the ladies to be an excellent dancer.   (TAP XII, 3, p. 9)

["Lofoten" is best remembered by this writer as a champion bread baker. He was a jolly old man whose favorite expression was "chick-a-bacca," but he never offered a translation. He left Unga in the early 1950s and spent his last years in the Pioneers' Home. Ed.]

"FRED THE WHALER"

Fred Pomian lived in Unga 49 years. He left Germany when he was fifteen years old on a whaling schooner. He whaled around Japan. Some people call him "The Whaler".

Fred (the Whaler) Pomian

Fred fished out of "Frisco" on a fishing schooner. He came to Unga as a codfisherman. Fred built his station around 1924. "Fred the Whaler" had a sailboat which he said that he was not afraid to sail around [the world] in. But then Fred says that there isn't anything to see going around the world, so he won't do it. Fred is very kind to everyone; his smoked salmon is a delicacy enjoyed by a few people here in the winter. He likes to have people come and see him.

Fred weighs 245 pounds and has a white moustache and hair. He is not too old to walk around the bay; he is 67 years old now and ought to make a hundred easily.

Fred is very capable at most things, but he has trouble making jam. His jam gets too watery, which is very sad, but he doesn't worry much about it. (Ha!)

Fred says that he enjoys his own singing almost as much as he does his own cooking. He says that he must be a good cook, because he never had any complaints from his favorite boarder (himself). (TAP XlV, 1, p. 8)

[Little is known about Fred Pomian's early history. The US Government Census reports that he resided in the Alaska Codfish Co. bunkhouse in 1920. He was then 36 years old. It is known that he had previously worked in the Apollo Mine and while there had presumably selected the site of his lifelong home, and there he built a cabin above the beach at the head of Delarof Harbor, less than a mile from the railroad spur that ran from the mine down to tidewater. "Fred da Whaler," as most locals knew him, was a long-time widower who raised two daughters, Lena and Annie. He died in Unga in 1962. Ed.]

"JOHN THE SNAILER"

John Berntsen, Sr. was born in Sandefjord, Norway, October 31, 1879. He is now 71 years old. He came over to this country on a sailing boat when he was 16.

After being in the States for awhile, he came to Alaska, where he got into the codfishing business at Unga.

John is commonly known to some people as "John the Snailer" because he used to be high liner at Kelly's Rock in the codfishing days. A high liner is a person who catches more fish than anyone else.

Since the codfishing business decreased, John Berntsen salmon fished around here and the last few years he fished up in Bristol Bay. Trapping in the winter was another one of his occupations.

Even though he is 71 years old, Mr. Berntsen is quite active for his age. Other things about him

are that he has bright blue eyes and a very neat white moustache. As he walks along, you will notice that he is smoking a curled pipe, which is the only kind he likes.

Mr. Berntsen is also a member of the town council. (TAP XIV, 3, p. 4)

["John the Snailer" lived most of his life in Unga. He married Margaret (Maggie) Creevden in 1910. The couple raised 13 children. John moved to Sand Point in the late '50s where he died in 1961. John Berntsen was 83 years old. Ed.]

Two Norwegians: Hjalmar Lauritzen and John (the Snailer) Berntsen

"FRENCHY"

Joseph Alcide, or "Frenchy", as he is very commonly known in the Shumagin Isles, was born in Corsica, France. He came over to this country while still a very young man. Before settling down, though, he had traveled extensively on windjammers and other sailing vessels throughout the seven seas.

During the early part of the century, he, like many of the other old timers around here, was engaged in the codfishing business. After the codfish industry started to dwindle and salmon fishing became the chief occupation, he would go to Bristol Bay every summer to get in on the rich harvest of fish there. He would make good money in Bristol Bay every year and had many an opportunity to go and live elsewhere, but after the fishing season was over in the fall the first one to step ashore off the boat would be Joe. When asked why he always came back, he'd give one a big grin and say, "Unga is my home, boy".

Today "Frenchy" is retired from the fishing industry and living comfortably on a pension provided by the government. He lives alone in a little house by the side of the road.

If one should meet him while he is taking his daily walks up and down the street, one will immediately notice that he has a cheerful smile and friendly greeting for everyone. Perhaps this is one reason that Joe Alcide, a real landmark in the community, is well liked by everyone.

(TAP XIV, 2, p. 8)

"GRISHKA"

George ("Grishka") Grassamoff was born and reared in Belkofski, which is a small village about fifty or sixty miles northwest of Unga.

While still a lad in his early twenties, he migrated to Unga because of the lack of work at his home.

With the gold mine at the head of the bay still operating, the town was still very active with its saloons and dance halls wide open.

At a local "pub", Grishka met up with two men, a Carlson and a Schmidt who had leased an island some time previously from the government. It was these men who chose his life work for Grishka. He was induced to go to Simeonof Island where they had a herd of cattle and a number of blue foxes put there by the late Andrew Grosvold.

Grishka stayed on the island and worked for these men for several years. During this time, he was not very happy because of the fact that he had left a girl back in Belkofski and wished to see her. He made arrangements to go back home on a small sailing vessel called the *Spray*. There were no motors on the *Spray*, so one traveled with the wind. He recalled the hardships involved in being caught by a stiff northwest wind while enroute. Reaching Belkofski, he again found the girl he had longed for. A marriage resulted and he brought his bride back to Simeonof.

While on the island, he trapped foxes and cared for the cattle.

Three of Unga's oldtimers: from left: Joe "Frenchy" Alcide, Viola "Bobbie" Nelson, and George "Grishka" Grassamoff.

Schmidt, who was in ill health during this time, passed away here in Unga. With the death of his partner, Carlson left this part of the country, never to return.

The island was then taken over by Adolph Petersen and Thomas Skulstad. According to Grishka, the new lessees treated him well and he was very happy in his work.

Throughout Mr. and Mrs. Grassamoff's long stay on Simeonof fourteen children were born to them.

Several years ago, after the death of Tom Skulstad, Grishka and his family moved to Unga to make their home.

It was here that he was to know deep sorrow. His wife had died during the diphtheria epidemic and his two sons were presumably frozen to death while out on their trap line.

Today, Grishka is settled down in a little house of his own. He is quite contented and takes great pride in his cat "Bobbie". He has been wanting a small pup for some time now, but hasn't been very successful in getting a canine of any kind.

(TAP XIV, 5, p. 6)

"HUNT"

Harrison Chandler Hunt was a doughboy in World War I. A Californian, he migrated to Alaska shortly after the war and entered the codfishing trade in Unga where he met and married Lena Pomian (Fred the Whaler's daughter).

They settled down in Unga and were blessed with twin daughters, one of whom died in infancy (see Historical Highlights, February '35).

Mr. Hunt was known by almost everyone as "Harry" but to his wife, Lena, he was simply "Hunt". Theirs was a stormy relationship. Lena was a strong-willed woman and Harry took life in his stride. In later years, they maintained separate homes, but Lena continued to care for Harry when the need arose.

So it was in the fall of 1953 when all those colorful old fellows died, one after another. First it was Frenchy, Joe Alisto (Alcide). My step-dad,

Andrew Foster, found him when he went to visit. Frenchy was on the floor, just inside the door. It appeared he suffered a heart attack while going for help. Harry had the dubious honor of preparing Frenchy for burial. Then he himself died shortly thereafter, presumably, as rumor had it, from drinking lemon extract, which he had purchased from the local store. It was suspected that he had been buying lemon extract by the case, the liquor store having been closed the year before.

With Lena's help, Grishka did the honor of getting Harry ready for burial. They got him all cleaned up and placed in the casket that Aleck Wilson had built. After getting everything "squared away", Lena left for home to cook dinner. Grishka by that time was, in her words, "half swacked". She told him to wait there, as she was going to bring him dinner. Upon arrival back at Harry's house (he was living at Fred Krone's house, across town from Lena's), she found Grishka to be "quite looped". She said she growled at him and got him to sit at the table to

The wedding of Lena and Harry Hunt

eat. Then Lena went over to the casket to check things out and immediately noticed that Harry's gold wedding band was missing. Lena turned and confronted Grishka. "Grishka, where's Hunt's wedding ring?" Grishka, who never could speak very good English, replied, "I no got. I no got!" "You give me that ring right now!" demanded Lena. Grishka got mad, jumped up and came over to the other side of the casket, still claiming not to have the ring. Lena, herself angry by this time, demanded again: "Give me that ring! YOU GIVE ME THAT GODDAM RING RIGHT NOW !", while reaching over the casket and grabbing Grishka by the collar. Grishka finally replied, "Him no need. Him dead!" To make a long story short Lena prevailed and said she kept an eye on that ring until the casket was closed and sealed.

Harry Hunt was buried in the American Cemetery, only a stone's throw from the tiny cottage on the hill where Harry and Lena raised their family.

Within a few weeks of his preparation of Harry for burial, Grishka himself died and was buried in Unga's Russian Cemetery.

[The foregoing account was relayed to this editor by Lena Hunt several years after this sad affair. A capsule summary of Lena's life after Harry is given in "Exodus," Part III. Lena Pomian Hunt died in Anchorage in 1983. She was 72 years old. Edward Melseth, Ed.]

EXODUS:

The Last Days of Unga

Unga's viability as a community was tested on several occasions during the first half of the 20th Century. The virtual closure of the Apollo Mine in the first decade and the collapse of the codfishing industry in the third saw the area's population plummet from a high of more than 300 to half that number by 1930. Yet, despite these jolts, Unga village thrived and continued to serve as the cultural and commercial center of the Shumagins through the fourth decade. Then came the Second World War and the disruptions it created in the community, and the destiny of Unga was forever sealed. The war's aftermath revealed a village gamely assessing its predicament in the face of an unrelenting population decline. As usual, the discerning staff of THE ALASKA PEN, keenly aware of its own survival, offered its view of the impending problem in the following editorial:

Under tow by the Garland

UNGA: BOOM OR BUST?

These two words describe many an Alaskan town at one time or another. Judging from remarks we've heard here and there, many people are ready to write Unga off the books as a town that is almost a "ghost". You don't hear people call it a ghost town yet, but you do hear them saying that it is "declining".

So far, no one has given any very good reason why this town should decline. No town ever had to die if the people in it didn't want it to. There are many ways to keep a town alive, of course. We know that they all depend on finding ways to earning a living. That would be the whole problem, since Unga people are mostly leaving to find other means of income.

It is no longer possible to earn a living here as before, but there may soon be other ways to gain security.

Unga has many possibilities, which are being investigated by outsiders. We wonder why more Unga people do not investigate these resources. There are plenty of capable men right here in Unga. There are men here who could experiment with livestock raising, new fishing possibilities and there may be many more.

Some communities have pooled their resources, and a group of ambitious men with some capital have formed development companies to attack their problem. The mention of capital may make some say, "There's a catch", for a little spare money is often hard to come by. But the biggest capital item on any list is willing alert minds and bodies. With some good men on deck, an undertaking can get by on very little capital.

It seems to us that a meeting should soon be called of any and all of the "adventurers" who think we could accomplish something together that would be more than we could do separately.   (TAP XIV, 1, p. 2)

Despite the optimism of youth, the exodus began in earnest in the fall of 1946 with the end of the salmon fishing season and the departure of the cannery crews—an annual happening that turned the Squaw Harbor cannery site into a ghost town. But on this occasion, the S. S. *Baranof* took with it ten percent of Unga's population as well. Granted that some of those leaving would return in the spring, but for most of those leaving, the move was to be permanent. THE ALASKA PEN in its September 1946 issue reported:

The S. S. Baranof *in Squaw Harbor preparing to leave for Seattle*

UNGA POPULATION DECREASES

...The S. S. *Baranof* took a chunk out of Unga by taking fourteen people to the States and two people elsewhere. The following left on August 28th:

Mr. and Mrs. Hjalmar Lauritzen, owners of the store at Unga, left for Seattle, as they needed medical care. Mrs. Lauritzen has lived here for the past 38 years, and Mr. Lauritzen lived here longer. He was engaged in the codfishing industry here. Their son, Thomas, also left for medical care.

Mr. and Mrs. Mike Galovin and family, George, Mary and Ray, who lived here all their lives, left for Bellingham, Washington, where they plan to make their home.

Evelyn Foster will live with the Galovins and go to Bellingham High with Mary and Ray.

Mr. William Harrover, who spent the summer with his daughter, Mrs. Robert Garlow, left for Arizona. He will spend a month at Palo Alto, California, and then proceed to his home in Phoenix.

Mr. and Mrs. Daniel Wilson left for Bellingham, Washington, to spend the winter. Future plans are undecided.

Ruth Lauritzen plans to attend high school in Kirkland, Washington.

Henry Berntsen will visit his sister, Mrs. Irene Hansen, of Seattle, Washington.

Ruth Lauritzen, Mary Galovin and Evelyn Foster, who helped publish THE ALASKA PEN the past two years, have always hoped to graduate from high school in the States. Your long-awaited-for chance has come, so we wish you lots of good luck, girls.

Mr. and Mrs. Andy Endresen moved to Sand Point where they will await transportation to Seward. They plan to make their winter's home there.

Gus England and Charlie Wood left as crew members on the cannery tender *Goodnews*. Charlie was bound for California to visit with his mother. Gus went for a trip to the States.

Ed Endresen left on the *Pansy* to visit in Cordova.

We all hate to lose such fine friends and neighbors, and to those who will return, we hope your vacation will be beneficial, and to those who have gone to stay, we can only say, "It was fine knowing you". Bon Voyage to you all.   (TAP XI, 1, p. 8)

Another seven residents left Unga in November 1946: Mrs. Laura Berntsen and children Bertha Jean, Louis (Buddy), Louise, Walter, Rosemary, and Trudy entered the Jesse Lee Home in Seward. Losing so many school-age children was rather traumatic, but the school was fortunate in picking up several student transfers from Squaw Harbor following the closure of its school. The Johansen family's move in 1946 increased the student body by two: Alvin entered the fifth grade class and Jennie went on to become the 13th and last graduate of Unga High in 1949. The most significant loss in 1946, however, was the transfer of Deputy US Marshal Allan Petersen to Kenai and the closure of the marshal's office in Unga—this on the heels of the loss of the US Commissioner's office to Squaw Harbor. Suddenly, Unga was left with no Federal representation or law enforcement, a situation not experienced by the village since the turn of the century.

Mrs. Allan Petersen and the Raymond Rodgers family (Raymond, Esther, and Raymond, Jr., and Arthur, Meryl, and Mildred Hansen) left Unga in 1947. Mrs. Petersen joined her husband in Kenai and the Rodgers settled in Seward. Esther Cushing also left to enroll in the University of Alaska. Others leaving were Carolyn and Mary Haaf, who entered the Jesse Lee Home, and Hilda Grassamoff, who moved to Seward. On the plus side, the Martin Gilbert family moved over to Unga from Squaw Harbor so that their children, Dorothy and Martin, Jr., could continue their schooling. Peter Calugan and Laura Berntsen also returned home. Peter's return was particularly noteworthy. Peter had been hospitalized for several years in the States. He quickly enrolled in school and was one of three UHS graduates in 1948.

The next two years saw little population change. The Alexander Calugans moved home from Sand Point in 1948 and the Andrew Krone family plus Maggie Kochutin and son Billy, and one of your editors (TL) left Unga in 1949.

In the fall of 1950, Mrs. Lena Lauritzen, daughter Ann, and Martha Hunt left for the States, and Ethel Cushing moved to Juneau. They were followed in November by the John Berntsen, Jr., children, Robert, Richard, and Patricia, who entered the Jesse Lee Home.

Lauritzen's store and residence, ca. 1948

Although these negative changes in population seem relatively minor, the net effect was beginning to be felt by the two local businesses that served the community with general merchandise. But in the end it was the untimely and tragic death of Thomas Lauritzen in 1949 followed by the death of his father in 1950 (see "Crossings," Part III) that sealed the fate of Lauritzen's—the smaller of the two stores—that had operated in Unga for more than 20 years.

Despite Edward F. Casey's departure in 1950, Sjoberg & Casey's continued to conduct business in an atmosphere of optimism following a surprising upswing in population with the arrival of three families in 1950 and 1951. William Torgramsen, who was born in Unga, returned with his wife, Phyllis, and their three daughters in 1950. Also arriving that year were Fred and Lucy Pesterkoff and their four children. In 1951, former UHS student Alma (Foster) Rudolph returned home with her six children to join her mother, Cecilia, and her several siblings. Hers was to become one of the last families to have moved to Unga. In 1952, Mrs. Rudolph gave birth to triplets—a newsworthy happening that was picked up by the Associated Press and caused great excitement in the village.

But the euphoria of a population upswing was short-lived. Unga continued to lose the very organizations that had marked it as a progressive community. The Women's Club, once the leader of social activities, disbanded in 1950 due to a membership decline. So also did the Girl Scout troop. The high school suffered a similar fate and closed its doors in 1951. This also spelled the end of THE

Triplets (Not 4) Born to Woman On Aleutian Isle

KODIAK, Alaska, Nov. 13.—(AP)—It's triplets for Mrs. Alma Rudolph of lonely Unga Island, 300 miles southwest of here. She has six other children.

The 30-year-old mother and her babies, two girls and a boy, were doing well after a Navy doctor and plasma were flown to her, the Coast Guard reported yesterday. She was attended only by neighbor women at their birth.

First reports from Unga were that quadruplets had been born to Mrs. Rudolph.

ALASKA PEN, the high school's and the village's mouthpiece for the past 17 years. In 1953, Sjoberg & Casey's folded, leaving Unga with no outfitters for groceries or supplies or a reliable central source of electricity. Viola and John Nelson left what remained of the store in the hands of Genevieve Foster and moved to Seattle.

Others leaving in 1951 included the Albert Cushing family, who moved to Chignik, Norman and Imogene Lauritzen and young son Conrad, who moved to Squaw Harbor, and Dorothy Gilbert, who went to the States to continue her schooling.

Rev. and Mrs. Densmore and son David arrived in 1955 to fill the void caused by the movement of Methodist Church operations to Sand Point in 1953. They remained until 1957 when they moved to Kodiak. Alvin Johansen returned to Unga in 1956 with his new wife, Marie. They stayed for two years, eventually resettling in Sand Point. Carol Larsen moved to Seward in 1956 to attend high school. During her time in Seward, Carol lived with her grandmother and old-time Ungaite, Mrs. Zenia Foster.

Another significant loss to Unga and its residents occurred in 1957 with the closure of the post office that had long served the community from a corner in Sjoberg & Casey's general store. Its last postmaster was Genevieve Foster. Also in 1957, the Peter Calugan and Buddy Berntsen families moved to Sand Point, and the town's population was reduced by nine. But this was only a prelude to things to come. In 1958 and 1959, at least 53 people pulled up stakes. Susie and Bert Lee and family moved to Kodiak, the Rudolph family resettled in Anchorage, John Berntsen and sons Howard and Henry moved to Sand Point, and Frieda and Charlie Wood found work in King Cove.

In 1959, the last full year of the Unga Territorial School, Laura and Aleck Wilson and five children transferred to Sand Point along with the Albert Krone family. Frances and Martin Johansen and son Arthur, and Norman Larsen, Jr., moved to Squaw Harbor, and Virginia Johansen's nine children helped swell the student body in Kodiak.

With formal schooling no longer available in Unga, the years following the Unga school's closure saw a rather general evacuation of the village. In 1960, the Andrew Foster family, including your editor (EM), the John Foster family, and the Martin Gilbert family moved to Squaw Harbor, and in 1961, the Glen Brandal family resettled in Kodiak, Ollie Krone moved to Squaw Harbor, and Axel Anderson, who lived "up the bay" near his old friend Fred Pomian (Fred the Whaler) for many years and helped him maintain his keg of elderberry wine, returned to his home in Sweden.

"Up the Bay" at Fred the Whaler's. From left: Axel Anderson, Fred, Fred's granddaughter Martha Hunt Fletcher, Martha's children, Aaron and Danetta, and Fred's daughter, Lena Hunt (summer of 1961)

After losing her father in 1962 and son Freddie in a boating accident two years later, lifelong Unga resident, Lena Hunt packed her rolling pin and resettled in Copper Center in 1964.

By this time, there were fewer than 25 people residing in Unga. Significantly, most of them represented one of the earliest pioneer families in Unga—a family that began with the arrival of William Foster, a sea otter hunter, in the latter half of the 19th century. William's son, John, was born in 1889 and he and his wife, Cecilia, spent their entire lives in Unga. After John died in 1934, Cecilia raised their seven sons and two daughters in a little house on the edge of the bay and remained there, the matriarch of the family, until her death in 1966. Harry had left Unga with his wife, Dolly, some years earlier but was always nearby. He lives still in Sand Point with his daughter Evelyn. Bruce and Kenneth and families moved to Squaw Harbor in 1965. Kenneth's neighbor, George "Bingo" Gilbert, left his sister Maggie's cozy cottage in 1966 along with Russell and Mary Foster and family. With Mary's departure, the only remaining civic organization, the Unga Community Library, stamped its final "Date Due" and closed its doors for the last time. In 1968, Thomas Foster finally succumbed to the exodus that had been underway for 20 years and joined his siblings in Squaw Harbor.

Forty years later, Unga is a ghost town still, and is likely to remain so. Much of the townsite is now owned by the Unga Corporation, an outgrowth of the Alaska Native Claims Settlement Act. The Corporation has recently constructed a modern cabin at McCann's Point to offer shelter for the occasional visitor. However, except for the fencing of the two cemeteries, the Corporation has made no attempt to preserve the townsite itself. Benign neglect has allowed what buildings remain to suffer the deterioration of time and weather. Yet the trees that were planted when this historical account began continue to grow, to thrive, and to mark the sites of houses they sheltered for more than half a century. But, since these trees have shown no evidence of propagation, they, too, will eventually fall and Unga will revert to the pristine wilderness it had been, long before the arrival of Aleut otter hunters, the Russian fur traders, the European codfishermen, and the American gold seekers. It is perhaps fitting that, at long last, the land of Unga has reverted to the control of those who sought shelter in its harbor long before history began. But it would be well to remember the time that Unga was a community of people who shared their hardships, their griefs, and their joys: people who built and maintained a village. With this book, we honor them: those who are living still and, in particular, those who live only in our memories. For those of us who grew up there, Unga was not only just a place. Unga was, and will always be, "home."

Central Unga in 1955. From left: the Foster family home, Harry and Dolly Foster's house, the remains of Mrs. Richard's house (Mrs. Richard was John Foster, Sr.'s mother), in the background, the John Berntsen house, and in the foreground right, the Albert Cushing house

Unga: Before and After?

VIOLA'S DEPARTURE: The end of an era.

It was a crisp, sunny September day when Viola left Unga in 1953. In her 40-odd years in Unga, Viola had left home numerous times but had always returned. This was to be her final departure, and villagers flocked to the dock to wish her a fond and teary farewell.

Viola Sjoberg was born in San Francisco, but spent most of her life in Unga, where her Swedish-immigrant parents had served as fish processors and merchants since the early years of the 20th century. Those who knew her as a child remembered her as a charming and vivacious girl with an easy smile and a friendly laugh. She was equally at home in Unga as in San Francisco, where she traveled to frequently to attend school and visit friends. On one of her trips to California, she married a young, handsome, and energetic San Francisco businessman, Edward F. Casey, and the couple planned to remain in the city. But the call of the north was persuasive, and shortly after their 1934 marriage, they returned to Unga to operate the family business, eventually renamed "Sjoberg & Casey's." On the eve of the Second World War, they became a family with the birth of Judith Ruth. The business thrived through the forties but changing fortunes eventually took their toll on both the business and the family. By the end of the decade, the marriage failed. Ed returned to San Francisco to resume his occupation in the insurance business, and Viola was left with the store. Shortly thereafter, Viola married John H. Nelson, like herself, a lifelong resident of Unga. But good fortune for her did not equate to a similar success in the business. After the war, the town's population began declining, and many families had begun to order their groceries and sundries directly from the "outside"—a euphemism for Seattle or, more specifically in this case, Ballard—where outfitters such as Bunsen and Davis would exchange barrels of salted salmon for their winter's supplies. Viola reasoned that the store could no longer support her and it was time to move on.

Preparing for her departure after more than four decades wasn't an easy or welcomed chore, except, perhaps, for the townspeople who flocked to her store and estate sale with wheelbarrows. She sold whatever remained in the store and all of her furniture, including her oil-fired heater and kitchen stove. All that was left in her house were the drapes in the windows, which were drawn as she prepared to leave.

I was not quite ten the day Viola left Unga, but I remember the occasion as if it were yesterday. A number of townspeople, including my mother and me, had assembled in the White House—a name given to the large two-story structure to distinguish it from the predominantly green general store and outbuildings comprising Sjoberg & Casey's—to share some final moments with Viola and John. As departure time approached, Viola asked everyone to leave and give her some time alone. She then walked slowly and silently from room to room, clearly reminiscing her life in Unga. We reassembled on the road adjacent to the house and watched as she appeared in the doorway, paused momentarily, dropped to her knees in prayer and, rising, strolled briskly down to the dock. Here were gathered the rest of the villagers—folks she served in the store, neighbors, old schoolmates, friends. Everyone in Unga liked her. They lived with her, danced with her, laughed with her, cried with her, even argued with her, and yes, drank with her. And now she was joining the exodus that had begun in the aftermath of the war. Everyone was hugging and kissing her goodbye. I don't believe there was a dry eye in the crowd. When they finally reached the *Southland* and the boat began to move out of the harbor, they stood together on the deck until the boat passed out of view. This was a sad day for Unga and, for Viola, probably one of the saddest days of her life.

Viola and John resettled in Ballard, where they were shortly joined by Judy. In a comfortable bungalow on 85th Street, they surrounded themselves with treasures of their many years in Unga and eagerly and generously shared these mementos with their many friends. Although John returned occasionally to the Shumagins as a fisherman, Viola never again saw the green hills of Unga. She died at 81 in 1988. EM

The wedding party: Robert Garlow, Newlyweds John and Viola Nelson, and Kathryn Garlow.

MARY'S STORY

Mary and Russell were pen pals in the early 1950s. Mary Purdy was born in Tennessee and moved to Sunnyside, Washington in 1944. Russell Foster was born and raised in Unga, the youngest son of Cecilia and John Foster, pioneer indigenous residents of Unga. After having corresponded for several years, Russell and Mary met in Sunnyside in 1955 and married. They moved to Bellingham shortly thereafter, on the first leg of their journey to Unga. In January of 1956, they boarded the mailboat *Expansion* in Seward for a rough three-day passage to Unga. Mary had mixed feelings about living in Unga: no grocery stores, no electricity, not much of anything. But, as a child of the Tennessee hill country, she knew about kerosene lamps and washboards and adapted quickly to these and other necessities of living in Unga.

During her eleven years in Unga, Mary served as librarian, postmaster, radio operator, and midwife, in addition to raising five children and assisting Russell as deckhand and fish packer. Mary ran the Unga Community Library, ordering many books and magazines during her seven-year tenure. The library was open from 1 to 4 P.M. each Saturday, and was the last public place in Unga to close. After the closure of the post office in 1958, Mary volunteered to sort incoming mail at her house and continued to do so for the next nine years.

One of the more interesting of her many activities was serving as midwife. Having never delivered a baby before, Mary relied on a medical book that she consulted on numerous occasions during her days in Unga, and assisted by Lena Hunt, she delivered a healthy baby boy for Bernice Brandal in 1961.

When Mary arrived in Unga in 1955, the village boasted 25 families or a population of just over 100. From 1957 to 1960, 17 of these families moved away and, with them, the school and post office. The two general stores had closed some years before. Mary and Russell resisted the urge to leave and, despite the lack of work and absence of essential services, they continued to live in Unga and to enjoy the life they had chosen. Mary home-schooled the children; Russell fished salmon during the summer and fall. After the commercial season, both would pack salmon for shipment to Bunsen and Davis in Seattle in exchange for their winter's supply of groceries. Mary became quite proficient in boatmanship, assisting Russell in running his boat, deckhanding, and taking her turn at the wheel. But landing the boat was a confidence she never acquired.

As the years passed and the children grew, Mary and Russell taught them to enjoy the flowers in spring, berries in the fall, trout fishing, clamming, and irrespective of season, beachcombing. It was an idyllic time, and Mary learned to love the land, the solitude and the satisfaction of living in Unga. But eventually she realized the need for more formal schooling for the children, and on one of the saddest days of her life, she, Russell, and the children became the last family to leave Unga. It was a short move in distance, but a giant step in their young lives. Their destination was Squaw Harbor, seven miles away—the site of the Pacific American Fisheries salmon cannery and a public school.

Here, Russell continued to commercially fish for salmon while Mary workd in the cannery and the children attended school. But this was to be not more than a way station, and three years later they left Squaw Harbor and settled in Mary's hometown of Sunnyside. There they purchased a house and lived happily for the next 34 years.

Russell reurned to the islands over the years to fish and provide for his family, but illness in the recent past forced him to retire. He died in 2003. Mary continues to live at home, surrounded by her children and grandchildren. She attends church every Sunday, goes to the local senior center for luncheons, and plays Bingo once a week. She still misses her life with Russell and always will, contending he was "one in a million." She reminisces often of her days in Unga. As Mary describes it, Unga will always be "home." Unga is where her heart is, and she will never forget it.

Russell and Mary Foster

...and part of their family

CROSSINGS

Crossing the Bar

...For tho' from out our bourne of time and place
The flood may bear me far,
I hope to see my Pilot face to face
When I have crossed the bar.

Alfred, Lord Tennyson

1946

ANDREW BRANDAL

On November 22nd, word was received from Kodiak that Andrew Brandal, a well-known resident, had passed away.

Susy and Andrew Brandal at their wedding

He was born at Chignik, Alaska, in 1907, the son of Mr. and Mrs. Sevard Brandal.

On August 27, 1929, he was united in marriage to Susy Pesterkoff, the ceremony being performed by Judge Driffield at the Judge's office in Unga. To this union were born thirteen children. The ten surviving are: Virginia, Norman, Nels, Nellie, Flossie, Glen, Christine, Sammy, Meryl Ann and Daniel.

Besides leaving his wife and children, he is also survived by two brothers, Aleck of Chignik and George of King Cove, and three sisters, Mrs. Alex Williamson, Bellingham, Washington, Mrs. Olga Wilkums, Seattle, Washington and Mrs. Pete Peterson, Chignik.

Andrew Brandal shall be greatly missed by all. He has done many fine things for the community and shall not be forgotten soon. Our deepest sympathy is extended to his wife and children.

(TAP XI, 4, p. 5)

1947

ANNA T. LAURITZEN

Mrs. Anna T. Lauritzen, a very dear friend of the high school, passed away July 25, 1947. She was very dear to everyone and her passing is regretted deeply.

At the age of 32, she came from Norway with her two sons, Harold and Conrad, to join her husband, who had entered the codfishing business in

Unga. Although she has traveled to the States, Unga remained her permanent home.

Four of her sons drowned in Unga bay before her passing. She left wonderful memories to her husband, Hjalmar Lauritzen, two sons, Thomas and Arthur, two daughters, Esther and Ruth, one daughter-in-law, Lena Lauritzen, one brother John Jacobson of Boston, and thirteen grandchildren.

(TAP XII, 1, p. 8)

Anna T. Lauritzen

[Anna Theresa Lauritzen, known far and wide as "Anna T" and affectionately as Grandma Lauritzen, was involved in numerous activities. She was instrumental in organizing the Unga Women's Club, the Library, and Sunday School, to name a few. She enjoyed playing the piano and singing, and was devout in her religion.

[At the time of her death, Mrs. Lauritzen was enroute to Seward to seek medical attention. She took ill in Squaw Harbor, where she died.

[A large contingent of mourners from Squaw Harbor and Sand Point came to Unga for her funeral. The Rev. Constance Erickson, pastor of the Unga

Methodist Church, of which Mrs. Lauritzen was a charter member, officiated at the service. She was laid to rest in the American Cemetery alongside her sons and mother. Ed.]

1947

PAUL LUDVICK

Paul Ludvick, who has lived in this vicinity a number of years, passed away at his Sand Point home during the first week in December.

Following Mr. Ludvick's request, the remains were taken to Unalaska where they will rest beside his wife, who died about seven years ago.

(TAP XII, 4, p. 9)

1948

NICHOLI PETERSEN

Nicholi Petersen, a resident of Sand Point, was found dead at his home on January 8th, of self-inflicted bullet wounds. He had been in ill health for some time.

(TAP XII, 5, p. 8)

HARRY BRUGMAN

Harry Brugman, a resident for many years in this area, quietly passed away in a Kodiak hospital on March 18th.

Harry was born in Holland and immigrated to this country during his young manhood. After sailing around the world in square riggers for a number of years, he grew tired of wandering and then settled down in this area during the golden age of the codfishing days.

It is believed that a sister survives him, but her whereabouts are unknown. (TAP XII, 8, p. 7)

TOM FOX

The people of Unga were shocked to hear of the death of Mr. Tom Fox, a well-known citizen of Unga. Mr. Fox, age 72, had been in poor health for several days but it was not thought to be serious. His body was discovered on the morning of September 20th in his house. It is assumed that Mr. Fox passed away during the night, as he had visitors the previous evening.

Mr. Fox was born in England in 1877 and, after serving in His Majesty's Navy, came to Unga in 1902 as a fisherman. He later married Nellie Gardner. They became the parents of nine children, who lived and attended school here.

Six children and his wife preceded Mr. Fox in death. Mrs. Fox passed away in 1940 and Lieutenant George Fox was killed in action in Italy in 1943.

Survivors of Mr. Fox are his daughters: Mrs. Katie Kashervarof of Unalaska, Mrs. Edna Larsen, of Wrangell, Alaska, and Mrs. Kay Koske, of El Cerrito, California.

Mr. Tom Fox was a member of the Roman Catholic Church. His funeral was held in the Methodist Church on September 22nd, where a large group of mourners gathered to pay their last respects to his memory. His remains were laid to rest in the American Cemetery. (TAP XIII, 1, p. 8)

ED PEARSON

Mr. Ed Pearson, one of Unga's oldest residents, 73 years old, passed away suddenly at Squaw Harbor in the latter part of May. Mr. Pearson died of a heart attack while working in the Pacific American Fisheries salmon cannery there.

During the early part of the 20th Century, the Shumagin Islands were the center of the entire Alaska codfishing industry and codfish companies had stations here and among the islands. It was at this time, in 1908, that Mr. Pearson arrived in Unga as an agent of the Alaska Codfish Company.

Mr. Pearson married Annie Cushing in 1914 and made his home here. He was a resident of Unga for forty years.

Mr. Pearson's funeral was held in the Unga Methodist Church on May 25th. He was buried in the American Cemetery.

Surviving Mr. Pearson are his daughters: Mrs. Clara Gilbert, of Squaw Harbor, Mrs. Frances Larsen, and Mrs. Genevieve Melseth, both of Unga, and thirteen grandchildren.   (TAP XIII, 1, p. 8)

NELLIE AND FRED KRONE

Word was received September 30th that Mr. and Mrs. Fred Krone passed away. Their deaths were less than a day apart.

Mr. Fred Krone was born in San Francisco, California, in 1883. Mr. Krone, age 65, passed away September 30th with a heart attack at the home of Mrs. Margaret Nelson of Sand Point.

Ed Pearson as a young man

Fred Krone

He came to Alaska to follow the fishing industry, and for many years worked as guard at the Shumagin precinct jail. In 1914, he married Mrs. Nellie Pesterkoff, to which union eight children were born, three of whom preceded their father in death. His survivors are: Albert and Andrew Krone and Mrs. Ollie Lindquist of Unga, and Mrs. Florence Gronholdt and Mrs. Margaret Nelson of Sand Point.

Nellie Krone

Mrs. Nellie Krone was born in Narkatak, near Sanak, Alaska, August 23, 1886, and was the daughter of Mr. and Mrs. Robert Gould, early pioneers of this community. She passed away at Fort Richardson Hospital near Anchorage, September 29th, at the age of 62. Mrs. Krone was a victim of vasomotor collapse.

In 1901, she was united in marriage to Mr. Fred Pesterkoff, to which union six children were born. Mr. Pesterkoff passed away in 1913, and the following year she married Mr. Fred Krone of Unga. From this marriage, eight children were born.

Her survivors are: Mrs. Irene Clements of Port Angeles, Washington, William and Johnny Pesterkoff of Bellevue, Washington, Mrs. May Still of San Pedro, California, Fred Pesterkoff, Mrs. Margaret Nelson and Mrs. Florence Gronholdt of Sand Point, Andrew and Albert Krone, Mrs.

Ollie Lindquist and Mrs. Susie Brandal of Unga. She has four sisters: Mrs. Mattie Galovin of Bellingham, Washington, Miss Anna Gould of Seattle, Washington, Mrs. Elizabeth Coon of Portland, Oregon, Mrs. Dolly Foster of Unga; and three brothers: Robert Gould of King Cove, Isaac Gould of Squaw Harbor and Rev. P. Gordon Gould of Philadelphia, Pennsylvania. Also surviving Mrs. Krone are 32 grandchildren and two great-grandchildren.   (TAP XIII, 2, p. 9)

BILL BOWMAN

Bill Bowman, who had lived in Squaw Harbor for many years, had been in poor health for some time and recently he became very ill.

One morning during the early part of December, he was found dead in his home. It is suspected that Bill Bowman committed suicide.

Since there is no cemetery where he lived, his body was laid to rest on a hillside near his home.   (TAP XIII, 4, p. 9)

1949

ANNA BERNTSEN

Mrs. Anna Berntsen (whose death notice was published in the PEN last month) was born in Unga on February 14, 1918, to Mr. and Mrs. Alec Wilson, Sr. She was reared and attended school here. On June 5, 1941, she was united in marriage to Mr. John Berntsen, Jr., by the Rev. Oscar Olsen, a former minister in Unga.

Mrs. Anna Berntsen passed away Tuesday, December 28th, of a cerebral hemorrhage. Her funeral, conducted by Rev. Constance Erickson, was held in the Greek Orthodox Church. She was buried in the Russian Cemetery.

Those who mourn her passing are: her husband, Mr. John Berntsen, Jr., three children, Bobby, 8 years old, Patricia, 5, and Richard, 4; her father, Mr. Alec Wilson of the Sitka Pioneer's Home, her mother, Mrs. Mike Galovin, of Bellingham, Washington, two brothers, Alec Wilson, Jr., of Unga and Daniel Wilson, of Bellingham; also, one half-sister, Mary Galovin and two half-brothers, George and Ray Galovin, of Bellingham.

Anna Berntsen

To those who mourn, we of the Unga High School extend our deepest sympathy.

(TAP XIII, 4, p. 7)

WILLIAM PETERS

While assisting with the funeral of Mrs. Anna Berntsen, Mr. William Peters passed away. It is believed that the cause of his death was a heart attack. Mr. Peters had been in ailing health for the past year.

Mr. Peters was born in Amsterdam, Holland, on December 8th, in the year 1886. In 1906, at the age of 20, he came to America. He landed in San Francisco, where he worked in the shipyards until 1908 when he came to Alaska on the schooner *John F. Miller*, which was wrecked in the Westward at Unimak Island. Mr. Peters happened to be on the schooner at the time of the wreck, but was one of the few fortunate folks who were saved. From then on, he followed the fishing industry.

In 1921 on August 7th, he and Mrs. Tania Torgramsen of Unga were married. He had lived in Unga ever since.

Mr. Peters was a member of the Roman Catholic Church. He belonged to the Alaska Fishermen's Union. Mr. Peters had taken a very active part in the community affairs of Unga. He also was the ex-chairman of the Unga town council. He became a citizen of the United States in 1941. Mr. Peters worked in the shipyards in Amchitka, Alaska, for the Army from 1941 to 1944.

Our sympathy is extended to those who mourn his passing.   (TAP XIII, 4, p. 7)

THOMAS LAURITZEN

Thomas Lauritzen, a very well known resident of Unga, met with a tragic death on January 7th, at the age of 28 years. It is suspected that he was accidentally drowned when he attempted to cross the ice-covered breakwater at the head of Delarof Harbor.

Thomas, the youngest son of Mr. Hjalmar Lauritzen, was born in Unga on May 5, 1920. He attended school in Unga and graduated from the Unga High School in 1937. Thomas later attended

Thomas Lauritzen and his limit (?) of ptarmigan

the University of Alaska, at College, Alaska, and the Seattle Pacific College, at Seattle, Washington.

Thomas was one of the first three men from Unga to enter the U. S. Army in 1941. After serving his four years in Alaska, he received his honorable discharge in 1945.

He returned home and followed the fishing industry and assisted his father in the Lauritzen's General Store.

Thomas was very active in community affairs, being Secretary of the Library Board and Chairman of the Unga Town Council.

His funeral was held at 2PM January 11th in the Unga Methodist Church, of which he became a member in 1941. His body was laid to rest in the American Cemetery. Four brothers and his mother preceded Thomas in death.

He leaves to mourn: his father, Mr. Hjalmar Lauritzen; two sisters, Mrs. Raymond Rodgers of Seward, Alaska, and Mrs. Ralph Soberg of Kenai, Alaska; one brother, Mr. Arthur Lauritzen of Seattle, Washington; a sister-in-law, Mrs. Lena Lauritzen of Unga; eight nieces and five nephews and a great number of friends in the Shumagin Islands.

In this recent sorrow, we extend to the bereaved our sincere sympathy.

(TAP XIII, 4, p. 7)

RUBY CUSHING

Miss Ruby Cushing, daughter of Mr. and Mrs. Albert Cushing of Unga, was born October 16, 1924, in Unga. She passed away at the Seward Sanatorium, January 24th at the age of 24.

Ruby was baptized in the Russian Orthodox faith. On confession of faith, she became a member of the Unga Methodist Church at Unga on Easter 1948. She was reared in Unga where she attended grade school and high school. She took sick in Bellingham, Washington in 1944. Ruby spent six months in the Cushman Hospital in Tacoma, Washington, and 18 months at home under faithful care. She entered the Seward Sanatorium in October 1948. Visitors always found her cheerful and cou-

rageous. Those who knew Ruby will miss her sunny disposition and thoughtfulness.

Funeral services were held in the Seward Methodist Church, Sunday, January 30th. The Rev. Paul Irwin officiated. Private memorial services were held for the family at the Cushing home in Unga on January 30th.

She leaves to mourn her death: her parents, Mr. and Mrs. Albert Cushing; three brothers, Albert, Jr., of Juneau, Aleck and Jackie of Unga; eight sisters, Julia, Juliette, Joan, Alice and Ethel of Unga; Florence and Esther (Mrs. Blair Brainard) of Kenai, and Anna (Mrs. Daniel Wilson) of Bellingham, Washington.

We of the Unga High School extend to the Cushing family our deepest sympathy.

(TAP XIII, 6, p. 6)

HJALMAR LAURITZEN

Funeral services for Hjalmar Lauritzen, seventy-five years old, were held on September 15th. He died in Kodiak on September 10th after a brief illness.

Mr. Lauritzen, a native of Norway, came to the United States in 1898 and settled here in Alaska. He has been well known and liked in this area of Alaska because of his friendliness and also because of his generosity. While living here the past five decades or so, he had been engaged in

Hjalmar Lauritzen

the mercantile business and, until recent years, the buying and selling of codfish.

Surviving are a son, Arthur, in Seattle; two daughters: Mrs. Raymond Rodgers of Seward and Mrs. Ruth Soberg of Kenai, and twelve grandchildren.

We of THE ALASKA PEN express deep sorrow and regret to those relatives who survive him.   (TAP XIV, 2, p. 5)

Sugarloaf or Hjalmar Mountain, Unga

A Final Crossing.......
THE ALASKA PEN: 1934-1951

The people of Unga, the Unga Territorial School, and their many friends throughout the country were saddened to learn in the winter of 1951 that the school's and the area's mouthpiece had published its last and final issue. THE ALASKA PEN, born along with the Unga High School in September of 1934, documented its activities and those of the lower grades throughout the latter 1930s and into the 1940s. THE PEN suffered a short hiatus in 1942, was replaced by PEN WHISPERS in 1943, and was reborn in 1944. It continued publication through the end of the Second World War and the early postwar period. An attempt to resume publication after a second hiatus (1949-50) failed after five issues, and THE ALASKA PEN passed into history. THE PEN was only 17 years old.

During its short but remarkable life, THE ALASKA PEN reported on the demise of gold mining, fur trapping, and codfishing in the Shumagins. It presented the area's vital statistics; it documented the diphtheria epidemic that threatened the health and life of Unga; it reported on the religious foundation of the community and followed the evolution of the several organizations that established and nurtured the social fabric of the village. Throughout its run, THE ALASKA PEN served as a sounding board for student journalistic endeavors. And, finally, it documented the sad decline of the village, but not its demise. (Unga outlasted THE PEN by some 15 years.)

THE ALASKA PEN was honored during its lifetime for scholastic achievement, having won First Place in its class by the Columbia Scholastic Press Association. (TAP II, 9, p. 4 Supplement) Its articles, essays, and even its tidbits of humor were widely praised in the many school publications with which it exchanged subscriptions. It enriched the lives of those who labored in its production. THE ALASKA PEN will be missed, but never forgotten.

[Ed. Note for those who wish to peruse the latter history of Unga in greater detail: The first issue of THE ALASKA PEN has been refurbished and reproduced full-size in the Appendix. This and the remaining issues of THE PEN (less three issues that have not yet been located), the full year's issuance of PEN WHISPERS, and the three UNGA NEWSLETTERS are now available on a single microfilm, produced by the Alaska State Library. The library served for many years as the repository of a major part of THE ALASKA PEN run—the Rodgers Collection—donated by its first editor-in-chief, Elizabeth Rodgers Gronholdt. Later editions were provided by your editors. We wish to applaud the library for producing and disseminating this collection, thereby ensuring that this chapter in Alaska's history endures. TL]

EPILOG

On the way to Unga...

"YOU *CAN* GO HOME AGAIN!"

There is an old saying that advises one wishing to return to the haunts of his childhood that "you can't go home again." The adage is meant to remind the would-be traveler that his childhood memories are just that: recollections of a youth long past. Try and relive those happy days by actually retracing those youthful paths and you will suffer grave disappointment. But tell that to former Ungaites who have made that journey, and more often than not, expressions of sadness will be overwhelmed by excitement and joy and a resolution to return once more. To be sure, most of the houses are now gone and the footpaths that joined them can no longer be discerned, but the town site remains as it always was: a hilly lowland hugging the bay, surrounded by pristine beaches, majestic cliffs, and mountains. The students of the Sand Point High School, many of whom could trace their lineage to Unga, understood this attraction when they named their epic 1982 annual "THE LAND-THE SEA." And it is this understanding that periodically draws together this dwindling band of aging Alaskans to reminisce about a place they all call "home." The Unga Corporation and The Aleut Corporation (TAC)—outgrowths of the Alaska Native Claims Settlement Act—were organized to advance the interest of native peoples of the Aleutians and, in so doing, serve to keep memories of lost communities such as Unga alive. The privately-chartered Pacific Northwest Aleut Council (PNAC) serves a similar function from its headquarters in Washington State for those living "outside." Robert Berntsen, a past president of PNAC and former board member of TAC, returned to Unga after a 45-year absence and Alice Knutsen Lauritzen Nilson, whose childhood memories of her birthplace prompted her return more than 50 years later, offer testimonials that loudly proclaim that you can indeed go home again.

ROBERT BERNTSEN'S STORY

My sister Patricia ("Tusa") and I had talked year after year about returning to the only place we both ever considered to be home. Our parents and three of their six children are buried there, along with many other family members. Now my sister is back home. She passed away last year and her desire was to have her ashes spread over Unga.

After 45 years: Bob revisits Unga in 1995. The ruins of his grandparents' house (the John Berntsen, Sr., residence) in the background.

This made me more determined to return to Unga, so after fishing in Bristol Bay this last summer, I flew to Sand Point and spent a week at Unga, and had plenty of offers to transport me, but this was fishing time as it usually is during the summer months. On my last day there, I had to charter an airplane and was finally able to spend only four hours back home.

My grandmother, Mattie Galovin, told me this story about my first arrival to the village of my conception, and I would like to share it with you. I was my mother's first child, so she decided to have me at the hospital at Unalaska. A few weeks after my birth on the 24th of October 1940, my mother, Anna, and my father, Skookum, returned home to Unga on the mailboat. My mother's cousin, Rachel, was also a passenger and was handing me to my father on the jacob's ladder when the boat rolled and over the side I went into the water. "Welcome to Unga, Robert John Berntsen!"

After being away from home for 45 years, I felt like jumping off the plane and swimming to shore. I've been to Hawaii, the Orient, and other places, but, believe me, there is no place like home, even if the whole town is falling down and no one lives there any longer. Returning to Unga had to be one of the most exhilarating days in the past 45 years, and I wondered why I waited so long...

Robert John Berntsen.

[Ed. Note: Bob, Patricia, and younger brother, Richard, left Unga in the fall of 1950 for the Jesse Lee Home. Bob graduated from Seward High School eight years later and took off on his own. He served a hitch in Korea with the US Army, honed his boatbuilding skills at various companies in the Seattle area, and eventually returned to Alaska. Following in the footsteps of his dad and grandfather, he began fishing for salmon in Bristol Bay, where he fishes to this day. In the off-season, Bob's home is in Seattle with his wife, Sharon, but as he says with pride and longing, his real home continues to be Unga.]

ALICE NILSON

Alice Nilson's recollections of Unga derive from a generation earlier than Bob's. Born Alice Sophia Knutsen in 1915 in Unga, Alice spent her entire childhood and youth in and around Unga where she reveled in the natural beauty of the land. She composed the following thoughts as a contribution to the "I Remember Unga" reunion held in Westport, Washington in 1993. They were later published in a monograph of the same name. Alice left Unga in 1941 and returned twice, in her "golden years," more than fifty years later. Her old friend, Harry Foster, ferried Alice and Peggy Petersen Arness to Unga on that last visit. It was summer in the year 1997 and the grass was green and tall and Alice, with her cane, waded through the lush undergrowth to the sites of memories—up to Flag Pole Hill, along the row of houses that faced the harbor, and finally to the cemetery where she brushed away the moss to reveal the marble tombstone of her husband, Arthur. It was a sad farewell, but Alice left Unga thankful that she completed the journey and anxious to share her experience with family and friends. Were she to be here today, she would surely have described her golden years as those she spent in Unga in her youth. Here, then, are some of Alice's memories of Unga:

ALICE'S STORY

What can I write about Unga?! I have so many precious memories of that dear place that it's difficult to zero in on just a few. Some are: picking violets on Violet Hill, sweet grass and white flowers on Flagpole Hill, kukurukus on Uglamya, picking bidarkis on Agate Beach. Playing "house" and making the most delicious-looking slurpy mud pies that looked just like chocolate pudding. Watching the gorgeous sunsets and knowing our little friend Norman Lauritzen (husband Arthur's brother) was letting us know that heaven was beautiful and he was happy there. An impression that lingers when I watch a beautiful sunset here. Precious, precious memories.

One picture flashes before my eyes so often, and I can see it so plainly. It also has a wonderful aroma connected with it: the smell of frying codfish with pepper! I'm about six or seven years old, and I'm just past the marshal's house, approaching Annie Olgin's, and I smell this wonderful aroma of fish frying—with pepper. I can hardly wait to get home. When I finally reach the house and enter the kitchen, I see Mamma "dishing up" BOILED CODFISH! What a disappointment! End of story.

I must add this: if I were ever asked about where I would choose to be born, I would choose Unga. We were all so lucky to have lived there as children with so many warm, loving, caring Ungaites in the peaceful, quiet town of our beloved Unga...   Alice Knutsen Lauritzen Nilson
(1915-2004)

A final farewell: Alice's departure from Unga, July 11, 1997

APPENDIX

THE

ALASKA PEN

Unga High School

Utility
Nobility
Gentility
Ability

SEPTEMBER 1934

The Alaska Pen

Vol. I   Published Monthly by the Students of the Unga High School   No. 1
Unga, Alaska

The Pen Makers

Editor-in-chief --- Elizabeth Rodgers
Associate Editor -- Clara Pearson
Literary Editor --- Catherine Gould
School Editor ----- John Nelson
Art Editor -------- Christine Cushing

Exchange Editor ---- Marie Gronholdt
Business Manager --- Thomas Lauritzen
Production Managers Andrew Krone
                     Hubert McCallum
                     Daniel Wilson

Introducing

THE

ALASKA PEN

We hope that you'll
    Be happy when
It is time for a new
    Alaska Pen.
It's your paper, you know,
And the news you see there
Is your news and our news
That we want you to share.
We'll have puzzles and jingles
And maybe some jokes,
Our very own stories
To read to home folks.
We'll try to draw pictures,
We'll tell what is new,
So please help us to learn
What has happened to you.
We know you're all with us;
We'll do our best, then,
So you can't do without
    THE ALASKA PEN.

TO THE POINT

THE ALASKA PEN

On September 14, at the close of the
school period, the election of staff officers was announced. The officers were
selected by the teachers because of the
difficulty in choosing the ones best a-
dapted to the various positions. The
names of those selected for the different tasks are listed above.

THE ALASKA PEN stands for the Alaska
Peninsula, PEN being short for peninsula
as well as indicating the literary nature
of our efforts. The departments of the
paper are named, as nearly as possible,
in accordance with the PEN. The feather
pen on the first page is a copy of the
map of the Alaska Peninsula from Lake Iliamna to Unimak Island. The location of
Unga is indicated. We realize, of course,
that we are not living on the Peninsula,
itself. Perhaps we should consider ourselves as bits of ink dropped by the
SUPREME WRITER.

THE ALASKA PEN . . . . Page 3.

APPRECIATION

We, the students of the Unga High School, send a vote of thanks to Mr. A. E. Karnes, our Commissioner of Education, and to the Alaska Board of Education, for their support in establishing our high school.

The Student Body,
Unga High School.

--:--

UNGA BASKET SOCIAL

The basket social for the benefit of Unga High School was held on the evening of August 27. Although it was a dark and rainy evening, the size of the crowd was augmented by a few young men who had walked over from Squaw Harbor and some of the men from the SS Starr which we were fortunate enough to have in port at the time.

Mr. Sjoberg kindly assumed the duties of auctioneer, and sold the beautifully decorated baskets at prices that certainly showed how loyally everyone is supporting our school. The amount realized from this source was $266.00.

The hall was very festive in its gay colors. We spent some time identifying the fish on the fish pond, salmon, halibut, and such. Everyone fished so assiduously that the pond was exhausted long before the fishermen grew tired.

Dancing was enjoyed all evening, music being furnished by Adolph Rodgers, Norman Larsen, and Louis Berntsen, and at last by the trusty phonograph.

Food for the social and trinkets for the fish pond were liberally supplied by interested friends. $49.60 were realized from these two sources. The total amount raised at the social was $315.65.

Besides the generous amounts spent at the hall, there were several donations by those unable to attend. Mr. W. P. Studdart, superintendent of the Sand Point cannery, sent a very generous cash donation to the school. Mr. Most, superintendent of the Squaw Harbor cannery, donated a ton of coal. Other contributors to the fund are Mrs. K. Knutsen, John Iverson, and Harry Hunt. Lumber for the partition was given by Laurita Pedersen.

Much credit is due the volunteer committee, Mrs. Hjalmar Lauritzen, Mrs. Conrad Lauritzen, Mrs. Zenia Rodgers, Mrs. Harry Sharpe, and Mr. Gustaf Sjoberg, for making the drive for high school funds a success. In this, they secured the cooperation of so many others that it would be impossible to record specifically the great number of helpful and generous acts.

Mrs. Zenia Rodgers and Mrs. Conrad Lauritzen have consented to work on a permanent committee, to work with the school treasurer, Mr. Gustaf Sjoberg, for the administration of these local funds.

--:--

SYMPATHY

We wish to extend our deepest sympathy to Nome, Alaska, for their recent great loss by fire. We hope for a speedy recovery in all lines of business.

--:--

THE PARTITION

The partition dividing the upper grade and high school rooms is giving satisfactory service, as classes do not disturb each other. The arrangement is very convenient as to the use of library and reference books. It is also very practical for the rapid changing of classes in departmental work.

to send in your DOLLAR if you don't want to miss a copy of THE ALASKA PEN.

All you have to do is to clip the coupon printed at the right, sign it, inclose a dollar bill, and mail it to Thomas Lauritzen, Business Manager, Unga, Alaska. Your PEN will be seeing you each month, via U. S. Mail.

Please do this NOW before you forget it!!

BELLS! BELLS! BELLS!

The new electric bell system aroused a great deal of mystification until all the bells and buttons were located. A game of "Hunt the Bell" was in progress during most of the recesses of the first day. Now, when one rings, it is just "bell time" again.

--::--

PLAYGROUND

The newly leveled playground on top of the hill has seen a total removal of tennis lines in favor of basketball and volley ball. The difficult problems now are: how to make the basketball goals stay erect during the severe wind storms since bedrock prevents planting the posts deep enough to insure stability, and how to coax Old Dame Nature not to cry on our playfield when we want to play.

The see-saw, or teeter, which was added to the school play equipment this summer, is still in service although it has seen quite heavy usage. The next teeter should be of somewhat heavier materials in order that the children might get the fullest enjoyment from it.

Of course, we can use other things on our playground.

FRESHMEN INITIATION
(Upper Classman's Viewpoint)

The initiation of the Freshmen of Unga High School took place September 14, 1934 at the school-house at eight o'clock in the evening.

The Freshmen entered the school through the basement door. Each one had a password and knock. In the basement they were blindfolded and led upstairs. Amid all the screams and stumbles they finally reached the stand where they placed their hand on a very familiar book and solemnly declared they would do everything we asked them to do, which they did. Then came the ice worms, which are very rare and, I am sure, the Freshmen enjoyed them. This was followed by the punch which caused many wry faces but they drank it like good fellows. The egg race was especially good because just what we wanted to happen did. They pushed their noses into the eggs. One thing that didn't turn out as well as we had expected was the mesmerizing stunt. Our ideas got all jumbled up and we should have tried it on all of them. However, the one girl we did try it on we give credit for being a good sport. Then came the

GREEN CAPS which every Freshman was glad to get. A few games were played, followed by the lunch which was served by the teachers, and enjoyed by all.

When the time came to go home, every Freshman went through the front door with a smiling face, glad that no bones were broken. Since they were the first to be initiated, I hope that they may have a chance to initiate the next group of Freshmen that enter and have just as much fun in doing it as we did.

                                    Elizabeth Rodgers.
          (Viewpoints of Freshmen)

                              Unga Public School,
                              September 17, 1934

Dearest Friend,

I must write and tell you about our "Freshmen Initiation Party". It happened the evening of the fourteenth of September. The Juniors and Sophomores of our school thought that it would be a grand idea to initiate the Freshmen of our class. Friday afternoon at school, our teacher told us to come to the party at eight o'clock, and bring with us a towel, a glass, and six sandwiches. He also said to come through the basement door of the school. Our secret knock was to be two short and three long, and our pass-word "swordfish".

We had heard of freshmen being initiated. It seemed as if they did some terrible things to them. This got us all to wondering what was going to happen to us.

At eight o'clock we all came. After standing around for a while, one of the boys finally got "nerve" enough to go in first. He knocked the secret way. The door opened and a white gloved hand reached out. A low voice said, "Your pass-word?" The boy answered, "Swordfish", and was pulled in the door closing behind him. After a few boys and one of the girls went in, I decided to try. I knocked and the same thing happened. After I got in, my sandwiches and glass were taken from me, and my eyes covered with the towel. Then someone took me by the arm and led me to the stairs telling me to step up. When we got to the top of the stairs, I was told to step up again. Thinking I was going up another flight of stairs, I did this. Instead, I heard a great rumbling sound. It was a can I had stepped on. They kept telling me to step up which I did, each time stepping on something. At last my hands were placed on a book and I was asked if I would obey all rules for one

week. Upon answering "yes", I was seated and told to take off my shoes. This I did and when I felt for my shoes, they were gone. Later, we were told to eat some worms, which we found out were only spaghetti. But, anyway, they surely tasted like worms. Next, our hair was "made believe" cut. Instead, it was rope they were cutting. After our eye bandages were removed, we played a few games, had lunch, and danced a while.

This was our initiation party and everyone had a lot of fun.

                                    Your friend,
                                    Anna Wilson.

"I sat and waited for all the rest to come in the same manner I did, only a little worse. Some of the girls were yelling and shouting because they were afraid."
                                    Hubert McCallum.

"The first thing I had to do was to shake hands with the dead.
"It was Thomas Lauritzen with a white glove on.
                                    Frances Pearson.

"While we were still blindfolded, we made a vow that we would do everything they told us for a week. The first thing was to take off our shoes (they did a disappearing act), then our blindfolds were taken off and we hunted for our shoes."
                                    Christine Cushing.

"They gave us a drink which, I think, was charcoal and water with a few drops of cod liver oil."
                                    Andrew Krone.
                          --::--

SCHOOL CITIZENSHIP

A good citizen in school will be truthful. He will not tell lies even if he is in the wrong. He will not try to lay the blame for some misdeed on someone else nor accuse someone else of a wrong unless he is able to prove the other guilty.

A good school citizen will assume responsibilities and do his duties cheerfully. He will be fair and broad-minded---not prejudiced.

By establishing a reputation of being honest and willing to do one's share, or a little more than his share, a person gains the confidence and respect of his fellow citizens, who, in school, are his playmates and classmates.

                                    Catherine Gould.

LUMBER DONATION

The arrival of the MS Beryl-E was very much appreciated by the students of the Unga High School. It brought a donation of lumber, over 3000 feet, from Mr. W. P. Studdart, superintendent of the A.P.S.C. cannery at Sand Point. The lumber is to be used for the building of a side-walk from the school building to the main walk. The lumber was landed at Mr. Sjoberg's dock. The students of the Unga High School wish to thank Mr. Studdart for this dona-tion.

The Student Body,
Unga High School.
By John Nelson, Pres.

--::--

THE QUILL

THE PTARMIGAN

Down in the valley
When the north wind blows,
All the ptarmigan lie nestled
In their holes in the snows.

But when the wind stops blowing
And the sun shines bright;
Then the foxy little creatures
Begin to seek the light.

And when the hunter sees them
Flying about so free,
He begins shooting at them,
And "packs" them home in glee.
Thomas Lauritzen

--::--

A CAKE FAILURE

One day when I was left at home alone, I thought that, to pass the time away, I would make a cake.

I made an Angel Food Cake, which takes one hour to bake. I put the cake in the oven at ten minutes before three, and took it out at ten minutes before four, for I thought it should be done. The top's being brown also made me think the cake was done. When I turned the pan over, a mess of raw cake batter fell out. I quickly managed to pick up the batter and to throw it back in-to the pan. Getting all the cake batter that I could, I put it back into the oven and hoped that it would be all right.

Fifteen minutes before five, I took the "cake" from the oven and threw it out to the chickens. The poor thing presented a very sad appearance and was so heavy in texture that, for a while, it seemed that even the chickens didn't care to eat it, but it finally all disappeared.

Catherine Gould.

--::--

DO YOU KNOW ME ?

I am the foundation of all business. I am the fount of all prosperity. I am the salt that gives life its savor. I have laid the foundation of every fortune in America, from Rockefeller's down. I must be loved before I can bestow my greatest blessings and achieve my greatest ends. I can do more to advance youth than his own parents, be they ever so rich. Fools hate me; wise men love me. I am represent-ed in every loaf of bread that comes from the oven, in every train that crosses the continent, in every newspaper that comes from the press. I am the mother of democ-racy. All progress springs from me. Who am I? What am I? I am WORK.

--::--

STUDENT'S LAMENT

Oral talks and written themes,
   Gives a fellow no time for dreams;
First we read, next we tell,
   Then we're asked if we can spell;
Books to read, writers to know,
   Oh! gee, but I'm feeling low;
Grammar drills, all those things,
   Another minute 'til the bell rings;
What class is this? You ask me that?
   English! O me! Oh my! O my hat!
No. 201978 (Get it?)

--::--

UNGA SEASONS

The gold, scarlet, and brown in the fall of the year means that the leaves and grass are "ripened" by the frosts and are dying away.

In the spring of the year, the new grass gives to the hills a greenish, veil-like, misty appearance.

In the summer, one can see great spots of bright blues, reds, and yellows inter-mingled with the green of the bushes and grass.

In the winter months, when there is snow, the ground looks as though it has been covered with a dazzling white sheet. The sun shining on it shows millions of star hues, sparkling, and dazzling with radiance.

Catherine Gould.

THE PEN REGISTERS

S C H O O L
September 4

School opens with a great deal of enthusiasm evident.

Several experience their first day of high school work.

- The strike on the West coast prevented the arrival of our school supplies but we are trying to "carry on".

Peggy and Jimmy Petersen, son and daughter of Mr. and Mrs. A. L. Petersen, formerly of Seldovia, entered school. Mr. Petersen is the local Deputy U. S. Marshal

Game of "Find the Bell" is in progress as mysterious electric bells ring.

September 5

Bells were all located so curiosity has subsided.

The Alaska Pen gets a boost as Mr. Sjoberg becomes first advertiser and subscriber.

September 10

Kenneth Knutsen enters the fifth grade, coming from his home in Kupreanof.

Thelma and Norman Lauritzen enter the second and fourth grades respectively.

September 12

Ruby Cushing was absent due to illness.

September 14

The Alaska Pen staff members announced.

September 17

Pearl McCallum was absent from the fifth grade.

Marie Gronholdt entered high school.

September 21

Student Body was organized with the following officers: President, John Nelson; Vice-President, Anna Wilson; Secretary, Clara Pearson; Treasurer, Thomas Lauritzen. School colors, blue and gold,w are chosen.

Robert Gilbert returned to school after an absence of two days due to illness.

September 24

All day rain prevented outdoor play, so quite a bit of uneasiness is evident.

Charles McCallum is absent this morning due to trouble with his teeth, but he is back with a smile in the afternoon.

September 25

Several meet their "Waterloo" in the Geometry class as a "test" is given.

September 26

Peggy has made her debut on the primary sand table.

September 27

First fire drill of year was held. The building was cleared in a half minute.

Several heads fell as General Science test papers were returned.

September 28

The last day of the first month of school.

An Alaska home for Peter and Peggy is being made on the sand table by the first grade. Peggy and her little white cat are now ready to move in.

Our enrolment by grades at the close of the month follows: GRADE 1: Alexander Calugan, Esther Cushing, Lee Demalt, Robert Gilbert, and Harvey Sharpe. GRADE 2: John Foster, Jr., Thelma Lauritzen, and Budilia Rodgers. GRADE 3: Henry Berntsen, Ada Gilbert, and Olive Krone. GRADE 4: Thomas Foster, Norman Lauritzen, and Emily Rodgers. GRADE 5: Margaret Berntsen, Isabel Calugan, Peter Calugan, Florence Cushing, Ruby Cushing, Alma Foster, Esther Gilbert, Kenneth Knutsen, Pearl McCallum, and Peggy Petersen. GRADE 6: Raynold Gilbert. GRADE 7: William Berntsen, Albert Cushing, Florence Krone, Donald McCallum, and Jimmy Petersen. GRADE 8: George Cushing and Olga Foster. GRADE 9: Christine Cushing, Catherine Gould, Andrew Krone, Betty McCallum, Charles McCallum, Hubert McCallum, Clara Pearson, Frances Pearson, Anna Wilson, and Daniel Wilson. GRADE 10: Marie Gronholdt, Thomas Lauritzen, and John Nelson. GRADE 11: Elizabeth Rodgers.

--:.:--
L O C A L
September 4

The opening of school is recorded.

September 7

Mr. W. P. Studdart, superintendent of the Sand Point cannery, was here with the pile driver repairing Sjoberg and Mentzers wharf.

The Elmer returned from Kupreanof Harbor bringing Kenneth Knutsen to enter Unga school.

September 8

Hans Hansen had the misfortune to severely cut his thumb while splitting wood.

September 10

The Blue Fox is in port. Later, it left for Seattle carrying as passengers Hans Hansen on his way to Seward to receive medical attention, Mr. and Mrs. Conrad Lauritzen and Mr. and Mrs. Paul Petersen for a visit in Seattle.

September 11

Territorial election was held with a fair number voting.

Judge F. C. Driffield and William Johnson visited Unga from Squaw Harbor.

September 14

The Freshman Initiation held the attention as the upper classmen gave them their "just" dues.

September 16

Mr. W. P. Studdart spent the day in Unga with his men while securing some of the mining machinery from the Apollo mine.

Marie Gronholdt arrived from Sand Point to enter Unga High School.

September 21

J. P. Hammer's dory was destroyed by the rough weather. Only the engine was saved, the other wreckage being strewn all along the beach.

September 22

Fishing proves popular as many local anglers wend their ways toward the trout streams. The run of salmon no longer bothers in the streams.

September 23

Father Neptune attempts to drive his white horses over our island. Boats were all safely sheltered behind the Sand-spit near the head of our bay.

September 25

The Neptune left for Squaw Harbor.

Harold Petersen and Louis Berntsen returned to Unga after being stranded at Coal Harbor by the storm. They brought a full cargo of coal on their boat, The Kingfisher.

September 26

Mr. and Mrs. Louis Berntsen are the proud parents of a nine and one-half pound son. He will answer to the name of Louis Hamilton.

Sjoberg and Hentzer today lost a loading platform at their saltery. The property at present is occupied by Carl and Hans Hansen. They also had slight damage done their wharf by the high seas.

September 27

Ed Pearson and William Gilbert arrived early this morning in the Milfred from a successful hunting expedition to Pavlof Bay.

September 28

The Elmer returned early this morning after a successful hunting expedition to Canoe Bay. This party consisted of Arthur and Harold Lauritzen, Raymond Rodgers, and Fred Pomian. They left Unga on the twentieth.

Mr. and Mrs. Harry Hunt returned from the mainland on a combined hunting and trap-line repair trip.

Fred Krone, Robert Golovin, and Thomas Foster returned from Pavlof Bay where they engaged in big game hunting.

September 29

The Beryl-E, Captain W. P. Studdart, came over with lumber for our new walk from its base, Sand Point.

Catherine Goull and Anna Wilson hiked to Squaw Harbor.

Work on the annex to the home of John Foster is progressing nicely.

Several roofs have been treated to new coats of paint.

Repair work on the home of Conrad Lauritzen is in progress.

September 30

Several took advantage of the beautiful day by hiking.

The arrival of the S.S. Starr is hourly expected.

October 1

THE S.S. STARR ARRIVED IN UNGA BRINGING MAIL AND FREIGHT. Were we glad to see it!!

--::--

WORLD

SEPTEMBER 8--The luxurious Ward Liner Morro Castle was burned off the New Jersey coast. More than 143 persons lost their lives in the disaster.

SEPTEMBER 17--Nome, Alaska was visited by a fire causing $2,000,000 property loss. A strip ten blocks long and three blocks wide through the business district was razed. A 22 mile wind helped spread the destruction. 1500 people were left virtually homeless, and, with only a limited food supply, hardships will be experienced.

SEPTEMBER 18--The U.S.S.R., or, in short, Russia, joined the League of Nations.

SEPTEMBER 21--1500 were killed and 500 injured in a typhoon which visited Japan.

SEPTEMBER 23--The daughter of Madame Curie announced a new cure for cancer.

(Continued on Page 12)

INSIST ON

PACKED BY

Alaska-Pacific Salmon Corporation

DISTRIBUTED BY

Skinner & Eddy Corporation

SKINNER BUILDING, SEATTLE, U. S. A.

................................THE ALASKA PEN........................Page 11

---THIS MONTH'S CROSS-WORD PUZZLE---

D O W N

1. Osmium: Combining form.
2. Cast out.
3. Cobalt: Chemical
4. Nigerian negro.
5. Dry up.
6. Commerce.
7. Moved swiftly.
8. Ireland: Poetic.
9. And: Latin.
10. Permit.
11. Local merchant.
13. Gleam.
14. College degree.
19. By means of.
22. Howls.
24. Ambush.
26. End of a lace.
28. One who dines.
30. A musical instrument.
31. Runs with ease.
33. Belar: Variable.
35. Word of refusal.
37. Hawaiian bird.
39. Local U. S. Commissioner.
40. Pertaining to the ear.
41. Large island near Unga.
43. Group of Danish Islands in Atlantic.
47. Designer of U. S. flag.
50. Local mining man.
53. Indefinite article.
54. Slide.
56. Out of: Greek prefix.
58. Clear profit.
60. The soil: Latin law.
63. Auditory organ.
65. Hebrew law-giver.
67. One that eases.
68. Tale.
70. Local miner.
72. Portable shelter.
75. Sailor.
77. It is: Portic.
78. Tin: Chemical symbol.
80. Greek letter.
83. Father.
86. Zirconium: Chemical symbol.

A C R O S S

1. A colonizer.
7. Tell again.
12. A local merchant.
14. Obstruction.
15. Afternoon function.
16. Personal pronoun.
17. Spoken.
18. Cut off at once.
20. Chinese measure.
21. Frosty.
23. Prepare for publication.
25. A tennis necessity.
27. A Sioux Indian tribe.
29. Register.
32. Important harvest of India.
34. Pale.
36. Prohibition.
38. Wager.
39. An English chemist.
42. Island near Unga.
44. Ezra: Abbreviation
45. Trick.
46. Measure of area.
48. Eye: Scotch Variable.
49. Capable.
51. Iridium: Chemical symbol.
52. Is furious.
55. A brightly colored fish.
57. Winnow.
59. Metal fasteners.
61. Call of a dove.
62. Run away.
64. Dialect.
66. Female sheep.
69. Game at marbles.
71. Plan.
73. A Burmese spirit of the woods.
74. A French conjunction.
76. Exposes to moisture.
79. One for whose use a thing is given.
81. True.
82. Overhanging flap.
84. Err.
85. Local merchant.
87. Rough sketches.
88. Stellar.

WATCH FOR THE CORRECT SOLUTION IN

NEXT MONTH'S ISSUE.

The first snow was reported in California. Our first is yet to fall. What is that about Alaska's being cold!

SEPTEMBER 25--Hugh S. Johnson's resignation as head of the N. R. A. was accepted by President Roosevelt.

SEPTEMBER 28--We gathered from the news that the name of the Richfield News Reporter is Sam Hayes. How many of you already knew that!

The sixth birthday of the noted comic player, Mickey Mouse, was celebrated.

SEPTEMBER 30--President Roosevelt delivered an inspiring radio message to the American people.

--::--

THE
TIP

If you always want your PEN, be sure that your subscription is in.

Rinse the cream pitcher with cold water before filling to prevent sticking to the sides. This is equally effective for molds for boiled puddings.

To remove egg stains from fabrics, wash first with cold water and then with warm water and soap.

If you find your soup too salty, add several slices of raw potato and boil for a few minutes.

Use a clean sheet of wrapping paper to roll pies and pastry on. It saves a lot of cleaning up later.

You need a PEN--We need your help--So lend a hand.

THE
PEN
SPRINGS

A brunette is a female bear.

A valley is a hill that comes down on one side and goes up on the other.

Evaporated means that all of the smell is out.

1420-1440 - Marco Polo walked to China and back.

Marco Polo discovered the Pacific Ocean.

Archeology is a study of the stars.

Vapor is water after it has all gone to steam.

Wind is air that passes by fast.

A whole wheat flour blooms in the spring.

False doctrine means giving people the wrong medicine.

--::--

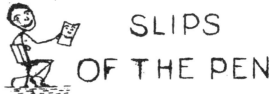

SLIPS
OF THE PEN

SMILES: You're a pig.
WILES: And you're my brother.

FRED: There's just one thing I miss when I don't go to school.
MR. SMITH: What is that!
FRED: Recess.

--::--

A FEW EXTRA COPIES OF THIS ISSUE FOR 15¢.
--The Editor.

DIP SAYS

I wonder what you think of The Alaska Pen!

I would certainly appreciate knowing. THANKS!

HISTORY AND CIRCULATION
"THE ALASKA PEN"

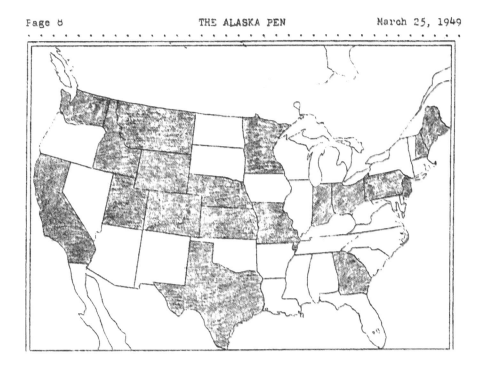

Because of numerous remarks and queries concerning our paper, "The Alaska Pen", its number of subscribers, and its circulation, we have decided to answer some questions that we think would interest our readers.

"The Alaska Pen" has a total number of 94 subscribers. In addition to this, we exchange with 24 other schools and institutions. The majority of our subscriptions are from various places outside of Unga. Town subscriptions number 25; 41 "Alaska Pens" are sent monthly to our Alaskan subscribers and exchanges. Of the 48 states in the Union, we send 52 "Alaska Pens" through subscriptions and exchanges to 19 states, namely: Washington (26), California (3), Idaho(1), Montana (2), Wyoming (1), Utah (1), Colorado (1) Nebraska (1), Kansas (2), Minnesota (2), Missouri (1), Indiana (3), Ohio (1), Pennsylvania (2), New Jersey (1), New Hampshire (1), Maine (1), Georgia (1) and Texas (1) To give you a vivid picture of the extent of the distribution of "The Alaska Pen" throughout the States, we have drawn a map of the United States shading the states which receive one or more "Alaska Pens".

"The Alaska Pen" has been published since 1934 by the High School students, and has been published every year with the exception of the 1942-43 school year when there was no High School in Unga. The name "The Alaska Pen" has appeared on the cover as the title of the paper every year except in the school year 1943-44 when it was changed to "The Pen Whispers" because the Freshmen who were the only High School students that year thought their publication would appear to be no more than a "whisper" as compared with the previous "Alaska Pens"!

As "the Alaska Pen" is the only paper published in this area, it has been the policy of the paper to not only publish school news but any local news which would be of interest to our readers. All-in-all, "The Alaska Pen" serves not only as a school paper but a town paper as well.

April 1945   Alaska Pen File

During the past month Mrs. French suggested we make a file—one issue of every Alaska Pen since the first publication in 1934. WE have been very unfortunate in that there are so many issues missing from our file and we would greatly appreciate, if anyone having the issues mentioned here, would return them as to help in making our file a complete set of all the Alaska Pens.

This file should make a good reference book of the history of Unga and vicinity during the previous 14 years which also includes brief summaries before that time.

Search through your old attics and see if you can salvage a few of these:

1934—The entire year's publication. 1936—February, April, September and December. 1940— March 1942—April 1942-'43-Nave none. It is not known if a paper was published this year. 1944— September , 1945---March and May 1946—March.

Our thanks go to Mrs. French and her Intermediate pupils for the organizing of this file which will be a great benefit to future makers of the Alaska Pen.

May 1948   To Our Exchanges

Once again we, the students of Unga High wish to extend our thanks to all the exchange papers which we have been receiving the past year. We appreciate any recognition given us during the year We feel that this part of Alaska is really a wonderful place in which to live and hope that by our articles you have gained a worth-while knowledge of our very fine land.

Thanks to Subscribers

Another school year is over and the school children's thought are once again turning towards summer plans. However our thoughts are not wholly concerned with the future. We are thinking of the past year and the many people who have subscribed to the Alaska Pen. Our thoughts are also of the many fine High School publications we have received from Florida to California and in and about Alaska.

Our thanks go to the many subscribers and may all have a happy and successful summer.

April. 1946   A Letter

`Dear Readers,

I sincerely hope the gripes are not contagious because this letter is lousy with them, (the gripes). Whether or not we have the right to complain is up to you.

Way back in September it was the paper. Too darn thin. If we wrote on both sides you couldn't see what you were reading, if we didn't we wouldn't have enough paper to go around.

Next came the stamp supply. We couldn't get any stamps so we could not mail the "Pen". Right about here we were running out of ink and paper. We were almost compelled to use anything for paper.

At the present it's the mimeograph that has our tongues lolling. Takes an hour to warm the darn thing up and then it's ready to be reinked. Ho-hum, no rest for the wicked.

To make matters worse this issue has been delayed one week by the diphtheria epidemic. Oh measles stay away from my door!

After this, we still have one more issue to put out. It sounds like plenty and then it doesn't. We'll pull through we hope.

The Alaska Pen

P.S. Do you know why the ink spot is so blue? Because his father just did a long sentence in the "Alaska Pen".

Evelyn Foster, Technician

September 1948   Alaska Pen Reorganized

       Congratulations, Alaska Pen on your thirteenth birthday! We, of the Unga High this year are few in number but feel worthy of carrying the responsibility of publishing our traditional paper.

       The staff for the publication was elected immediately after school opened. Our new Editor is Thorwald Lauritzen; Associate Editor, Jennie Johansen; and acting Business Manager, Norman Brandal.

       The opening of school this year was delayed two weeks and thus threw the publishing date into October. We shall endeavor to publish another paper the latter part of October. From then on, the Alaska Pen will appear every four weeks as usual.

(six high school students)

THE PEN-MAKERS:
Jennie Johansen, Associate Editor
Nora Berntsen, Exchange Editor
Alice Cushing, Typist
Thorwald Lauritzen, Editor
Martha Hunt, Business Manager
Harold Pedersen, Humor Editor
(not shown)
(March 1949)

Credits for Photographs and Illustrations

122   On the boardwalk: EMC.

123   Christmas Boat, the USFWS *Penguin*: LFC

126   The *Elmer* in her heyday, late '30s: Ibid.

       The *Elmer* in drydock, late '40s: Ibid.

127   "Marriage by Midnight" program: TL

128   "Billy," "Wanda," and "Kitty": Photo by Edward F. Casey, courtesy Judy Casey Cross.

       Part of the cast, "Marriage by Midnight": Ibid.

129   Norman Lauritzen and the *Anna T*: Photo by Ray Krantz, Photographic Illustrations, Seattle, Washington.

135   The PAF tender *Glenwood*: TL.

136   The medical corps in Unga: PAC

137   A somber souvenir of Unga's devastating epidemic: TL.

139   The *Hygiene*: TL

140   The crew of the M. V. *Hygiene*: PAC.

141   The *Hygiene* riding at anchor at Unga: TL.

142   Freddie and his pals: LFC.

143   Donald V. and Opal Lawvere and Mrs. Allen Petersen: PAC.

144   Budilia B. Rodgers: Unga High School Graduation Announcement.

       Emily M. Endresen: Ibid.

145   Esther Cushing and her schoolmates: Girl Scout Scrapbook, courtesy Martha Hunt Fletcher.

146   An Unga sunset: An Allan L. Petersen Panoramic, PAC.

147   Harold and Lillian French: Ibid.

148   Ethel Cushing: LFC.

       Kenneth Foster: Ibid.

       Peter Calugan: Photo courtesy Polly Calugan.

149   Jennie Johansen: Photo courtesy Jennie Johansen Berntsen.

150   The Squaw Harbor School: LFC.

       The Pacific American Fisheries salmon cannery at Squaw Harbor, mid-1930s: Photo by Lee Isaacson.

151   The *Garland* at Unga: Drawing from "I Remember Unga"; Drawing courtesy Robert D. McCausland.

152   The Unga Methodist Parsonage and Church: Ibid.

       Roberta Hill: Photo courtesy Robert Hill Allen.

153   Evert Tigner: Photo courtesy Evert Tigner.

       Mr. Tigner's students, 1955-56: Ibid.

154   Evert Tigner on the dock in Unga: Ibid.

155   The Unga Community Library: PAC.

157   Library artifacts: Contribution courtesy Robert Galovin, Jr.

158   To Peugh or not to peugh: Photo courtesy Carol Larsen Smith.

160   The Apollo Mine, ca. 1910: Photo postcard by J. E. Thwaites.

161   The Apollo Mill, late 1930s: Photo by Edward F. Casey, courtesy Judy Casey Cross.

162   The Locomotive *Apollo*: Ibid.

       The Apollo dam, late 1940s: TL.

163   The cyanide plant in 1915: PAC.

       Remains of the Cyanide Plant, ca. 1948: TL.

       The Apollo Hospital, ca. 1948: Ibid.

Selected Bibliography

Although some of the sources listed below were not quoted or referenced in the present work, their importance in presenting other aspects of Unga's history demand that they be called to the reader's attention, should one wish to pursue this subject further.

Students of the Sand Point High School, *"The Land...The Sea,"* Sand Point School Press, Sand Point, Alaska (1982).

> Of all the literature that was reviewed in the preparation of *THE ALASKA PEN: An Illustrated History of Unga,* the book that we hope our present efforts will emulate is *"The Land... The Sea."* This yearbook, prepared, printed and published entirely by the students of the Sand Point High School, is a treasure trove of historical information on the Shumagin Islands. It is a beautiful book and a credit to the entire Sand Point community for the skill and devotion that made this project possible.

B. Shepard & C. Kelsey, *"Have Gospel Tent Will Travel: The Methodist Church in Alaska Since 1886,"* Conference Council on Ministries, Alaska Missionary Conference of the United Methodist Church (1986).

> This publication discusses the growth of the Methodist Church in Alaska from its first outpost in Unga in 1886. After a hiatus of more than fifty years, missionary work in Unga resumed and continued until the early 1950s. This book presents a concise summary of that work.

JRB Pels, Coordinator, *"I Remember Unga,"* Hardscratch Press, Walnut Creek, California (1993).

> This small monograph presents a collection of autobiographical sketches of former residents and friends of Unga. The booklet was an outgrowth of a reunion of the same name, held at Westport, Washington, in August of 1993. Forty-five people attended the reunion. Of particular interest are the pencil drawings of R. D. McCausland that illustrate the book.

JRB Pels, *"Unga Island Girl: Ruth's Book,"* Hardscratch Press, Walnut Creek, California (1995).

> Jackie Pels' nostalgic walk down memory lane honors the life of her mother and, in so doing, presents a detailed biographical account of the extended Lauritzen family of Unga. Interwoven through this account are interesting historical tidbits of life in early 20th century Unga.

Susan Meredith, *"Alaska's Search For a Killer,"* Alaska Public Health Nursing History Association, (1998).

> Meredith and her co-authors, Kitty Gair and Elaine Schwinge, visited Unga in 1946, as members of the medical staff of the M. V. *Hygiene.* Their work documenting the prevalence of tuberculosis in coastal Alaska communities and their efforts to educate the people on its prevention and treatment won the hearts of many. Their description of Unga was included verbatim in the present work.

Lydia T. Black, *"The History and Ethnohistory of the Aleutian East Borough,"* The Limestone Press, Kingston, Ontario and Fairbanks, Alaska (1999).

The research that this historical account of Unga and its neighboring communities represents is awesome. Black details Unga's history from the Bering voyage of discovery in 1741 to the present day. Her search into the archives documenting the period of Russian occupation is impressive. For anyone interested in Unga's early history, this is a must read.

J. Pennelope Goforth, *"Sailing the Mail in Alaska: The Maritime Years of Alaska Photographer John E.Thwaites, 1905-1912,"* CybrrCat Production!, Anchorage, Alaska (2003).

The venerable S. S. *Dora* played a crucial role in the development of Unga in the early years of the 20th century, and its mail clerk, Thwaites, documented that role prolifically and with great distinction. His postcards filled many a family album. One of the reproductions was used in the essay on mailboats in the present work. This and other photographs were incorporated into Goforth's riveting story of life on the Westward Run. A great historical nautical read.

Microfilm, *"The Alaska Pen: September 1934-Febraury 1951," "Unga Newsletter: November 1938-May 1943,"* and *"Pen Whispers: September 1943-May 1944,"* Unga Alaska, Positive Microfilm Second Generation, Alaska State Library (2004).

This microfilm record of the Unga Territorial School's publications from 1934 to 1951 form the basis of the present book. The single microfilm was produced by the Alaska State Library and can be viewed and copied at the main library in Juneau or at selected libraries in the State of Alaska. The microfilm can presumably be loaned to out-of-state libraries as well. Since all of the issues published by the Unga school were mimeograph or hectograph copies, some reproductions on the microfilm are difficult to read, but the large majority of issues are quite legible and offer a unique glimpse into the everyday life in Unga and surrounding communities.

Index

ABOUT THE EDITORS...

All three co-editors spent their formative years in Unga. **Thor Lauritzen**, who shepherded this project, lived in Unga from 1932 to 1949. He served on the staff of both PEN WHISPERS and THE ALASKA PEN, assuming the role of editor-in-chief of the PEN for the 1948-'49 school year. He left home to attend his senior year of high school in Seward. He then went on to the University of Alaska and Stanford University. He has never returned to Unga. Thor lives in retirement in Westport, Washington.

Peggy Arness lived in Unga from 1934 to 1944, served on the staff of THE ALASKA PEN during the 1941-'42 school year and graduated from Unga High School in May, 1942. That fall, she enrolled in Pacific Lutheran College in Tacoma, Washington. The next year she accepted a teaching position in Unga along with her mother, Mrs. Allan (Jettie) Petersen. In addition to her teaching duties, Peggy was instrumental in the publishing of PEN WHISPERS, THE ALASKA PEN's war-year surrogate. She left Unga in 1944 to attend the University of Washington. As a life-long Alaskan, Peggy has visited Unga several times since her 1944 departure, her last visit being in the spring of 2004. Peggy lives with her husband, Jim, in Kenai.

Edward Melseth was born in Unga in 1943 and attended Unga Territorial School from 1950 to 1958. He attended high school in Tacoma. Edward has lived in and around Unga for most of his life. After Unga's demise, he and his family moved to Squaw Harbor and eventually to Sand Point, where his mother and several of his siblings live today. Edward is a member of The Aleut Corporation, The Unga Corporation, and The Unga Tribe. He currently lives in Anchorage.

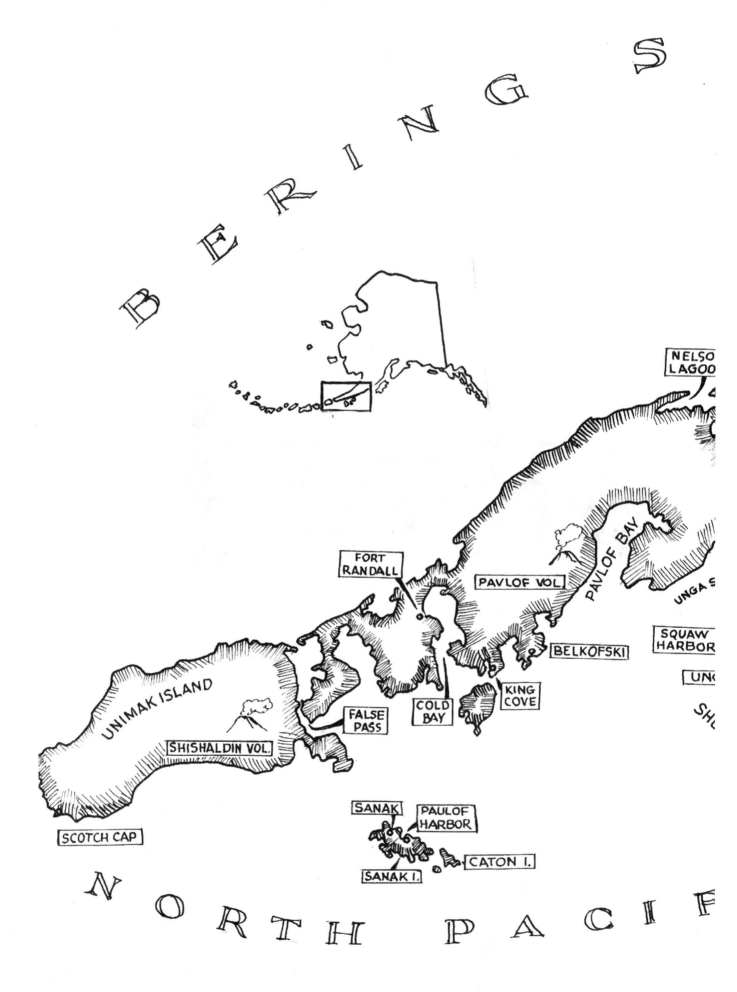